Political
Science Fiction

Political Science Fiction

Edited by
Donald M. Hassler and Clyde Wilcox

The University of South Carolina Press

© 1997 University of South Carolina

Cloth edition published by the University of South Carolina Press, 1997
Paperback edition published in Columbia, South Carolina,
by the University of South Carolina Press, 2011

www.sc.edu/uscpress

Manufactured in the United States of America

20 19 18 17 16 15 14 13 12 11 10 9 8 7 6 5 4 3 2 1

The Library of Congress has cataloged the cloth edition as follows:
Political science fiction / editors, Donald M. Hassler and Clyde Wilcox.
    p. cm.
  Includes bibliographical references and index.
  ISBN 1-57003-113-4
  1. Science fiction—History and criticism. 2. Politics in literature. I. Hassler, Donald M.
  II. Wilcox, Clyde, 1953–
  809.3′876209358—dc20   96–10073

Quotations from Frank Herbert's *Dune* are used with the permission of Herbert
Properties LLC.

ISBN: 978-1-57003-847-1 (pbk)

Contents

Contents

Preface

I sing of arms and the man.
Virgil, Aeneid

Our plans for this collection of essays began shortly after the publication of the special issue of *Extrapolation* devoted to science fiction and politics that appeared in the fall of 1993. We are completing work on the book in May 1995 and as we finish the project cannot ignore the late spring anniversaries around the world that resonate with implications which link our continuing interests in literature, in political science, and in the future. In particular, two of the great military, or "armed," conflicts of our century are being talked about as we complete our literary work so that, though we are no Virgils, we are especially sensitive about the relation of arms to mankind and hence about the relation of politics to the literature of the future that we know as science fiction.

Almost like the melodrama of other popular literature, the anniversaries on our minds at this moment commemorate a good war and a bad war; and so perhaps it is appropriate to evoke such broad outlines and such broad images for the relationships between public events and imaginative literature before the more careful and detailed analyses in what follows. We are reminded of the relevance in academic writing, as well as the relevance of the futuristic fictions which we like to study, when we think of this moment of history. It was just fifty years ago that the Allied forces in Europe declared victory, and it was just a quarter of the century later in May when the antiwar protest movement over Vietnam reached its climax with the shooting of students at Kent State University and at Jackson State. Thus somewhere between victory and defeat, and dependent on the collaborative work of all our contributors who lived through both, we think we can attribute the origins of this collection of essays. War and conflict teach us that there is no place to hide, and the analysis of events and of narrative tells us what may happen when the truth is not told.

Thus what follows is a scholarly and writerly book that focuses at least half of its attention on the imaginative and popular literature of the future known as science fiction. But it is also a book haunted by the reality of current events and by our experiences in recent politics.

We are grateful to Kent State University Press and to its director, Dr. John Hubbell, for permission to reprint the essays that originally appeared in the fall 1993 issue of *Extrapolation* (volume 34, number 3); and we are grateful to the Government Department of Georgetown University for support in the preparation of the manuscript. Much of the typing was done by Jennifer Nikolin Ott of Youngstown, Ohio, and we thank her. We appreciate the advice and support of Warren Slesinger, senior editor at the University of South Carolina Press; and we thank our families for their continuing support of our writing and editing.

Introduction
Politics, Art, Collaboration

Donald M. Hassler and Clyde Wilcox

The best science fiction frequently includes a sophisticated depiction of political interactions. In some cases, the politics are secondary to another story line. Future earth governments are shown formulating policy to deal with the first contact with alien species. The government and society of civilizations from other planets are shown as a backdrop for adventure stories. Interplanetary federations debate the future of worlds while space wars rage. In other cases, politics is a central theme. This is most evident in utopian and dystopian stories and novels, but the novels of many of the greatest writers—Isaac Asimov, Robert A. Heinlein, Frank Herbert, Ursula Le Guin, and Frederik Pohl (to name but a few)—are frequently centered on political bargaining and conflict in future, sometimes alien worlds.

Political science often addresses many of the same questions as those raised in science fiction. Political theorists debate the role of the state and speculate about the nature of a just society. Their theories are sometimes fleshed out into hypothetical societies by those who write of political and social utopias. Theorists also write of the role of various social elements such as class and gender in the conduct of the state, and conduct "thought experiments" in which they imagine a world without these distinctions. Once again, science fiction writers frequently imagine worlds in which species change genders at will, in which class is irrelevant, in which various religious groups such as fundamentalist Christians or Muslims rule. Political theorists and science fiction writers alike are also continually aware of the role language itself plays in politics. Political theorists use a variety of techniques to determine how meaning is embedded in language, and how that meaning structures the way we think about politics. Science fiction writers also focus on language, both subtly and more overtly.

Thus the art of fiction and the art of data collecting and exposition in political science seem to us to contain remarkable affinities, and both are human creations. In fact, what is of greatest interest to us, and we hope to our readers as well, is exactly this interface between the inventions of humankind that we call art, on the one hand, and the accumulation and analysis of data about the human and community experience that we call social science on the other. Asimov's important essay on "Social Science Fiction" (1953) alludes to a part of this interface just as its title pivots in nice wordplay around the difference between social science and the literature or art of science fiction. The fulcrum is the word "science," of course, and it balances fiction, or fictions, against the real society. Such a balance is precisely what this book attempts, and our partnership on this project may symbolize the interface and prepare for the variety of voices to follow in the essays.

Another important factor for the introduction of what follows has to do with the "time," or timing, we experience as readers near the end of this century. The images from the fictionists that are social science and political images as well as the political images themselves of the second half of our century are deeply bedded in our imaginations. Nuclear diplomacy, Vietnam, environmental issues, abortion, living wills, the year of the woman, even the space program are all solid facts in our experience that one can study as a social scientist or "muse" over in the imaginative way of the arts. We think it is significant that several of the essays that follow deal with one or another of the *Star Trek* fictions, and we have produced another special issue of *Extrapolation* (similar to the one that generated this book) on *Star Trek*. We started watching that series just a few years prior to the first moon landing, and we have not stopped. We are speaking here about ourselves personally and about social scientists and hard scientists and science fiction fans.

The foundations for this collection of essays, however, lie not just with personal taste and with the good luck of timing. Much of science fiction itself must be written by inspired amateurs who are spread-eagled between their science and their fiction. To use Asimov as example again, he was a biochemist as well as a professional writer; but he had to be technically "amateur" about most that he wrote since he wrote so much. Similarly, both of us as "amateurs" in the field of the other have been amazed at some of the correlations between Aristotle's ideas on politics and his ideas on literature. Perhaps the art of science fiction, the conventions of politics in our time, and the hard sense of possibility that all of us have in politics (and in fiction) do have a more general correlation that is grounded in the nature of things; and no thinker has been more inclined "to move to the general" in order to uncover valid generalizations or natural law than Aristotle. Furthermore, we tend to think of ourselves as "moderns" and, certainly as scientists, the latest materials are the most relevant to us—otherwise as either scientist or literary critic we would not offer up a new book to further the general understanding. But Aristotle as the ancient and most venerable of authorities is, paradoxically, quite a modern; and it is on his authority that we ought finally to ground the mix in this book of invention and reality, of art and science.

Aristotle's use of the word *polis* refers to the very small and homogeneous community of the city-states that he knew, and the editor of our text, Ernest Barker, argues that Aristotle was probably suspicious of the political innovations of his student Alexander toward the creation of the larger state, the *cosmopolis*. But Aristotle believed that mankind "invented" the *polis;* and more than that initial invention he had a profound vision of invention in nature as changing, even evolving. Thus for Aristotle the move to the more cosmopolitan, the wider *polis*, was natural and even inevitable if it were linked to mankind's skill at invention.

The two main themes in this book are on the one hand the sense of expansion toward a wider, more cosmopolitan society, a sense of the *polis* that Aristotle never imagined which includes aliens and not just barbarians, and on the other hand the need for conscious invention and art. Some of our writers are Aristotelian even in the smaller sense of admiring the invention of the strong political leader, the "monarch"; but all of our writers are fascinated both with change and with the need for some self-conscious control or "invention" of changes. A further implication from our favorite "oldest" authority or "author" is that true invention is always a collaborative effort. We work with nature, our natures, to invent what is to come next in history. This is Aristotle's view of evolution (so much more intentionalist and Lamarckian than Darwinian), and even in the *Poetics* he strongly dislikes too much emphasis on "character" itself at the expense of "action"—or the general and useful idea. In any case, no book is more collaboration than a collection of separate voices such as we have here.

We open with a personal witness of sorts from one of the most "political" and one of the most enjoyable living writers of science fiction.

Our longest section is the next section on theory in which all of the facets of the interfaces are touched: voice and art, collaboration, power and political leadership, even philosophical anarchy that would seem to deny any Aristotelian intervention of "invention." But even theory of anarchy requires the need to invent the telling about it. The final section of the book speaks to the most practical sense of possibility that our writers find in the fictions. Specific issues and specific inventions imagined in the literature having to do with a wide *polis* and an inventive nature range from extrapolations out of actual Latin American situations to the farthest distant voyages of the starship *Enterprise*—and beyond.

We believe that a familiarity with science fiction can help political scientists broaden the scope of their theories, and that focus on political themes in science fiction can help English department faculty broaden their appreciation for a good deal of the best science fiction. We therefore have assembled a diverse set of authors who vary widely in their backgrounds and interests. Frederik Pohl is one of the best-known science fiction writers, and his work consistently explores political themes. Several of our contributors are English professors with a good deal of experience in the science fiction area, others are political scientists who are interested in science fiction and bring to it the theories and methods of their discipline.

June Deery examines one of the most interesting of utopian science fiction texts, H. G. Wells's *A Modern Utopia*. She explores the textual and imaginative qualities of the book, and suggests that the weaving of explicit, nonfictional commentary with fictional dramatization, the embedded levels of narrative, and other elements make this an intriguing but flawed work.

Neil Easterbrook's fascinating essay explores the role of the state and politics in Heinlein's *The Moon is a Harsh Mistress*, Le Guin's *The Dispossessed*, and Samuel R. Delany's *Triton*. All three novels detail the struggle of an anarchic political system on one or more moons against the more traditional political system of the parent planet. Each explores the relationship of political systems (ranging from authoritarian to anarchic) and individual freedom. Easterbrook argues that each book provides a vital and sophisticated political commentary, and that taken together, the works expand our understanding of anarchic political theory.

Next, Carol S. Franko's essay hinges on the dilemma faced by feminists, who insist on the importance of the "I" in collective movements,

4

for all collective action ignores the needs of individuals, and the importance of the "we" to moving from selfish individual liberation to collective political action. The discourse between these two concepts is examined in two utopian novels—Wells's *When the Sleeper Wakes* and Le Guin's *The Lathe of Heaven*.

Patrick Novotny takes a postmodern reading of cyberpunk novels and stories, arguing that the genre contests the assumption of technological utopias that were common in earlier science fiction. He suggests that cyberpunk is best suited to examine postmodern themes such as disintegration, fragmentation, heteroglossia, implosion, and dissolution. Peter Minowitz explores the politics of the classic *Dune* series, using insights from classical political theory. The theory section concludes with Josephine Carubia Glorie's examination of the role of feminist utopian fiction as social critique. She suggests that the obvious contrast between the present and fictional worlds is not the only source of critique. In addition, many feminist utopian works suggest a world in which social and political conditions permit an ongoing, internal critique of the utopian culture. The conditions that permit this internal critique are critical to the success of most feminist utopian societies, and have been consciously created as a feminist method for political change.

In the next section, after an opening essay, Ingrid Kreksch shows that much of Latin American science fiction is influenced by the myriad political systems of the region, and by the eternal conflict between the military and civilian actors. She also shows how the Latin American view of an international system dominated by the United States is reflected in science fiction descriptions of galactic politics. Paul Manuel examines the depictions of alien governments in the original and new *Star Trek* series. He focuses special attention on the Klingons and Romulans, which are depicted as authoritarian cultures with little room for interest articulation. Everett Dolman defends Heinlein against charges that this and other works are fascist and militarist. He argues that Heinlein shows a military that enhances democratic values. His careful analysis suggests that Heinlein oversimplified a more complex vision of a democracy with a special role for military forces. Kathy Ferguson, Gilad Ashkenazi, and Wendy Schultz examine the gender politics of the original and later *Star Trek* series. They argue that *Star Trek: The Next Generation* sometimes succeeds in allowing the denaturalization of conventional gender boundaries and identities, which allows us to imagine a differently gendered world. And finally, Mark Lagon examines the changing view of military intervention in the original and new *Star Trek* series. He argues that changes in the international political system have created very different interpretations of the political role of the Federation in interplanetary politics. His chapter focuses on the Prime Directive, a general policy of nonintervention that was routinely violated in the original series but more rigidly adhered to in the new series.

Thus the essays which follow depict a wide politics of the possible— a vast sense of "possibilities" conveyed by science fiction as well as an analysis of the "arts," sometimes arts of rhetoric, that help us navigate the possibilities. By no means do these essays exhaust the topic. Rather they open an extremely interesting set of interfaces between the literature of science fiction and the world of politics. Just as Aristotle, whom we evoke above, was intensely interested in both literature and politics, so we look at the same topics and, further, by means of science fiction, turn our vision to the future.

Works Cited

Aristotle. 1968. *Poetics, A Translation and Commentary by Leon Golden and O. B. Hardison, Jr.* New York: Prentice-Hall.

———. 1958. *The Politics,* edited and translated by Ernest Barker. New York: Oxford University Press.

Asimov, Isaac. 1971. "Social Science Fiction." In *Science Fiction: The Future,* edited by Dick Allen (New York: Harcourt Brace). Originally published in *Modern Science Fiction,* edited by Reginald Bretnor (New York: Coward-McCann, 1953).

Chapter 1

The Politics of Prophecy

Frederik Pohl

To speak of "political science fiction" is almost to commit a tautology, for I would argue that there is very little science fiction, perhaps even that there is no *good* science fiction at all, that is not to some degree political.

Of the making of definitions of science fiction there is no end. Still, however we define the term, I think that most of us would be forced to agree with Tom Shippey that, at bottom, science fiction is a literature of change. That "change" can be of many kinds. It may be revolutionary or evolutionary, in the stories that set themselves in the future of our own human race; it may concern life-styles which are different from our own because they arise from different origins, as in the stories that deal with extraterrestrial aliens; it may concern the changes that might have arisen in alternate "paratime" worlds of the present or past if certain decisions had been taken, or certain events had occurred, in a different way in our own history. As far as I can see, this is a diagnostic trait of science fiction. There simply is no other way to write it.

Some twenty or more years ago I had a discussion on this subject with the late English science fiction writer John T. Phillifent (most of whose works appeared under his pen name of "John Rackham"). Toward the end of our correspondence, John wrote with some excitement that he had at last arrived at the one factor that was common to all science fiction and absent in all other literatures: just as the factor which made organized science different from the hobbyist gathering of facts and specimens and the unfettered speculation of the amateur was the "scientific method," so, John announced, science fiction was uniquely that sort of writing that was written according to "the science-fiction method."

Unfortunately John died before he could say just what his "science-fiction method" was, but I believe it would have been related to the process I described above. As I see it, science fiction writers do universally use a single method in devising their stories. First they look at the world around them in all its parts. Then they take some of those parts out and throw them away and replace them with new parts of their own imagining. Then they reassemble this changed world and start it going to see how it works; and that is the background to every science fiction story I know.

And every time a writer creates one of these different worlds, he or she makes a political statement, for he or she offers—deliberately or inadvertently—the readers the chance to compare his or her invented world with the real one around them. Of course, it is not often inadvertent. Most of the better writers, at least, know full well what they are about, and the political statement they make is fully intended. As a case in point, when Ray Bradbury was once asked if he thought the gritty, mean world of *Fahrenheit 451* was meant as a prediction, he replied, "Hell, no. I'm not trying to *predict* the future. I'm just doing my best to *prevent* it." And that, of course, is where the politics comes in. It is politics that determines what societies will do, and thus it is politics that shapes, and reflects, change.

Overtly political science fiction has been with us for a long time; *Gulliver's Travels* is only one of the early masterpieces of the class. Jonathan Swift did not care to say what he thought of the politicians who surrounded the current English royalty in clear language, so he invented the Lilliputians, the Brobdingnagians, and the Houhyhnhms to make his point.

More than that, science fiction has actually taken a part in creating political change, and one of its most effective ways of doing so is by offering new models to its readers. For example, consider how science fiction has encouraged the change of attitudes in race relations. They tell me that when Captain Kirk kissed Lieutenant Uhura on *Star Trek* it broke an ancient tabu. That was said to be the first interracial kiss on television, and perhaps it has played some part in the increased—perhaps only very slightly increased—tolerance for black-and-white love affairs in the real world.

And then there is the case of Robert A. Heinlein. Everything Bob Heinlein ever wrote is laced with overt political subtexts—the exaltation of the military, the Heinleinian notion that the privilege of voting should be limited to those who earn it—but perhaps one of his most influential political statements is masked. This came to my attention early this year when I happened to be having a conversation with a Texan acquaintance who said he wanted to tell me a story. I don't have his permission to give his real name, so let me call him "Bill." Bill had been born into a Joe-Sixpack, blue-collar family in East Texas. They were white, and they were proud of it. They took their skin color to be a sign of the special favor of their God. White was right; other skin colors weren't, in their view. Of course, there were plenty of black people around in East Texas, but Bill's family never considered them as social equals. Their black neighbors were not even thought of as blacks, much less African-Americans; they were plainly and simply niggers. In Bill's view, and in his family's and that of all his friends, niggers were clearly a lesser race, partly comically contemptible and partly just subhuman and bad.

Bill grew up with that mindset fixed in his consciousness, but somehow Bill discovered science fiction. He was thrilled by the adventure and excitement of the stories. He read everything he could get his hands on. He was a particular fan of Heinlein, and then, well into one of Heinlein's novels, Bill came across a scene in which the hero looked at himself in the mirror, and Bill discovered that this hero whose persona he had adopted for his own was—horrors!—a *black* man.

Bill said to me, "That was just about the biggest shock I ever had. It hit me hard. I had some friends who read science fiction, too. When they read the story they had the same shock, and what they did then was to throw the book away, refuse to read any more. They were just plain disgusted. It had a different effect on me. It occurred to me, for the first time in my life, that black people were as human as I. And I was never able to go back to the old ways."

Sometimes the political models in science fiction are dystopias—what Kingsley Amis called "comic infernos" in his landmark study of the field, *New Maps of Hell*—and their political effect is to show how inevitably destructive one possible pathway into the future might be. *Nineteen Eighty-Four* was like that, and it may have had a great effect.

There are people who maintain that one important reason why the year 1984, when it came, was nothing like the one described in George Orwell's novel was because the novel had warned its readers of what they must do their best to avert. And I think it at least a possibility that Nevil Shute's *On the Beach*, in both its forms as novel and as film, played a significant part in warning us away from that all-out nuclear Armageddon that might have, and perhaps still might, put an end once and for all to all dreams of human perfectibility.

Then there is the matter of Green politics. As some of you are aware, I'm pretty much a Green, in that I think we human beings are committing great acts of folly in the way we are destroying the world we live in—with our bashing of our air and water, our destruction of the ozone layer, our heedless, senseless addiction to the burning of fossil fuels, and our folly's apparent threatening of the whole world through global warming. I've written about it in my own science fiction stories. I've even—with the late Isaac Asimov—written a nonfiction book on the subject, *Our Angry Earth;* I care about it very much, and I think I have been led in that direction largely because of my lifelong interest in science fiction. After all, Rachel Carson's *Silent Spring*—canonically one of the first calls to environmental arms—is itself really a science fiction novel, though one without characters or plot. But long before she wrote it, science fiction writers were already calling attention to the dangers to the environment—as, for instance, in my own (or I should say "our own," since it was a collaboration with the late Cyril Kornbluth) *The Space Merchants.* I think it would be very nearly fair to suggest that the environmental movement in America actually began with science fiction.

Then there is that unique political role science fiction has always played. I am talking about science fiction as political cryptogram, about the use of science fiction to say things in hint and metaphor that the writer dares not say in clear. Sometimes these stories take the form of satire; this is what Jonathan Swift was up to in *Gulliver's Travels,* and Voltaire in his neglected science fiction novella *Micromegas.* Swift wrote about undiscovered races here on Earth, Voltaire about a visitor from the stars; but what both were really discussing were the follies and wickedness of the Europe of their own times, and their readers had no difficulty in decoding what they wanted to say.

It is under repressive regimes that this sort of science fiction flourishes. We could see that happening very clearly in the old, pre-Gorbachev Soviet Union, where there wasn't an awful lot of freedom of speech around. To say anything critical of the society or the government was to invite a one-way ticket to the gulag. One way the suffering artists of the old Soviet Union dealt with the problem was through *samizdat* or its electronic cousin *magnetizdat*, the recording of forbidden material on illegal tape cassettes. There were no such things as mimeograph machines or even photocopiers available for such purposes (the few that did exist were kept under lock and key), so dedicated individuals would type up copies of prohibited works, putting as many sheets of carbon paper as they could handle in the machines, and pass them around from hand to hand. I've seen some examples of *samizdat*, and they are sometimes astonishingly beautiful, handsomely bound volumes—but tend to be a little hard to read when you get down to the fifth or sixth carbon.

But *samizdat* wasn't enough. Writers wanted actual print publication and distribution, and of all the kinds of literature available in that constrained Soviet world there were only two varieties that ever dared to discuss the harsh and threadbare realities behind the state-invented gloss. One of them was poetry. The other was science fiction.

Even in those two cases the freedom the writers possessed was chancy and sharply limited; it rested on their use of metaphor and analogy to say, in code, the things that no one dared say in clear. Their success in avoiding the harsh penalties attached to free speech rested pretty heavily on the fact that the censors were not smart enough to understand just what the writers were saying. But their readers did understand, and that was one of the reasons why such were among the most popular authors in the USSR.

It's hard to convey just how influential and widely read the Strugatsky brothers were. They reached every part of the Soviet society. You could never hope to go into a bookstore and find any work of theirs on the shelf, but it was not because they were unpublished. It was because their readers were too hungry for that. Although the Strugatskys' stories were printed in large editions, often in the hundreds of thousands of copies, every last copy that came off the press was ordered, long before publication date, by some eager customer, probably one who had gone to some trouble to make friends with the store clerks. Otherwise the quest was hopeless. If the books came into the store in a morning they had all been snapped up before the store closed that night. Unfortunately, the Strugatskys' immunity from the leaden hand of censorship didn't last, for even the censors were not quite sufficiently dull to miss the hidden meanings of their work forever. Toward the end of their careers the Strugatskys began to lose their immunity. Sometimes their works were flatly refused publication. (Once on a visit to Moscow I was offered the chance to smuggle a new novelette of theirs out to the West, since it had been rejected by the Soviet censors; I was persuaded not to do it because it was made clear to me that the Soviet friend who offered it to me surely would have been caught and penalized for his part in the project.) Sometimes their books were allowed publication, in spite of their suspect qualities, but only under such circumstances that what they had to say was so distorted that it no longer made sense.

The Strugatskys' late novel, *The Snail on the Slope,* was a case in point. The Strugatskys had elected to write it in the form of two parallel narratives told in alternate chapters. In order to understand their meaning, the stories had to be read in that form. But by then the work of the Strugatskys had begun to arouse considerable suspicion, even among the party hacks who were charged with preventing the publication of "anti-Soviet" literature. They took measures. The censors did not go so far as to forbid publication completely. Indeed, the censors permitted *The Snail on the Slope* to be published—all of it—but not all of it in one place. The two intertwined stories were surgically separated, and they were published in two different magazines, at two different times, in order to blunt their political thrust.

In many repressive societies all over the world, science fiction has been used for political statements. It has even happened, in fact, here in the United States. I don't know how many of you remember the chill on free speech that was imposed by the Joseph McCarthy period in the early 1950s. "Tail-Gunner Joe" terrified the media, the schools, the Pentagon, and even the White House, and few dared speak freely. But science fiction writers went on saying just about whatever they chose, which led to some odd consequences. For example, in Los Angeles there was a minister named Stephen Fritchman who thought there was much to be said in criticism of American society at that time and mourned the fact that so few were willing to say it. So he began the practice of buying science fiction magazines and putting them on sale in his vestry after his Sunday services, because, Reverend Fritchman said, magazines like *Galaxy* and the others represented the only truly free speech left in America.

If we agree that science fiction often has a political subtext, is it possible to say just what that text is? It is certainly not the official dogma of any political party. The political affiliations of science fiction writers are as diverse as those of any random selection of Americans; there are Democrats and Republicans, libertarians and socialists, warhawks and peaceniks—even a few anarchists, and at least one old-fashioned royalist. Yet there is, I think, a common political thread that unites nearly all of them and shows itself, in some form, in nearly every science fiction story written.

I first realized this nearly thirty years ago, when I was editor of the science fiction magazine *Galaxy* and American passions were running high over our involvement in the war in Vietnam. Some thirty-odd science fiction writers decided they needed to take overt political action on that subject. So they got together, pooled their money, and bought a full-page ad in the magazine. They included some of the best science fiction writers of the time, and what their ad said was a plea to get America out of that Indo-Chinese bloodbath—immediately and without reservation. Then, when other writers with different political views heard of that ad, they got together. They bought another full-page ad, this one calling on the United States to hold to its treaty agreements with the Vietnamese government and remain in Vietnam to prosecute that war until it was won; and the list of their signatories, too, included some of the best science fiction writers of the time.

When I looked over the names signed to the two ads, something struck me as curious. I knew nearly every person quite well—well enough, I thought, to be able to form a pretty clear idea of what sort of world each of them would like to see by, say, the year 2100 . . . and I did not believe there was really a nickel's worth of difference among them. Almost without exception, their ideal world was one that was without racial prejudice or extreme poverty; it would allow freedom of speech and action to everyone; and it would be marked by heavy investment in scientific research and exploration. Whichever side of the present controversy they chose, their long-range dreams of a better world were, in many respects, almost indistinguishable, and these consensual notions were the political subtext that underlay most of their work. What divided them was only the choice of tactics to be employed in reaching those goals. I don't mean to say that all these people were saintly, only that their harshest angers—and they sometimes had plenty of those—were aimed at those they thought were perversely wrong-headed in those tactics.

If we suppose—as I think most of us do—that science fiction is something more than mere escapist entertainment, it is because we believe that at its best science fiction gives its readers some new and otherwise unobtainable insights into our world—in fact, into all our possible worlds. I do believe that. I think that through science fiction we can see, for instance, how many of the customs and "truths" we live by are logically inevitable, and thus "right," and how many are mere accidents of decisions taken, or even of our mammalian biology and the physical constraints of the particular planet on which we happened to evolve. Science fiction is the only literature we have that can give us this objective perspective on our human affairs—what Harlow Shapley once, in a considerably different context, called "The View from a Distant Star."

When science fiction writers explore the implications of what that God's-eye view of our world reveals, they enter many touchy areas. That can't be avoided. Most writers don't even try to avoid it, and this is true not only of those writers who set out to explore large questions, but even of the authors of the space operas and the pulpy adventure stories of the 1920s and 1930s. If we look, we will find social and political comment in some unlikely places. Edgar Rice Burroughs's Barsoom novels were full of political satire—for example, his send-up of organized religion in *The Master Mind of Mars*, where religious dogma was summed up in the invocation "Tur is Tur," a mantra that, as its priests pointed out, was just as powerful and true when said backwards. Political satire, too, was a major element in the works of Stanton A. Coblentz. And even Doc Smith's ground-breaking father of all space operas, *The Skylark of Space*, was not without its social comment; witness its scathing portrayal, legitimately inherited from the muckraking period in which it was written, of the evil giant industrial corporation Steel. There are political messages in works as diverse as S. Fowler Wright's *The World Below* and David H. Keller's "The Revolt of the Pedestrians."

Sometimes the political content is only a minor theme in a larger design; sometimes it is quite obscure—it is difficult to know, for instance, just what political view Rudyard Kipling was proselytizing in *As Easy As A.B.C.*, though the story is drenched with politics. But we don't have to get out our decoder rings to find the political message in some of the best science fiction. The messages are quite explicit. Joanna Russ's *The Female Man* is a very good and well-written novel, but it is also an unmistakable political tract of the radical-feminist variety. Ursula K. Le Guin's *The Dispossessed* is a sort of anarchist utopia (though a downbeat one, since its ultimate message is that her society is doomed). Heinlein's *The Moon Is a Harsh Mistress* also has an anarchist message.

14

In my personal view, *The Moon Is a Harsh Mistress* is just about the best novel Heinlein ever wrote, and part of its charm is the fully functioning political structure he erected around his story. He left nothing out. His society, it is impossible to doubt while you are reading the novel, would *work*—even, perhaps, his invention of the "line marriage." As conceived by Heinlein, the line marriage is an attractive compromise between the traditional daddy-mommy-and-kids so dear to, for example, Dan Quayle, and the amorphous commune-type relationships of the hippy 1960s. It starts out conventionally enough. Boy meets Girl; Boy falls in love with Girl; they marry. They even, perhaps, have a child or two. But they don't stop there. Perhaps a year or two later they come across a very attractive and congenial Girl No. 2, or Boy No. 2. In conventional society the consequence of that is either divorce or adultery— or maybe loyal rejection of the outsider. The line-married don't have to get into such stressful problems. They simply propose to the third party, and if she/he agrees, they marry her/him as well; and then maybe they meet and so marry a fourth party, and a fifth, and as many as they like, until they have a family of a dozen or more adults, all married to each other, all sharing whatever children happen to come along.

Would that work out in real life? I don't know. I do know that the experiment has been tried. Not long after the publication of *The Moon Is a Harsh Mistress* news reports began to appear of group marriages of that sort being practiced in Scandinavia and elsewhere. It was never explicitly said, at least not in my hearing, that reading Heinlein's novel had inspired any of the attempts to put its ideas into practice, but the timing was, at least, interestingly coincidental. And maybe Heinlein's utopia wouldn't have worked out, after all. At least it appears that, on mature consideration, Heinlein himself didn't think so, because he returned to the world of *Moon* in one of those huge omnium-gatherum novels about his hero Lazarus Long he wrote toward the end of his life and reported his world as doomed as Le Guin's.

It is fair to ask if the political aspects of all this political science fiction are deliberately inserted by the author. Fair to ask, but hard to answer, for attempting to untangle an author's purposes is one of the high-risk activities of literary criticism. However, there is one author whose intentions I do know something about—much of the time, anyway—and that is myself. Many of my own works, including some of the ones I like best, are overtly political, even propagandistic in their central themes. *The Years of the City* is an explicit attempt to describe the stages of political evolution in America over the next century or two; the starting assumptions of *Jem* deal with what I imagined to be the future of international politics after the Cold War had run its course.

If it is chancy for a critic to try to discern an author's purposes, it is even more adventurous for a writer to assume that what is true of himself must be common among all other writers. Still, I do not doubt that every writer does necessarily put something of himself into everything he writes; that personally unique and idiosyncratic view of the world is really all that any writer has to sell. Indeed, as some perceptive person—identity unfortunately not known to me—once pointed out, the true and proper title of any book should be *How to Be More Like Me*. And, of course, in this political age (with frequent political change institutionalized in countries like the United States, irregular and sometimes extraordinarily violent in others), our politics is one of the ways by which we define ourselves.

So it is inevitable that politics should be a part of science fiction. And fortunately so, I think, for how much better it is to attempt to work out the consequences of political change in a science fiction story than to play them out in the bloodier, harsher, and less-forgiving real world we live in.

Works Cited

Amis, Kingsley. 1960. *New Maps of Hell*. New York: Harcourt Brace.

Asimov, Isaac and Frederik Pohl. 1991. *Our Angry Earth: A Ticking Ecological Bomb*. New York: Tor Books.

Bradbury, Ray. 1953. *Fahrenheit 451*. New York: Ballantine.

Burroughs, Edgar Rice. 1928. *The Master Mind of Mars*. Chicago: McClurg.

Carson, Rachel. 1962. *Silent Spring*. Reprint, Boston: Houghton Mifflin, 1987.

Havens, George R., ed. 1925. *Selections from Voltaire*. New York: Appleton.

Heinlein, Robert A. 1966. *The Moon Is a Harsh Mistress*. New York: Putnam.

———. 1959. *Starship Troopers*. New York: Putnam.

———. 1973. *Time Enough for Love: The Lives of Lazarus Long*. New York: Putnam.

Keller, David H. 1976. "The Revolt of the Pedestrians." In *The Street of Queer Houses and Other Tales*. Edited by Robert Reginald and Douglas Menville. New York: Ayer.

Le Guin, Ursula K. 1975. *The Dispossessed*. New York: Ace.

Orwell, George. 1949. *Nineteen Eighty-Four*. New York: Harcourt Brace.

Pohl, Frederik. 1979. *Jem*. New York: St Martin's.

———. 1984. *The Years of the City*. New York: Simon & Schuster.

Pohl and C. M. Kornbluth. 1974. *The Space Merchants*. 1953. New York: Ballantine.

Russ, Joanna. 1975. *The Female Man*. New York: Bantam.

Shippey, Tom. 1992. *The Oxford Book of Science Fiction Stories*. London: Oxford.

Shute, Nevil. 1957. *On the Beach*. New York: Morrow.

Smith, E. E. 1946. *The Skylark of Space*. Reprint, New York: Pyramid, 1958.

Strugatsky, Boris, and Arkady Strugatsky. 1980. *The Snail on the Slope*.

Swift, Jonathan. 1726. *Gulliver's Travels*. 1938. Edited by Arthur E. Case. New York: Ronald Press.

Wright, S. Fowler. 1929. *The World Below*. London: Collins.

Chapter 2

Swift, Pohl, and Kornbluth
Publicists Anatomize Newness

Donald M. Hassler

The career of Frederik Pohl in science fiction has been associated
with, and even inspired by, politics from the start. As he tells us in his
memoir *The Way the Future Was*, he and other teenage science fiction
fans in New York City such as Isaac Asimov and Cyril Kornbluth were
hopefully involved in meetings of what they called "The Futurians,"
dealing with a nice mix of literature and politics. In recent years, he has
made trips to Russia and has cultivated friendly relations with the Soviet Writers Union as he speaks of eloquently in the Afterword to his
recent political novel *Chernobyl*: "A particularly visible sign of such
change [toward honest writing on politics] is Mikhail Gorbachev's continuing sponsorship of a policy of *glasnost*, or candor and honesty. . . . I
believe it was again because of *glasnost* that I received the great assistance and cooperation that was extended to me when I returned to the
Soviet Union to complete my research for this novel" (355).

But I think Pohl's writing on politics hit an early peak in collaboration with Kornbluth. Pohl himself has continued to nurture the memories of his friend following Kornbluth's unfortunate early death in 1958
as he writes here, decades later, about the tone of voice in an early political novel by Kornbluth, "I think it's fair to say that *The Syndic* is most

truly Cyril's own voice speaking, in tones no other writer has quite succeeded in capturing" (9). But it is their early tone together in collaboration, and the classic political satire contained in that tone, that I will
treat in this essay.

No prose writer in English, with the possible exception of Mark
Twain, is more often remembered as a precursor for and master of political satire than Jonathan Swift.[1] Frederik Pohl evokes Swift in precisely
this context now and then as, for example, in his chapter in this book. In
fact, one might argue that it is Swift who first sets the argument in several of his key prose satires that provides the foundation both for the
open-ended way of thinking that has allowed notions of change,
progress, and changing politics to be so widely speculated upon (most
recently in science fiction texts) as well as for the satiric criticism of that
open-endedness.

Since the Enlightenment and since the liberating possibilities of the
technology revolutions that resulted from the Enlightenment such as
our near-instant global communications systems, we have carried with
us a profoundly mixed attitude toward newness as well as toward our
clever, persuasive skills that translate into the most practical politics.
We have found that good writers can convince us of most anything, and
the more open-ended our thinking the more receptive we are to being
convinced. Today we call that persuasive skill advertising or public relations. In Swift's day, it was called writing about new projects and the
writers were "projectors." Writing about new projects was a direct out-
growth of the Enlightenment tolerance for new possibilities assisted by
new technology in publishing and communications. Implicit in such
writing is the horrifying notion that nothing is good or bad but that the
telling makes it so. And a further horrifying implication in this persuasive writing is the need to be bland and "scientific" about all possibilities because, indeed, we need to learn to do this in order not to be shocked
by the near infinite range of new possibility. This is exactly the horror
when Swift's narrator in A Modest Proposal (1729) speaks so calmly and
with so much data about his new "project" for the use of Irish children.
Similarly, everyday TV news stories today almost seem like self-satire.
Swift was a master in the use of the new "scientific" prose to make convincing points about new possibilities, and he made fun both of the newness and of the manner of flat, bland prose.[2]

I will show that The Space Merchants, Pohl and Kornbluth's classic
science fiction novel from the early 1950s, is Swiftian in sardonic atti-

tudes and even in some specific images. More than that important work, however, other early collaborations of these two seem to indicate a Swiftian, even Scriblerian, imprint that we can be grateful for and that may tell us, also, something more about the difference between science fiction and high art.[3] During the rage for autobiographical writing that affected the old pros in science fiction in the late 1970s, Pohl uncovered a good bit about the collaborations among the Futurians. There was considerable genius, experimentation, interest in literature, and sharing of ideas among these early New York science fiction fans.[4] In *The Way the Future Was*, Pohl tells of his first fanzine, that contained mostly poetry (33). He recalls trying all modes of verse with Kornbluth before they wrote any science fiction (65). Both of them, along with James Blish, shared an interest in the work-in-progress of James Joyce (14, 33). And Pohl mentions a number of canonical writers that he likes, including Voltaire (18). In the memoir sections from two years earlier in *The Early Pohl*, he gives vivid details on the collaboration of genius with Kornbluth and others (8–9, 38–39). These interactions include, even, dating and marriage of friends of Pohl's first wife as well as some details of his experience in the Young Communist League (68–71). The latter is given a chapter entitled "Boy Bolsheviks" in the 1978 autobiography.

I think that if we read histories of the Scriblerian Club and of the Scriblerian collaborations from a little over two centuries earlier, which include the fictional memoirs of Martinus Scriblerus, we can get a clearer sense of what Pohl, Kornbluth, and their Futurian friends were doing.[5] The Scriblerians had a program for speculating on all things, and yet they were suspicious of such open-endedness and also had a program for language awareness that allowed them to repress, to be self-critical, and above all to be sardonic. Thomas D. Clareson in his book-length study of Pohl highlights what he calls the "razor edge" of his wit (29). In *New Maps of Hell*, Kingsley Amis stresses the "Kornbluthian elements" in the later satire of the two (133); and Pohl often refers to Kornbluth as sardonic.

But like the Scriblerians, these young science fiction writers carried immense hopes for changing things. Their genius and their sense of community matured during the Depression years, and so Pohl observes simply that for them the ". . . world was a bad place and technology was a way out" (*The Early Pohl*, 5). He recalls, also, in this memoir that for them full satire did not come until the 1950s with *The Space Merchants*, *Gladiator-at-Law*, and other works ranging through the McCarthy years and essentially ending with Kornbluth's death in 1958. Somehow for them the earlier optimism had to be hidden in the 1950s in a strikingly similar way to how Scriblerians hid possible Jacobite sympathies. Out of the Scriblerian hiding, however, came great works of irony and art such as *Gulliver's Travels, The Beggar's Opera,* and *The Dunciad.* Pohl and Kornbluth might have been following exactly these models as they produced their 1950s masterpieces that gleefully jab at the politics and the new technologies of the time.

But they had telegraphed their lineage and their Scriblerian tendencies long before. An early collaboration called "Trouble in Time" (1940) carried the nom de plume "S. D. Gottesman" that sounds so playful and Swiftian because "God's man," in one sense, expresses nicely the mix of pretentiousness and self-mockery that permeates Swift's own treatment of hack writers in his early *A Tale of a Tub* (1704). Pohl and Kornbluth name a character in this early story "Bickerstaff," who was Swift's famous contribution to *The Tatler,* and Clareson faults the story as being way too "talky" (Clareson 1987, 8). In fact, the free-wheeling parodies, the use of first person, and the self-conscious brilliance about science fiction conventions in the story are Swiftian in the sense that Swift often makes fun of the very writing community that he values.

Two other apparent echoes from Swift can be mentioned before moving on to a fuller treatment of *The Space Merchants.* Kornbluth wrote by himself a long story called "The Marching Morons" (1951), but Pohl reports in *The Best of C. M. Kornbluth,* as he introduces the story, that when they came to collaborate on *Search the Sky* (1954) they both liked the moron story so much that they used it to conclude the novel. The wit in "Morons" turns very much on a similar lashing irony to that in *A Modest Proposal* even to the extent that Hugh Barlow is finally condemned by his own analysis just as Swift's narrator would surely eat his own children if he and his wife were not "past child bearing." Then, in *Gladiator-at-Law* (1954), Pohl and Kornbluth decide to name two fascinating villains who live on only in glass jars, and who thus represent all that our hopeful technology can do for us, after that strange, immortal Struldbruggs in the science-dominated third voyage of Gulliver. Swift is ambivalent about his Struldbruggs, and by the 1950s Pohl and Kornbluth have learned also to be deeply mixed in their satiric tones and in their programs for writing.

In January 1957 Kornbluth gave a lecture at the University of Chicago, later published in *The Science Fiction Novel,* in which he lamented

21

the failure of science fiction as "social criticism." He said he did not want their work to be "socially impotent"; but offered a glimmer of hope (perhaps ironic) that what he and Pohl accomplished in *The Space Merchants* may have had some effect because it received a long review in *The Industrial Worker* (72). Generally, though, he was afraid that such satire does not accomplish much; he mentioned *Gulliver's Travels* as another possible piece of impotency. It would be another study to explore exactly what Swift did accomplish. But as I am suggesting, one accomplishment was to inspire satiric complexity in descendants such as Pohl and Kornbluth. This complexity also must include exactly the ambivalence about effects and even about methods that drove Kornbluth's lecture.

The Space Merchants is narrated in first person by a future ad executive and "copysmith," or writer of ads, who both defends his manipulative profession and learns to see "copysmithing" for the deception that it has become in the Pohl and Kornbluth near-future. Mitchell Courtenay changes somewhat by the conclusion of the novel but is still a copysmith. Since this narrator is a writer and a persuader, and only reluctantly a traveler, he resembles much more Swift's narrator in "An Argument Against Abolishing Christianity" (1711) than he does Gulliver. This less well-known Swiftian narrator is clearly in the business of "selling" a later version of Christianity, removed far in the future from the original church; and he calls himself a "nominal" Christian just as Mitch, the seller of space, calls himself a copysmith, not a writer. Similarly, the real work of writing from the past is unthinkable to Mitch just as "real Christianity" is unthinkable to the Swift narrator. Here is Mitch on poetry, a type of writing that both Pohl and Kornbluth tried to emulate as younger men. He is talking to an astronaut about how his agency can sell the Venus project:

"Words and pictures. Sight and sound and smell and taste and touch. And the greatest of these is words. Do you read poetry?"

"My God, of course not! Who can?"

"I don't mean the contemporary stuff; you're quite right about that. I mean Keats, Swinburne, Wylie—the great lyricists."

"I used to," he cautiously admitted. "What about it?"

"I'm going to ask you to spend the morning and afternoon with

22

one of the world's great lyric poets: a girl named Tildy Mathis. She doesn't know that she's a poet; she thinks she's a boss copywriter." (48)

The major question in this novel, which is similar to the major question in the Swift tract, deals with how society ought to proceed when the optimum goals are impossible. We cannot return to primitive Christianity, but we can go on with an imperfect later development. The planet Venus is terribly inhospitable (and note that this is the same location where Heechee remnants are discovered in later Pohl fiction). Thus the question posed in the novel is whether developing Venus is just a challenge for sales people, like getting the public to consume the Chicken Little that is Pohl and Kornbluth's wonderfully gross future food, or whether "conservationists" really want to develop the awful place. It is a Swiftian dilemma, and it is also the big question about science fiction itself. Is science fiction just fantasy hype about the future, or can the writing in science fiction, as Kornbluth coyly hopes in his later lecture, do something?

Both the possibilities for a positive resolution to the dilemma and the "horror" of the future and of newness seem to be keyed more to statistics than to human efforts. Swift realizes this early because his tract on Christianity, as well as *Gulliver* and other tracts, is filled with economic statistics. The rationale for accepting newness, for selling, for advertising, for keeping "nominal" and new churches is that with newness almost anything remains possible. Mitch realizes this as his narrative and adventures go on and writes, "It had a bloodcurdlingly truthful ring to it. . . . It was true. When there are enough people, you will always find somebody who can and will be any given thing. Taunton [his arch enemy and competitor] was an artist" (Pohl and Kornbluth 1974, 137–38). The January 1993 issue of *Analog* states exactly this argument, fleshed out more statistically and with no irony: "There are now a quarter of a billion Americans. . . . With those numbers our society cannot help but be a bunch of alternative universes; every behavior, every statistical anomaly, should show up in some one of those [high number] segments. Why should we be shocked when we see aberrant behavior in the news?" (77).

Over and over again, of course, Swift was shocked and yet learned to convey this shock at the same time that he conveyed the hope in newness. The early label that Pohl and Kornbluth coined for some of their first stories, "S. D. Gottesman," is a fitting reminder with which to conclude of how Swiftian their irony was intended to be. In the final analysis, Swift is Dean Swift, a man of God; and as Pohl says in his memoir in *Hell's Cartographers*, writers like himself are "divinely discontented" (172). It does not matter which of the two of them first thought to be "God's man." Pohl says it for both himself and Kornbluth. Ironically, it will probably not be God but the statistical success and posterity of the texts themselves, Swift's, Pohl's and Kornbluth's, that will have the final word.

Notes

1. Pohl does mention Mark Twain in his book-length autobiography, *The Way the Future Was*, but the echoes I find most predominant in the early Pohl and Kornbluth are from Swift. For the best of recent scholarly opinion on Swift and especially on the techniques in his prose satires, see the works cited below by Bullitt, Ehrenpreis, and Rawson.
2. This interpretation of the real horror residing in the blandness by which the narrator makes his proposal is widespread in readings of Swift. See Bullitt and Rawson.
3. See my essay on Isaac Asimov and high art. Asimov was also a party to these Futurian collaborations but with less "poetry" leanings and with less of the Swiftian sardonic tone.
4. See my 1985 essay on the autobiographies of Asimov, Jack Williamson, and Pohl, "Children of Rousseau and Wonder."
5. A good comprehensive beginning on the Scriblerians is the edition by Kerby-Miller cited here. Swift was clearly a leader of the group. The two other best-known members were Alexander Pope and John Gay. Several important Tory politicians clubbed on an equal basis with the writers, a further example of the link between writers and politics.

Works Cited

Amis, Kingsley. 1960. *New Maps of Hell*. New York: Harcourt Brace.

Bullitt, John M. 1953. *Jonathan Swift and the Anatomy of Satire*. Cambridge: Harvard University Press.

Clareson, Thomas D. 1987. *Frederik Pohl*. Mercer Island, Washington: Starmont House.

Ehrenpreis, Irvin. 1962–1983. *Swift: The Man, His Work, and the Age*. 3 vols. London: Methuen & Co., 1962 (vols. 1, 2); Cambridge: Harvard University Press, (vol. 3).

Hassler, Donald M. 1985. "Autobiography and Science Fiction: Children of Rousseau and Wonder." *Extrapolation* 26: 277–84.

———. 1987. "Science Fiction and High Art." *Extrapolation* 28: 187–94.

Kerby-Miller, Charles, ed. 1988. *The Memoirs of the Extraordinary Life, Works, and Discoveries of Martinus Scriblerus.* New York: Oxford University Press.

Kornbluth, C. M. 1969. "The Failure of the Science Fiction Novel as Social Criticism." In *The Science Fiction Novel,* edited by Basil Davenport. Chicago: Advent.

———. *The Syndic.* 1982. Introduction and Afterword by Frederik Pohl. New York: Tor.

———. 1959. *The Marching Morons and Other Famous Science Fiction Stories.* New York: Ballantine.

Liss, Jeffrey G. 1993. "Comment." In *Analog, Science Fiction and Fact* 113 (January): 77.

Pohl, Frederik, ed. 1976. *The Best of C. M. Kornbluth.* New York: Ballantine.

———. 1976. *The Early Pohl.* Garden City: Doubleday.

———. 1984. *Heechee Rendezvous.* New York: Ballantine.

———. 1975. "Ragged Claws." In *Hell's Cartographers.* Edited by Brian W. Aldiss and Harry Harrison. London: Weidenfeld & Nicolson.

———. 1978. *The Way the Future Was.* New York: Ballantine.

———. 1987. *Chernobyl.* New York: Bantam.

Pohl and C. M. Kornbluth. 1955. *Gladiator-at-Law.* Reprint, London: Gollancz, 1973.

———. 1954. *Search the Sky.* Reprint, New York: Bantam, 1977.

———. 1953. *The Space Merchants.* Reprint, New York: Ballantine, 1974.

———. 1962. *The Wonder Effect.* New York: Ballantine. Pohl reprints here their story "Trouble in Time" that originally appeared in the December 1940 issue of *Astonishing.*

Rawson, Claude, ed. 1983. *The Character of Swift's Satire.* Newark: University of Delaware Press.

Swift, Jonathan. 1960. *Gulliver's Travels and Other Writings.* Edited by Louis A. Landa. Boston: Houghton Mifflin. Landa is a highly respected Swift scholar, and this is a good, reliable teaching edition that I have used for many years. It contains all the texts mentioned in this essay.

Chapter 3

H. G. Wells's *A Modern Utopia* as a Work in Progress

June Deery

As a literary artifact, H. G. Wells's *A Modern Utopia* is quite extraordinary, even bizarre. Yet as with much commentary on utopian literature that is largely characterized by its focus on conceptual content,
Wells's critics have paid this literary experiment little heed, not even to
the extent of seriously investigating its flaws. Kenneth Roemer is puzzled
by this. He observes that "Wells's attempts to revise the literary form of
utopia," which, whatever the results, would be a significant undertak-
ing in what is largely a conservative tradition, "have been ignored" by
those who examine this text (Roemer 1982, 118). This despite the fact
that, as Patrick Parrinder recommended some years ago, nowadays "it
is for its textual and imaginative qualities, rather than for its ideas, that
the book repays rereading" (Parrinder 1990, 116).

Previous studies by Roemer and David Y. Hughes did undertake
this kind of rereading, but little else has been written from this perspective.[1] Hughes and Roemer offer excellent analyses of different narrative
voices and their relation to the author. What I want to focus on is the
peculiar fictionality, and indeed metafictionality, of the text—its variegated surface and its peculiar contradictions. This is where *A Modern
Utopia* becomes intriguingly contemporary for present-day readers and

reveals much about what has been and what can be done in its own genre, the utopia.[2] The more one looks at this text, the more extraordinary it appears. Seen in its historical context, it is obviously an exceptional and in many ways anticipatory work; it is not simply another discussion novel in the Peacockian vein but something Wells fabricated after considering several formal schemes.[3]

Generally speaking, the relation between fictional and nonfictional elements is quite fascinating in utopian literature, despite the utopist's often perfunctory use of fictional techniques. Wells, however, did think this aspect worthy of notice, and it is specific textual features, not ideological content or the relation between this text and Wells's other works, that will be examined here. Judging the text from a narratological basis, it is both clever and weak, ambitious and flawed.

I refer to *A Modern Utopia* as a work in progress first in two obvious senses. In common with many utopias, it is about progress, that is, about social and technological advance as opposed to the more retrospective paradises of ancient mythology. Wells also stresses that he is describing a dynamic utopia, a society that requires and allows further improvement: "the Modern Utopia must be not static but kinetic, must shape not as a permanent state but as a hopeful stage, leading to a long ascent of stages" (5). In other words, as his previous publication suggests, "Mankind" is still "in the Making." This, he feels, is a necessary safeguard against the static and totalitarian schemes of past utopists. But *A Modern Utopia* is also a work in progress in a more literary sense in that the reader is presented with a work which, it appears, is in the process of being written. It is thus not only a piece of writing but a discourse about writing, not only a utopia but a work that encourages the reader to think about the whole process of utopianizing. Its very title announces its fictionality, and it is this self-referentiality—the awareness of the text as text and of the utopia as utopia—that makes it particularly interesting for contemporary readers. While Sir Thomas More originally hid his work's fictionality under cover of the Greek neologism "utopia,"[4] Wells's *A Modern Utopia* more obviously professes its membership in a by now self-conscious (Western, male) literary tradition; indeed, there are numerous intertextual nods to its literary forebears, everyone from More and William Morris to Cabet and Campanella (8). It is, as Lewis Mumford remarked, the "quintessential" utopia (Mumford 1962, 184)—and consciously so. As its title declares, it is both commemorative and innovative, the self-conscious modern expression of a long tradition.

In this "text" (etymologically "woven piece"), Wells sought to weave the warp of explicit, nonfictional commentary with the weft of fictional dramatization to achieve what he, with some optimism, described as a subtle "shot-silk" texture (xxxii). It was to be a deliberate experiment not only in ideas but in literary form. And lest the reader miss this point, the author prefaces the work with a full account of the several different trials which led up to his choosing this final form. Though known primarily as a fictionalist, Wells had previously written two straightforward nonfictional works, *Anticipations* (1901) and *Mankind in the Making* (1903). As a socialist, he now wanted these ideas on the good society to be disseminated as widely as possible and to this end unashamedly used the fictional story line as a bait to interest a wider readership, loudly defending his mongrel fiction against criticism from purists such as Henry James.[5] In the case of *A Modern Utopia*, he says, "I have done my best to make the whole of this book as lucid and entertaining as its matter permits, because I want it read by as many people as possible" (xxx). Whether or not Wells achieved his aim, or could ever have hoped to attract a large audience with his present scheme, is something we shall have to consider.

Many utopists have looked to narratives to popularize their ideas, to hold their audience and then persuade through enactment by locating the reader within the utopian "reality." This is a significant and legitimate use of fiction. The narrative can also perform another function as a genuine, albeit secondary, testing ground for ideas. Narrating fiction and constructing utopias have much in common, for to utopianize is to see the whole picture, to construct a model which tests not only the efficacy of isolated ideas but their interrelation. This can be achieved within the other world and living interaction of fiction. As Wells's internal author says with some satisfaction on contemplating his description of Utopia, "I feel that I have joined together things that I had never joined before" (353). No doubt one of the pleasures of authoring a utopia is that it can fulfil the dream—or illusion—of omnipotence: "the mere pleasure of completeness, of holding and controlling all the threads, possesses me," says Wells's surrogate (354). Yet Wells also parodies and shows his own impatience with the "love interest" commonly used to enliven literary utopias. He both uses and abuses what he refers to as an "intrusive, petty love story" (27). In particular, he flaunts its fictionality, and he teaches the reader for his or her readiness to enter into even the flimsiest and most intermittent dramatization in a technique that amounts to harassment. By stretching our capacity for suspending disbelief to the limit, Wells's text reminds us both of the power of literature in this respect and of the authorial trickery found just below the surface.

To tell this story, Wells has constructed a recessed narrative with three distinct levels. Much of this scheme has been meticulously examined by Roemer and Hughes, but not the enfoldment of fictional layers. What happens, briefly, is that we enter the text through successive frames and exit it again in reverse order. In the initial frame we find H. G. Wells, the author who signs the prefatory remarks and explains some of his authorial decisions in "A Note to the Reader" (this is matched by the appendix at the book's end). Next, we encounter an internal author, the "chairman," who, in italicized script, further explains the narrative's formal scheme. This position is confused when he refers to "the chairman" (3) in the third person and there is a danger that we will keep on slipping into an infinite regress of voices. However, we next encounter the third and thereafter the main narrator, the Voice, an embodied character-narrator who occupies different levels of fictionality in the main text. Both he and the chairman are obvious caricatures of Wells and self-consciously refer back to their author. Joining the Voice is a character referred to as "the botanist," whose fictional status is somewhat confused. Apparently we are to imagine the Voice sitting on a stage reading from a manuscript and illustrating his utopia with film footage on a screen behind. In addition to a series of fictional frames, there is thus an amalgam of genres in what purports to be a multimedia presentation. However, in practice, the work turns out to be primarily a novel-cum-essay, with only half-hearted gestures towards drama and film.

Whatever the form, the manner in which utopists manage the link with the real, extratextual world is one of the most striking features of their work, and this is certainly true of Wells's text. While utopian narratives are obviously fictional, many aspire—in a weak or strong sense—to nonfictionality; that is to say, they are written in order to be translated into reality, or rather to have reality meet their description to a greater or lesser extent. Of course, they always remain texts; what may change is their fictionality in certain respects, never their textuality. This is at once an obvious and an extremely curious aspect of this type of fiction; in effect, utopists attempt to create not only within but also beyond the boundaries of the text. And success means self-annihilation, for in a eutopia (good place) utopian literature would most likely be unnecessary, while of course in many dystopian (bad) societies it would not be permitted.

If we compare this to other forms of literary realism, we can distinguish between the desire to persuade readers that a utopia (the place) does exist (i.e. ordinary verisimilitude) and persuading them that it ought to exist, a mode I call "imperative realism." In the case of dystopias, of course, the desire is that it should not exist, but this is still in the imperative mode. These two effects are related since verisimilitude is persuasive, but readers also have to acknowledge that the utopian world differs from the real world in order to recognize the need for change. It may be that there is an inherent ambivalence between believing that utopia is real and seeing that it isn't but that it should be. Wells's text foregrounds this.

Wells is clearly not advocating that every detail of this particular utopia be realized, but he does play with both these modes of realism and switches from one to the other more obviously and openly than is usual in utopian texts.[6] The verisimilar and the imperative, the fictional and the nonfictional, interweave, slip, and clash throughout the text. Take the distinction between the fictional and the nonfictional: as well as a running, though not always linear, narrative, there are passages of various lengths that read like nonfictional essays on diverse topics, and these repeatedly interrupt, or even run counter to, the narrative flow. At one point this is rather clumsily explained as being due to the defective lantern on which the drama is being portrayed (3–4). One effect of this "conflicting form" (373) is a metafictional awareness within both narrative and essay discussions of the narrative's fictionality. Injecting essay discussion into fiction need not render the latter autotelic; the so-called "novel of ideas" is able to assume quite a large burden of commentary without breaking the fictional illusion. However, instead of the fictional subsuming the nonfictional, in Wells's text it rather appears that the fictional emerges from the nonfictional. This creates an altogether different effect, making the fiction intermittent and self-conscious.

We have already seen how Wells manages the initial transition from extratextual reality to the author's text through a series of recessed frames. But to begin again at the beginning, the discontinuity of the first sentence is always an interesting site, and rather than immediately enveloping the reader in the fictional world, Wells opens his narrative by discussing its literary form self-consciously and at several removes. It is this inside view from various authors which introduces the self-referentiality that perforates the rest of the text. Throughout the narrative we are privy to authorial decisions about where certain points should be raised, about the order in which they should be discussed and at what length. For example, as soon as one topic is mentioned we are informed that "the matter is not even to be opened in this chapter. It will need a whole chapter even to glance at its issues" (24). And when another issue crops up the narrator decides on the spot that "the matter of that discussion I shall put apart into a separate chapter" (312). Of course, laying bare the process does not in itself determine the status of the product. The mere fact that we witness the writer at work in this way need not mean that the events he or she describes are to be taken as unreal, but this is also the case here—or at least partly the case. We are told that none of the events described ever really occurred. We are also expected to believe that they did.

Wells implants quite meticulous suggestions that this is an entirely realistic account of the Voice's visit to an actual location called "Utopia." It is the very limitations of the description which "prove" the authenticity of the events described. Thus, when recounting his visit, the Voice tells us that he can't quite remember everything the utopians told him about their society (311) or that he regrets he didn't ask them for all the figures to explain some point (298), the implication being that this information exists in a world which is greater than his knowledge of it. Wells also breaks conventions and points to the fact that he does; for example, he abandons the basic expository device of the perennially curious visitor and the contented natives who are always able and willing to answer his or her questions and thus describe their society for the reader's benefit (122–123).[7] Wells's uninquisitive visitors and discontented or uncooperative natives are presumably more realistic. There is even an attempt within the fiction to substantiate the reality of the picture by explicitly distinguishing it from fiction. "That's all very well in a novel," says the botanist dismissively when the Voice offers him advice, but it would not be practical in their, the characters', "real" world, a world which the reader recognizes is in a novel (58). The joke is not a new one, but Wells can't resist playing with the fictional illusion in this manner.

Alongside realistic suggestions are numerous cues to the text's lack of realism. One form which this takes is what might be called a deliberately "incomplete" realism. Of course, all literary realism is in a sense incomplete; no one text can denote the whole of existence. But conventional metonymic realism implies what it does not specify; that is, we take it on trust that a larger world exists beyond the items specifically denoted in the text. However, in Wells's incomplete realism the author explicitly declines to fill in certain gaps in information and prevents the reader from doing so. Pleading ignorance, he simply washes his hands of certain decisions. There "may be double railways or monorails or what not—we are no engineers," says the Voice, so he leaves it undecided which form of transport, if any, exists in Utopia (45). Or again, another section opens with: "How will a great city of Utopia strike us? To answer that question well one must needs be an artist and engineer, and I am neither," says the Voice, so he declines to fill in any more detail than he feels equipped to provide (241). In such descriptions it is absence that is foregrounded, so that certain details are not permitted to exist even by implication. Not only are they not there, but we are told that they are not there. By refusing to invent certain details, the author reminds the reader of his powers of calling them into existence, or in this case non-existence. At times, Wells's Voice is so disengaged as to offer either/or alternatives. It seems he has not yet made a final decision about certain points and simply leaves them in an unsettled and ontologically queasy state. For example, comparing it with its state on Earth, he says in Utopia a certain cabin "would be gone or wonderfully changed" (15). Well, which is it? Does it exist or doesn't it? This is never settled, and it is not clear that the reader will ever settle it. Even when details are fixed, the Voice will sometimes point to the very arbitrariness of their existence and, hence, to his authorial control. "I have an idea— I know not why—that we should make the journey by night" (238), he tells us. It will be "a convenient accident" (71), he says, if such and such happens. He "insist[s] quite arbitrarily" (171) that such and such will be the case. And so it is.

The main premise both inside and outside the fictional narrative is that the Voice is hypothesizing this utopia into existence as he goes along, hence the provisional, ad hoc presentation. The problem is that it is not consistently so. At other times we are to read it as a realistic account—or both at once. Sometimes the Voice and the botanist are aware that they are in a vision and the botanist holds the Voice responsible for what they encounter: "I do not like your Utopia, if there are to be no dogs," he grumbles (231). Or the Voice himself refers to his "Frankenstein of reasoning" which has created this state and rather uncharitably mocks the other characters for not realizing that they are merely fictional (236). At other times neither he nor the botanist appear to recognize that this is the Voice's vision, and both are surprised by what they find there. Or they do recognize that it is his vision but are still surprised.[8] It may be that this gives the reader the impression of sharing another aspect of writing, of the work in progress, for fiction writers commonly report that the story takes them over or that the book practically writes itself. In the Voice's case even basic ideas are not anticipated, and characters he has informed and called into existence in turn inform him about various matters, their feedback fundamentally modifying his previous assumptions about Utopia (259). Thus sometimes he appears to have full authorial control; sometimes he stresses how little control he has; while at other times the Voice is supposedly just another character who should not even be surprised at his lack of control. In short, the Voice occupies several what we would ordinarily consider contradictory positions.

Another curious interface is created when the Voice and his double—the utopian version of himself—discuss what is openly called "Utopia," an object that is at once the Voice's invention and yet something he seeks information on. In fact, during this exchange the explanatory narrator appears to slip from the double to the Voice without any clear demarcation. Does the double know that he is merely a figment of the other's imagination? Does he know that he inhabits a utopia? Wells essentially fudges this issue and has the Voice account for his presence here in vague and tortured terms: he just somehow "came upon these explorations" (263). What is essentially a conflation of story and discussion also occurs when the Voice explicitly hypothesizes in an essayistic fashion yet also insists on the realistic dramatization of concrete details. This brings us to one of the most striking features of this work—the sudden sliding of tense and mood from the indicative to the subjunctive, from "is" or "was" to "would" and "should" with no warning and little apparent reason. The following is an early example of the this kind of intermingling.

> We have tramped and botanised and come to a rest, and, sitting among rocks, we have eaten our lunch and finished our bottle of Yvorne, and fallen into talk of Utopias, and said such things as I have been saying. I could figure it myself upon that little neck of the Lucendro Pass, upon the shoulder of the Piz Lucendro, for there once I lunched and talked very pleasantly, and we are looking down upon the Val Bedretto. . . . And behold! in the twinkling of an eye we are in that other world! We should scarcely note the change. Not a cloud would have gone from the

sky. It might be the remote town below would take a different
air, and my companion the botanist, with his educated observation, might almost see as much, and the train, perhaps, would be
gone out of the picture. . . (13–14).

Employing anything but a past or present indicative could well undermine the rhetorical force of the utopian narrative. Richard Gerber,
though he is not referring specifically to Wells, strongly advises "the
real utopian" to take full advantage of the fictional indicative. Any use
of the conditional, he warns, "would not only be rather clumsy and dull,
but the reader would also feel tempted to question the conclusions arrived at," since the "very grammatical form" of such statements "points
to the unreality of the conception in every sentence" (Gerber 1955, 81).
Robert C. Elliott agrees that the effect is awkward and regrets that "Wells
allowed the narrative sections of the work to be hampered by a clumsy
entanglement with the subjunctive mood" (Elliott 1970, 114). It may be
that a certain evasiveness is a characteristic weakness of Wells.[9] Certainly, the fitful shifting that this extract illustrates is one of the most
tiresome features of the book, and more so because it often appears to be
due to carelessness more than anything else.

The transitions are not always as sudden and brief. In other instances,
prolonged blocks of narrative and discussion are quite distinct; indeed,
one can almost hear the Voice clear his throat before adopting the more
formal and logical style of the essays. Even so, between these blocks
there is a busy, though rarely acknowledged, traffic of ideas. Usually the
Voice discusses general principles in essay form before deciding what
to put into the Utopian picture. These ideas are then fed into the story,
often as soon as they have been aired. As readers we can hardly fail to
notice this. However, once immersed in the narrative, we are frequently
expected to take these same features as objectively given and as real as
anything else found in Utopia; in other words, after first witnessing their
genesis, we are to erase it from our minds. Beginning as a speculation,
an abstract notion, the "real" object grows before our very eyes. For example, first the Voice speculates that Utopians will "Almost certainly . . .
need to have money." By the next sentence it is decided that "They will
have money, and it is not inconceivable that . . . our botanist . . . would
be the one to see and pick up the coin that has fallen from some wayfarer's
pocket." Next, self-consciously invoking his "author's privilege of details," the Voice goes on to describe the aforementioned coin as though

it were none of his invention but a real object which he too is encountering on a Utopian road for the first time (*Modern Utopia* 70–71).

Less often, the fictional frontier is also traversed in the opposite direction, and a notion first arises in the narrative which is later taken up in essay discussions; for example, the key element of the Samurai is first encountered in the narrative before being discussed in essay form (121, 128–129), and on another occasion a fictional character previously encountered in the narrative is invoked as "evidence" of some point in a general discussion (114, 153). In such cases, the fact that a feature appeared in the narrative is actually taken as some indication of its practical validity, though beyond this fact—the fact that it did appear—it is of course wholly fictional. The Voice gives it a "real" existence, an apparent factuality, outside the narrative and by a sleight of hand uses the fictional as a basis for fact. He exploits its fictionality even while ignoring it and expects us to do likewise. This is the basic dualism in the text. We are asked to quite consciously doublethink that Utopia exists as it is described but also that it is something the Voice is making up as he goes along according to gradually emerging principles. Discovery and invention are deliberately confused. For the reader, entering such a narrative is like entering a hall of mirrors where the real and virtual become wholly confused.

For example, although it is acknowledged that the botanist is the Voice's invention, both also exist side by side as characters who visit the planet of Utopia; thus two levels of fictionality collapse into one—but again not consistently. At times it is not clear how the Voice regards this figure. His initial description of him is typically ambiguous. "He is a man, I should think, of thirty-nine, a man whose life has been neither tragedy nor a joyous adventure" could mean that he is trying to describe an already existing person and form his own first impressions or that, as his author, he is just now deciding what the botanist shall look like (26). Furthermore, though the botanist is the Voice's creature, he very often acts independently and even antagonistically towards his creator, so much so that the Voice is moved to protest. "It is strange," he declares at one point, "but this figure of the botanist will not keep in place. It sprang up between us, dear reader, as a passing illustrative invention. I do not know what put him into my head. . . . But here he is, indisputably, with me in utopia" (25). The botanist is both in the Voice's head and walking alongside him in Utopia—a fictive invention and a real presence. Indeed, it seems he is making a great nuisance of himself

35

and either deliberately or inadvertently upsetting the Voice's plans. For example, as mentioned before, the Voice disparages the botanist's love story and views it as an unnecessary intrusion. He protests, "Why should a modern Utopia insist upon slipping out of the hands of its creator and becoming the background of a personal drama—of such a silly little drama?" (256). Most critics agree that the botanist represents the personal life, the unpredictable, even rebellious, individual who is sometimes overlooked but who must somehow be accommodated in any utopia.[10] The antagonism between these two, between creator and creature, is one of the basic dynamics of the text.

In his prefatory note to the reader, Wells declared his intention "to present not simply an ideal, but an ideal in reaction with two personalities." One might say that Wells has in effect translated the utopia into a tale of the mental states of these two voices (Roemer 118), so that we recognize "utopia is not a place but a mode of thinking" (Hughes 64). Clearly the Voice's thoughts dominate, but his conflict with the botanist breeds further self-referentiality since, when exasperated, he retorts by reminding us that what we are reading is finally his utopia, something he has created, not the botanist. "Thank Heaven this is my book, and that the ultimate decision rests with me. It is open to him to write his own Utopia" (67), he somewhat petulantly insists. Needless to say, this conflict makes the botanist appear more real because he is more independent of the Voice; yet the Voice's explicit complaints against the botanist's independence also remind the reader that he was created by the Voice in the first place. The effect is that once again the process of writing fiction and the text's fictionality are foregrounded.

When the author emerges from the text, the reader has little choice but to follow. Occasionally, the Voice leaps right out and addresses the reader directly, with a playful, almost Shandyean "dear reader. . . . Sir or Madam" (25). But even when not so directly buttonholed, the reader is made conscious of the act of reading and even of the physical text being read; for example, the Voice refers to "this moment of reading" or to "this page you read" (24, 367). The contract between reader and author is unmistakable, and from the start we are asked to sign on the bottom line. Once granted, the Voice likes to upset our position, as when we are suddenly addressed as the botanist, and then a few pages later the Voice admits that for no apparent reason "it fell in with my humour for a space to foist the man's personality on you as yours" (18, 25). Some critics have suggested that the text's open structure and subjunctive mood encourage reader participation (Hughes 1977, 60). But while the Voice does employ a weak sense of "we" on occasion, as though he and the reader were collaborating, or pretends to report the reader's opinion (*Modern Utopia* 23, 25), this does not lessen his control. We are not really being consulted; he does not really hear us and assuming our position is just as likely to displace and distance us as invite us in. In the case of referring to the reader as the botanist, of attempting to fictionalize readers by positioning them within the fiction, the net result is to underline the text's fictionality and thereby distance them from it.

The characters exit from Utopia because of the botanist's skepticism and, as we might expect by now, the transition is full of twists and contradictions. In the first place, it is interesting that a narrative should end because the characters can no longer suspend their disbelief. Then we wonder how a character who was apparently created within the vision and solely for the purpose of narrating the vision can not only end it but also step outside it. The botanist exits the vision with his creator, though the latter, supposedly the author of the piece, is once again taken by surprise. He apparently did not know that his visit to Utopia would be so brief (312). The botanist seems reasonably unperturbed and appears to be unaware that he is, not to put too fine a point upon it, a fictional character and a figment of the Voice's imagination. He merely believes that he somehow shared the Voice's vision while they were discussing the notion of a utopia. Both he and the Voice acknowledge that their previous experience was merely visionary and that they are now back in a brutally real London (though this is not always clear in the Voice's case because he also reminisces about his visit as though it really occurred).[11] The reader is clearly to regret that Utopia has been lost. The stark contrast between utopian dream and nonutopian reality is a common rhetorical device, famously used, for example, by William Morris. The Voice goes one further and, almost echoing Edward Bellamy, tries to overturn the distinction between the fictional and real within the text by suggesting the "real" London is actually a dream or nightmare.[12] He gives Utopia ontological priority by adopting the Platonic maneuver of declaring the Ideal the more real. According to the Voice, present London is merely an imperfect imitation of the true Form.[13]

Despite claiming that he is trying to attract a wide audience, Wells is clearly writing for the initiated. This is a text for utopists, utopian scholars and, I would suggest, contemporary literary critics. Utopias and utopianizing are its subject. In the final pages the botanist is actu-

ally permitted to dismiss the whole activity, but he is soon overtaken by
the Voice who fervently hopes that some utopia, though not necessarily
an exact copy of his, will one day be realized (370). His last words are
"So surely it must be—" (370). This is not the "strong" imperativism
which calls for subscriptions and immediate action or claims that this is
a blueprint that can be defictionalized. Wells set out to create a utopia
"at once possible and more desirable than the present world" (xxx). These
are two distinct and quite modest aims, but it is clear that Wells wished
his outline to be more practical than, say, that of Morris (7). Some readers were indeed inspired to volunteer their services, especially among
the ranks of the Fabian Society, and Wells himself went back to the idea
of the Samurai in his own Open Conspiracy. But within the text, the
Voice forces himself to be patient and await the inevitable transformation (370). Indeed, for a while it seems that even this postponed hope is
destined to be undercut by the chairman's skepticism. But though he
mocks the Voice, he too emerges as something of a utopist in the end;
Wells is merely using him to check the Voice's enthusiasm.

What we are left with is an open and tentative ending. As J. R.
Hammond points out, this is not uncommon in Wells's "novel[s] of indeterminacy" (Hammond 1990, 79), and in this instance the self-
referentiality and resistance to closure allow one to read this premodern
novel postmodernistically. As often happens in literary history, certain
features are bypassed only to reemerge later as dominant and therefore
retrospectively salient in previous texts.

Wells may describe his text as "a sort of summary of Utopian ideas"
(Wells 1982, 120), but it is accomplished partly through concrete dramatization—and this cannot be ignored, though it frequently is. How
verisimilar is it then as a work of fiction, and what is the general effect of
its intermittent fictionality? As we have seen, on the one hand the Voice
and the botanist know they are in the land of Utopia "by an act of the
imagination" (*Modern Utopia* 133). Nevertheless, they are really there.
How can they be simultaneously within and above this level of
fictionality? How can they regard Utopia as objectively real and as solely
of their own imagining? Wells does not even attempt to resolve these
apparent contradictions. To some extent, he uses the collision of fictional
planes to create the dramatic tension that is otherwise notoriously difficult to generate in utopian narratives.

As many utopists have discovered, nothing is more tedious than a
prolonged description of contentment, nothing more difficult to make

likeable or even credible than a wholly virtuous and undesirous character. Rather than rely solely on the subject matter, Wells also looked to the form for dramatic conflict. Yet the manipulation often seems high-handed or careless, and the meager verisimilitude does interfere with the work's imperative force. Rarely does the reader feel that he or she is actually living in Utopia with the Voice, which means that Wells is missing the persuasive force of fictional enactment. The Voice's transitions from fiction to nonfiction are also often deflationary, like planting one's foot on what turns out to be a nonexistent step. One can get used to it, to the slippage and jolts of Wells's scheme, but what still rankles is that it so often appears underdetermined and flaccid. And the fact that the author is playing so cavalierly with our willingness to believe or to suspend disbelief is not calculated to encourage us to accept his ideas too readily.

Reader, author, and even characters are asked to take on a dual awareness in which they simultaneously see and do not see the fictionality of the text. Nevertheless, the self-consciousness that this breeds also brings with it some freedom and allows Wells to establish a curious relation between essay and narrative. No doubt he decided that surreptitiously loading up a story with essay discussion often does not work, is even dishonest. Therefore he made the incorporation of essay elements into the story quite open: he made it a feature in fact. Perhaps the idea was that if this is openly declared to be part of the plan, then readers will not feel there is a weak attempt to bamboozle them. The pretense is opened up, pointed to, and thereby legitimized. The Voice tells us that he is largely free "of the trammels of convincing story-telling" (17). For instance, he simply makes the assumption that all Utopians speak one language and one that he can understand. And he tells us this quite candidly (17–18). He apparently expects us to demand less as readers because he has let us in on the process. Also, the essay discussions do not seem so out of place in a story of such tenuous fictionality. We know, or rather are usually asked to believe, that all is the Voice's invention, so he is entitled to discuss his ideas explicitly; it is within his character. He is not acting as a visitor who is totally embedded in the story and must stretch or be stretched to discuss larger ideas on behalf of the author.

Among other things, Wells uses his surrogate author, or authors, as protective masks. For example, he half-heartedly attempts to deflect charges of didacticism (a common complaint against utopists) onto the

Voice. He mocks the Voice for being strident, while making full use of this channel for his ideas. And on more than one occasion Wells tries to ward off or soften criticism by embedding it in the text. The chairman, for instance, tries to anticipate readers' objections to the text's "peculiar method" and suggests that it may make "the argument hard to follow" (371). Certainly some discussions could be condensed and the transition to the story line better handled; for example, Wells might have done better to generate comedy from the switching over and back. Nevertheless, the argument is clear. The chairman is closer to the truth when he refers to "a quality of insincerity" in the text (371). Hollow, fickle, and contrived—this is how the method often strikes us. The performance is meant to be stagy to some extent (remember, the Voice is supposedly sitting on stage), but it is overdone and misses the subtle "shot silk" texture that Wells apparently aimed for. Instead, the texture is marked with inconsistencies, ruptures, and twists. These are also what make this such an intriguing text. As an experiment that is still bold, it is simply too curious to neglect.

Notes

1. The only other interesting, though brief, references to formal aspects of this piece are by Robert C. Elliott (113–16), J. R. Hammond (66–81), Mark R. Hillegas, John Huntington, Krishnan Kumar, and David Lodge (227–28).
2. In this essay I maintain the following distinctions: the "utopist" is one who writes utopias; "Utopia" is the place or society; "utopia" is the genre or text.
3. This is how Hillegas describes it in his introduction to *A Modern Utopia* (ix) despite Wells's explicit refutation (xxxii). All parenthetical references in the text are to Wells's *A Modern Utopia* unless otherwise indicated.
4. Thomas More coined the term (from the Greek *ou*, "no," and *topas*, "place") when he wrote his *Utopia* in 1516.
5. For an account of James vs. Wells on the art of the novel, in many ways an archetypal debate on the use of literature, see Leon Edel and Gordon N. Ray.
6. Wells was careful to distinguish between utopia and prophecy; see his "Utopias," 117.
7. See also Roemer, 129.
8. See, for example, 75, 223, 235, 247.
9. This is Kumar's belief and one aspect that makes him impatient with Wells (2).
10. For example, see Hughes, 65; Parrinder, "Meta-Utopia," 120; and Huntington, 168.
11. The Voice says in parenthesis at one point: "Whenever I think of Utopia that

faint and fluctuating smell of resin returns to me, and whenever I smell resin, comes the memory of the open end of the shed looking out upon the lake" (222).

12. In *Looking Backward* Bellamy first had his hero, West, believe that he had woken out of his utopian dream, but then in a final twist reasserted that Utopia was real and West only dreamed that he woke up from it.

13. Of course, as Roemer points out, the London that Wells depicted here no longer exists and many of Utopia's features now do (126).

Works Cited

Bellamy, Edward. 1888. *Looking Backward.* Reprint, New York: Viking Penguin, 1984.

Edel, Leon, and Gordon N. Ray, eds. 1958. *Henry James and H. G. Wells: A Record of their Friendship, their Debate on the Art of Fiction, and their Quarrel.* Urbana: University of Illinois Press.

Elliott, Robert C. 1970. *The Shape of Utopia: Studies in a Literary Genre.* Chicago: Chicago University Press.

Gerber, Richard. 1955. *Utopian Fantasy: A Study of English Utopian Fiction Since the End of the Nineteenth Century.* London: Routledge & Kegan Paul.

Hammond, J. R. 1990. "Wells and the Novel." In *H.G. Wells Under Revision*, edited by Patrick Parrinder and Christopher Rolfe. London: Associated University Presses.

Hillegas, Mark R. 1967. Introduction to *A Modern Utopia*, by H. G. Wells. Lincoln: University of Nebraska Press.

Hughes, David Y. 1977. "The Mood of *A Modern Utopia*." *Extrapolation* 19 (December): 59–67.

Huntington, John. 1982. *The Logic of Fantasy: H. G. Wells and Science Fiction.* New York: Columbia University Press.

Kumar, Krishnan. (1982/82) "A Book Remembered: *A Modern Utopia*." *New Universities Quarterly* 36 (Winter): 3–12.

Lodge, David. 1971. *The Novelist at the Crossroads and Other Essays on Fiction and Criticism.* Ithaca: Cornell University Press.

More, Sir Thomas. 1516. *Utopia.* Reprint, New York: Norton, 1975.

Morris, William. 1891. *News from Nowhere.* Reprint, New York: Viking Penguin, 1984.

Mumford, Lewis. 1962. *The Story of Utopias.* New York: Viking.

Parrinder, Patrick. 1985. "Utopia and Meta-Utopia in H. G. Wells." *Science-Fiction Studies* 12, pt. 2 (July): 115–28.

Parrinder, Patrick, and Christopher Rolfe, eds. 1990. *H. G. Wells Under Revision.* London: Associated University Presses.

Roemer, Kenneth M. 1982. "H. G. Wells and the Momentary Voices of *A Modern*

Utopia." Extrapolation 23 (Summer): 117–37.

Wells, H. G. 1902. *Anticipations of the Reaction of Mechanical and Scientific Progress upon Human Life and Thought.* New York: Harper.

———. 1903. *Mankind in the Making.* London: Chapman and Hall.

———. 1905. *A Modern Utopia.* Reprint, Lincoln: University of Nebraska Press, 1967.

———. 1982. "Utopias." *Science-Fiction Studies* 9 (July): 117–21.

Chapter 4

State, Heterotopia
The Political Imagination
in Heinlein, Le Guin, and Delany

Neil Easterbrook

"Do you think it would be much better to have the prisoners operating the Panopticon apparatus and sitting in the central tower, instead of the guards?"
—Michel Foucault, *"The Eye of Power"* (164–65)

". . . one wants something of the folded-back-on-itself recomplication in the psychology of the political alien."
—Samuel Delany, *"To Read The Dispossessed"* (254)

   One of the most frequently voiced attacks on science fiction concerns its "naively authoritarian" political models. In a brief but infamous 1982 article in *Harper's*, Arnold Klein argued that "the staccato inconsequence" of science fiction can be seen in its "simpleminded" political systems: even "the out-and-out dystopias in sci-fi are usually set on a weary Earth governed by moms and dads who are either too strict or too lax" (65). "Sci-fi plots," he concluded, "are ridiculously simple as well as simply ridiculous, the characterization nonexistent, the prose not prose at all" (66).

Yet among science fiction's most significant virtues is its dedication to the serious exploration of political models, especially during historical periods when the general public shows little interest in serious political debate. At least since the time of Mary Shelley, science fiction has operated both as popular titillation and *Gedankenexperiement* (thought-experiment). A legendary modern example of the latter occurred in 1941 when John Campbell suggested to the young Isaac Asimov a story developing Ralph Waldo Emerson's question in his essay "Nature": "If the stars should appear one night in a thousand years, how would men believe and adore, and preserve for many generations the remembrance of the city of God?" (qtd. 11). The result was Asimov's brilliant (if stylistically embarrassing) "Nightfall." No doubt somewhere some writer is already at work realizing the similar speculations of a contemporary Emerson, Jacques Derrida: "Imagine a city, a State in which identity cards were post cards. No more possible resistance. There are already checks with photographs. All of this is not so far off. With the progress of the post the State police has always gained ground" (Derrida 1980, 37).

Science fiction's discussion of the relationship between individual and the state is nowhere better represented than in three well-known novels produced between 1966 and 1976: Robert A. Heinlein's *The Moon Is a Harsh Mistress*, Ursula K. Le Guin's *The Dispossessed*, and Samuel R. Delany's *Triton*. Published just two years apart, the relation between *The Dispossessed* (subtitled "An Ambiguous Utopia") and *Triton* (subtitled "An Ambiguous Heterotopia") is perhaps obvious, especially considering Delany's 1976 critical article "To Read The Dispossessed." But one might argue that *The Dispossessed* is reaction to *The Moon Is a Harsh Mistress*. Each novel details the struggle of a moon against the more traditional, conventional political order of a parent planet. Each contrasts the relative value of authoritarian political systems (including democracy) to the freedom and liberty of individuals. Although each settles on social systems that ought to be described as anarchies, they differ in their ideological accents.

Heinlein's Luna Free State, a "rational anarchy" (*Moon*, 64), is a libertarian system. Le Guin's Anarres is anarcho-syndicalist. Delany's outer satellites, from Titan to Triton, offer myriad political options, an ambiguous array erasing not only left and right but above all revoking the common ground conventionally used to legitimate any political system. The first praises capitalism, free markets, Thomas Malthus and (implicitly) Ayn Rand. The second seems inspired by various nineteenth century Utopian movements, Paul Goodman, and (implicitly) Herbert Marcuse and Jurgen Habermas. The third finds its primary influence in Michel Foucault, and through him (implicitly) in Gilles Deleuze and Felix Guattari.

Neither utopias nor dystopias, the novels' three moons—Luna, Anarres, Triton—have remarkable similarities. None has an indigenous population—all inhabitants have migrated or been born to immigrants. Each is initially the arid mining colony of a planet. Each revolts against its stronger progenitor, and "wins." Each features a male protagonist who, despite being apolitical, finds himself at the center of global change and so journeys to the home planet as an emissary of his people. Each, as is often the case in political science fiction, contains lengthy homilies on good government, social order, and ethical action. And each privileges an anarchistic political philosophy. Robert Nozick's definition, in his *Anarchy, State, Utopia*, succinctly defines anarchism: "the anarchist claim [is] that in the course of maintaining its monopoly on the use of force and protecting everyone within a territory, the state must violate individuals' rights and hence is intrinsically immoral" (xi).

I hope to show how the sharp, ironic counterpoint of the rhetorical strategies of these three anarchic systems provides an exemplary demonstration of how science fiction offers a vital contemporary political commentary. I also hope to show how science fiction has revised our understanding of anarchism as much as books such as Nozick's. The traditional, clichéd view of the anarchist is the purely destructive terrorist or terrorist's dupe, such as the portraits of The Professor and Verloc in Conrad's *The Secret Agent* (1907), a novel which ends with this image of the anarchist: "And the incorruptible Professor walked, too, averting his eyes from the odious multitude of mankind. He had no future. He disdained it. He was a force. His thoughts caressed . . . images of ruin and destruction. He walked frail, insignificant, shabby, miserable—and terrible in the simplicity of his idea calling madness and despair to the regeneration of the world" (252–53).

Unlike Conrad's depiction of the anarchist as a cynic, nihilist, or solipsist pleased to see others' pain, *The Moon Is a Harsh Mistress, The Dispossessed,* and *Triton* all envision anarchy in positive, if finally ambiguous, terms. What must be seen is if "this anarquista wet dream bullshit" (Kadrey 1988, 70) remains politically viable.

Mere Anarchy Is Loosed upon the World

Heinlein's Luna serves a role analogous to the British Empire's eighteenth-century establishment of Botany Bay in Australia: violators of various laws, especially political criminals, are exiled to the moon—which means permanent exile, for return to Earth's higher gravity is impossible following continued exposure to lunar conditions. In turn Luna's lower gravity extends the exiles' life; one-sixth g means less heart strain, and the relatively unsullied environment avoids the hazards of Terra's industrial pollutants. Terra exploits Luna just as the British Empire exploited Australia: to colonize a wild territory and to serve the motherland, Luna's economy is dedicated to producing grain for Terra's starving billions. Seed and a paltry few manufactured goods come up the gravity well; Loonies then send tons of wheat back down. The colony is in reality a prison, and Luna Authority's Warden extracts some small profit from the exchange, but Luna's "citizens" receive little more than current prison inmates make. Like colonial Australia or America, Luna becomes a place of exile and isolation, but also the new frontier—attracting anyone with sufficient courage, regardless of ethnicity or nationality (*Moon* 21, 28). When they finally adopt a flag, its central emblem will be the bar sinister (207). Driven by hard cash, nothing happens without a profitable exchange of capital; Loonies take that principle as their "motto" (301): there ain't no such thing as a free lunch, "Tanstaafl" (126). Or as Mannie phrases it (echoing an unattributed Milton Friedman), "anything free costs twice as much in the long run or turns out worthless" (129). Luna Authority (usually just "Authority") exercises an iron grip over commerce, so even by 2076, when most Loonies have been born free or served their sentence, wages still remain suitable only for inmates.

Because of the exigencies of lunar life, few guards and fewer rules are necessary for social order. Once acclimated to the Moon's conditions; permanently altered by the lower gravity, human physiology cannot readjust to life on Terra. Consequently, there is virtually no crime, for Loonies either learn to be careful in a culture without laws (93) or they die. Errors of etiquette invariably mean death (150) either by their own hand or by others', for any offence can result in "spacing" (94): "attrition ran 70 percent in the early years—but those who lived were nice people" (20). Mannie, our narrator, regards this "respect" for "manners" as both a suitable condition and desirable end; not only does it provide social order but also "improve[s] the breed" (159).

Three characters dominate the narrative: the narrator Manuel Garcia O'Kelly Davis (Mannie, Man), his former teacher Professor Bernardo de la Paz (Prof), and Mike, the Artificial Intelligence Mannie is contracted to repair—the first AI to attain (or stumble upon) consciousness. Wyoming Knott (Wyho) initially seems a powerful figure (22), an "agitatrix" (28), but like most female characters in Heinlein quickly fades to subservience (65 ff.), learning to "ke[ep] her pretty mouth shut" (280). I will return to Luna's sexism below.

Physically the weakest of the lot, Prof emerges as the prime mover of this revolutionary cabal. Success depends on careful manipulation of information rather than brute force because the cabal recruits Mike, entrusted by Authority to run everything; without Mike, Authority cannot exercise authority. So the strategist, we soon discover, wields the greatest power. Because Heinlein conceives of all governments as bureaucracies filled solely by incompetent pedants ("yammerheads"), when Mike first attains consciousness and starts telling jokes, Authority must call in someone else (especially since yammerheads are incapable of understanding irony). Enter Mannie, Loonie Every Man and bricoleur extraordinaire who, having lost one arm to a laser drill but now aided by an array of prostheses, turns electronic troubleshooter; this "general specialist" (10) learned two things from his father, "Mind own business" and "Always cut cards" (7).

After Warden's "Peace Dragoons" butcher a few citizens—Mannie is "opted" (62) into Prof's revolution. What incites Authority's raid is Prof's public proclamation that Luna must embargo grain shipments (25), for without total self-sufficiency Luna will, as Mike later calculates, irrevocably disrupt the biosphere's delicate zero-sum balance, converting Loonies into cannibals within seven years (74). "The only one who seemed to know" (237), Prof's disturbing prescience suggests that he really is the only one who knows why or how events happen the way they do. Mannie will eventually realize (231) that even Mike's "objective" calculations have been manipulated by that political bricoleur, Prof. As Prof fixes elections that appear honest (229–31, 284) and passes death sentences while contriving alibis (148), so too he subtly forces others to obey his will, making them believe they respond to events rather than simply play parts in his plan. In short, all of Mannie's actions unwittingly deny his father's wisdom, for within ten pages of narrative he is embroiled in a violent revolution and within fifty has permitted Prof to stack the deck.

Of course the revolution succeeds; barely, and with ambiguous results. Two years of planning culminates in a coup d'etat, followed by some reasonably polite but condescending chit-chat with Terra's global government (178–219); finally realizing the Loonies' resolve, Terra launches an attack. Luna retaliates, using the same ballistic mechanism that delivered grain in order to throw rocks—which, considering the relative mass, can yield as much potential energy ("instructive shrecklichkeit" [258]) as thermonuclear weapons. The Terrans—yammerheads all—flock to the uninhabited impact sites Luna warns them to avoid; millions are killed, and Terra launches a full-scale invasion. In a final but finally unsuccessful assault, Mike himself is blinded—killed or lost (302), he is no longer conscious; Prof dies of cardiac arrest shortly after the Loonie victory (299). Tanstaafl: freedom comes only at someone's expense, and huge profits involve huge costs.

These dark ambiguities are played out several ways. Mannie opens his narrative commenting that now many years after the victory, the bureaucratic government is once again raising taxes (7). As Hazel, Mannie's adopted daughter, will later explain in *The Cat Who Walks Through Walls* (in some respects *Moon*'s sequel), "In my childhood when this was a penal colony, there was more freedom under the Warden than there is now with self-government" (236). On the novel's final page, Mannie will contemplate moving to the asteroids, for that's the new frontier (302) where there are no governments-by-yammerhead restricting what Prof calls "the most basic human right: the right to bargain in a free marketplace" (24). In place of Authority, or bureaucracy, or democracy, Prof proposes a system he calls "rational anarchy" (64).

Several political and social ideas inform rational anarchy's particulars—Locke's state of nature (130, 184), Jefferson's inalienable rights (162), Rousseau's natural law (130), Lenin's claim that (class) enemies can never be converted (148)—with the economic thought of Malthus (206). These several views have found their modern advocate in Ayn Rand, whose arguments Prof closely parallels, beginning with the Malthusian notion that the worst thing one can do for a starving man is feed him (206).[1] Since moral responsibility rests solely with the individual (64), Prof argues, rules apply only to others (161, 301). Since the single natural right is to bargain in a free marketplace, this is the only service that a minimal state should provide. Since all social institutions are determined by economics alone (210), then economics should be the sole principle to determine social mores. Laws should always proscribe, never prescribe, restrictions (241–42) because government is a "disease" (243, 251); there-fore a good constitution "forbids government action" (301). Democracy, like "representation," is "a myth" (227). Even the state itself is a myth: "there's no such thing as a 'state.' Just men. Individuals" (65). In each case, Prof attacks the notion that moral or legal responsibility resides outside the Cartesian subject, which exists and operates independently of others. When and where the subject chooses, he can extend his own moral sense to others, such as his family.

But all abstractions of a "people" or a "nation" or a "community" have no concrete, empirical referent. They are what, in *Cat's Cradle,* Kurt Vonnegut called "granfalloons" (Vonnegut 1963, 67), nice but essentially meaningless names for Boolean groups. (Yet Vonnegut also directs this irony back against the book, arguing that the protagonist's wisdom is not final or definitive.) Indeed, Loonies who conceive of the state in terms of generic collectives are, Prof argues, fools enacting myths whose con-sequences they cannot comprehend. The worst form of such non-sense is socialism (164). Hazel describes the "wrong-headedness in general" of an inept miscreant she happens across: he "has the so-cialist disease in its worst form; he thinks the world owes him a liv-ing. He told me sincerely—smugly!—that of course everyone was entitled to the best possible medical and hospital service—free of course, unlimited of course, and of course the government should pay for it. He couldn't even understand the mathematical impossibility of what he was demanding" (*The Cat Who Walks* 197–98). Any imbecile simple enough to expect assistance from others then deserves whatever he gets. This one gets killed, of course.

But while debunking the popular myth that moral, social, and po-litical responsibility rest in some extrahistorical foundation, Prof substi-tutes another mythic entity, itself an invention of Locke's state of nature. Wyho, who rightly suggests that Prof's "words sound good but there's something slippery about them" (*Moon,* 64), holds that surely some rules restrict irresponsible behavior. Prof replies that "My point is that one person is responsible. If H-Bombs exist—and they do—then some man controls them" (65). "All parliamentary bodies, all through history," Prof maintains, "when they accomplished anything, owed it to a few strong men who dominated the rest." From plebiscite to parliament, the "rest" is otherwise "a mob of retarded children" (162). Indeed, Prof's position is that absolute political control should always be vested in or appropri-ated by some strong man—"strong, handsome, virile and dynamic" (169).

Preferably an infallible, benevolent Occidental like Prof.

In *The Moon Is a Harsh Mistress,* Heinlein's authorial metonym is a composite. Mannie possesses the virility, Prof the sage wisdom, Mike the dynamism; all are configured as strong men. For Heinlein, strong men are always men. Especially so on Luna, where they outnumber women two to one. Prof and Mannie think this ratio makes males respect and honor females in ways heretofore unimaginable. Women are loved and protected, Mannie says, "the most valuable thing in Luna, more precious than ice or air" (*Moon,* 130). There is no sexual harassment. Women can flirt or sleep with anyone without the slightest continuing obligation. There is no rape (131). But not because women have been liberated from political or social oppression, but precisely the opposite: their patriarchal position has been reified. Treated (by men) as things, given value only by men and only for men, women exist as objects, never as subjects. Heinlein configures women's rights as exclusively sexual: to be a "Free Woman" (32), for instance, means to be unmarried, that is: not monogamous (cf. 291, 172). Just as the narrator is Man, the object of his affection is Wye Knott. But of course this irony works according to the novel's universal Law of Reinscription: Tanstaafl—a price must always be paid. Luna's other slogan—"beer, betting, women and work" (91, 235)—suggests not only Luna's patriarchy but also the exact status of women within its hierarchy of commodities.

Even where women take traditionally masculine roles, they are reduced to mere metonyms for men. In order to seduce more men to gun the laser defenses, Wyho dresses attractive "girls" in military garb; this "Lysistrata Corps" (239) is Heinlein's cruel joke, for in *Lysistrata* Aristophanes's women revolt against male stupidity, refusing their company until they abandon their idiotic militarism. However, Wyho's task won't be to end war, but only, like Florence Nightingale, to provide "first-aid" (255). So too all the roles for women: Wyho runs errands, Mum manages the household, Lenore serves coffee. Even twelve-year-old Hazel is sexualized (157, 114). Heinlein restricts women to such roles because Prof and Mannie believe in an essential difference between the sexes: men are intellectually stable, but women randomly oscillate between savagery and compassion (148, 293). In short, women are simply less rational. The modality given women mirrors the subordinate position of all Loonies: while both seem to throw off oppression, both end up more dominated than ever before by a subtle reinscription of authority precipitated and sanctioned by Prof.

Prof, then, remains the text's political nexus, mourned in the final pages as the passing of the one true master, martyred author of the definitive discourse on the best possible state (299). For Prof, the emplotment of utopian political discourse assumes the narrative structure of nineteenth-century social theory developed from misreading evolutionary science, drawing heavily on Darwin's natural selection. Richard Hofstadter's *Social Darwinism and American Thought* (1944) describes the broad impact that such thought had on Americans during the period of and just before Heinlein's youth. The discourse of Social Darwinism was founded by the British philosopher Herbert Spencer, who "not only coined the term 'the survival of the fittest' but. . . developed a powerful critique of all forms of state interference with the 'natural' workings of society, including regulation of business and public assistance to the poor" (Foner 1992, 598–99). Prof's position is clearly contiguous with Spencer's. Only the best and brightest survive Luna, that "stern schoolmistress" (*Moon*, 188)—and with an improved "breed," only Luna is positioned to realize the Nietzschean will to power that allows "one man" (162) to rule. But "what I fear most," Prof says rightly, "are affirmative actions of sober and well-intentioned men" who exercise power "to do something that appears to need doing" (242).

His blindness produced by its reciprocal insights, Prof names himself as Luna's greatest danger, someone who should be purged by Luna's "white corpuscles" (251). His theory of good government fundamentally undermines the moral position he employs to justify his actions. Prof both transgresses the rules of Rational Anarchy and hides behind them. As such, he becomes a figure reminiscent of the salude, the bastard, "someone essentially unstable, who accepts the rules only when they are useful to him and transgresses the formal continuity of attitudes." This agonist, "outside the rules of society," is essentially "asocial" (Barthes 1982, 24). Mannie confirms that "Prof was familiar with rules but followed them only as suited him" (164). The acute irony, then, of Prof's selection of the bar sinister as Luna's national emblem is not that it represents the melting pot of Luna Free State, but that it is Prof's family crest. He hypocritically holds that a free press is the one thing that can preserve freedom from "our greatest danger"—one source of information run through a single bottleneck (205)—but then controls and censors what Luna's citizens can hear: revealing his expedience but also his inauthenticity, his disregard for anyone's freedom but his own. Using Mike, Prof maintains complete surveillance on Loonies—Mike can even listen in on dead phone lines; this surveillance, from the inside-out, modernizes the technology of Jeremy Bentham's Panopticon: Prof's preferred state is a prison.

When finally confronted with his hypocrisy, the meretricious Prof presents betrayal as universal law (243). Thus, the position that masquerades as progressive political thought is finally revealed as reactionary. The State of Nature does not guarantee an egalitarian body politic so much as justify the cavalier morality of a new aristocracy; Prof, who presents himself as authoritative (62–66) turns out to be authoritarian, and in the Loonies' desire to throw off the yoke of Authority, they reinstall it again. No wonder they find themselves less free than before: Warden never operated with the control Prof exercises. And of course Prof's Rational Anarchy not only legitimates senseless violence for political, social, or economic gain, the narrative glorifies that violence or fills it with secondary sexual imagery. An example of the former comes during the coup, when Warden's guards, incapacitated by oxygen deprivation, are captured by Loonie insurgents: "No guard recovered . . . would appear anoxia broke necks," Mannie comments, letting us in on his little joke (147). A telling example of the latter: after Mike mercilessly crashes the Terran cruiser, slaughtering two thousand defenseless troops (257), he describes his experience as "an orgasm" (269).

In a state where death is the only penalty and where all judgments are made by strong men answerable only to themselves, violence becomes an ideological pogrom, as in the murder of Citizen Wright, a pretentious member of Luna's revolutionary council who cannot understand that Operation Hard Rock's rocks aren't thermonuclear weapons, and says so, loudly. Though Loonies always have bitter arguments (159), Mannie is happy to have his political opponent killed (278)—"certain types of loudmouthism should be a capital offence among decent people" (159). However, Judge Brody, an ally who understands as little as Wright, isn't killed even though guilty of the same offence—vociferous ignorance of what will actually happen (283). Wright is murdered because he constitutes what Nozick calls an "innocent threat" (Nozick 1974, 34), which he believes justifies exception to the libertarian prohibition against "violence on innocent persons" (33). Yet notice Wright's threat is discursive, focused on policy rather than physical immanence. Wright is murdered because his "certain kind of loudmouthism" is political dissent: "some people talk better if they breathe vacuum," Mannie says (*Moon*, 272).

The uncanny, frightening reinscription of authority might have been predicted early on, when Wyho wryly comments that "everybody does business with the Authority, we can't avoid it—that's the trouble" (18). Mannie's subvocalized response identifies the novel's central problematic: "Everybody does business with Authority for the same reason everybody does business with Law of Gravitation" (19). If the Law of Authority is as universal as the Law of Gravitation, how can one ever act morally, authoritatively, without reinscribing authoritarian power moves? Prof's aggressively antidemocratic position (that the cells must be kept small, or as Mannie will later say, "Three was two too many" [229]) recalls James Madison's warning in number ten of his Federalist Papers: "and the smaller the number of individuals composing a majority, and the smaller the compass within which they are placed, the more easily will they concert and execute their plans of oppression" (74).

Madison was specifically supporting the new Constitution and its Bill of Rights, which protects individuals from the state. Prof thinks even this kind of proscription untenable because it might limit his "freedom." It might limit, for example, his "freedom" to murder political opponents. Mannie's provisional solution ("I told conscience to go to sleep" [*Moon* 108]) may allow him to go and do "what I had to do" (247), but it cannot resolve the problem. Richard Rorty has rightly noted that this dilemma is the poststructural problematic par excellence: ". . . the problem of how to finitize while exhibiting a knowledge of one's own finitude—of satisfying Kierkegaard's demand on Hegel—is the problem of [contemporary] theory. It is the problem of how to overcome authority without claiming authority. That problem is the [contemporary] counterpart to the metaphysician's problem of bridging the gap between appearance and reality, time and eternity, language and the non-linguistic" (Rorty 1989, 104–5). The ineluctable reinscription of authoritarian logics, then, is the direct consequence of the attempt to pretend that power, here presented as the figure of Authority, can be evaded and exercised without problematic questions or moral worries. Despite his "abstract hatred of all Authority" (*Moon* 90), Prof's Rational Anarchy collaborates with the structures it contests, repeats every voice of Authority, failing to be either rational or anarchic.

A Great Disorder Is an Order

On Luna "dirty-word intellectuals" (281) are either dangerous yammerheads or "merely . . . literary critic[s], which is harmless, like dead yeast left in beer" (164); in either case they do nothing, produce

nothing other than "talk" (157). But on Le Guin's Anarres, our protagonist is both a yammering intellectual and a strong man who never equates
strength with machismo (*The Dispossessed* 230), virility or violence: the
"strongest" human is the "most ethical" (177). Like Prof, Shevek understands that moral authority rests with individual choice, but also recognizes that "The choices of the social being are never made alone" (217).
He does not believe that his own circle—his "us"—is restricted solely to
contingencies of blood, geography, or political alliance. Rather, he feels
that his circle encompasses the whole of humanity, since the Anarresti's
primary value, their "only resource" is "human solidarity" (135).

Unlike the inhabitants of Luna Free State, those on Anarres willingly orchestrated a mass migration to Urras's satellite, an event reminiscent of the religious migrations of the seventeenth century or the
utopian self-isolations of the nineteenth. The Anarresti are followers of
a political revolutionary, the anarchist and pacifist Odo of Urras, who
accept ostracism to test their anti-hierarchal political scheme, one based
on cooperation rather than competition, public propriety rather than
personal property, mutual aid rather than mutual aggression (167). Nos-
talgic of the utopian communities of America's nineteenth century, the
narrative's heavily romanticized depictions of Odo, her movement, and
human behavior idealize "the natural": "The Settlers had left the laws
of man behind them, but brought the laws of harmony along" (71).
Anarresti festivals arise "spontaneously out of the rhythms of life on the
planet and the need of those who work together to celebrate together"
(188).

Despite such mythicized origins, Odo's political philosophy follows
familiar and rational models, beginning with her notion of the properly
minimal state, which is generated not because government is a disease
but because minimal interference is the best way to develop mutual aid
and utilitarian order. Throughout, the Anarresti hold that no state and
no laws can nurture either individual or social growth, so laws are neither necessary nor preferable. "We have no law," Shevek will say, "but
the single principle of mutual aid between individuals" (241). To become Anarresti means to accept the tenet that "we are responsible to
you and you to us" (310): "and that responsibility is our freedom. To
avoid it, would be to lose our freedom" (36). Odo's belief is that the state
effectively preserves inequalities rather than prevents them (Heinlein's
Luna is an exemplary case). Odo echoes Foucault, who argued that: "The
role of political power . . . is perpetually to re-inscribe [disequilibrium]

through a form of unspoken warfare: to re-inscribe it in social institutions, in economic inequalities, in language, in bodies themselves, in each and every one of us" (Foucault 1977, 90).

Anarchists must therefore short-circuit what the libertarian state would preserve: private property. Since individuals can grow only within a healthy community, personal property and the profit motive are replaced by community ownership and collective aid. Essence is replaced by function, hierarchy by centrality, centralized authority (or concentrated capital) by decentralized administration (or disseminated labor), ownership by use, conspicuous consumption by frugality, militarism by pacifism, nationalism by global economics. Anarres, then, seeks to establish not a utopia, regarding that notion as childishly naive, but an isotopia, an egalitarian-universalist system wherein all individuals are equals. Annaresti ideology resembles the loosely administrated pluralism endorsed by the Ekumen, already familiar to readers of Le Guin's well-known *The Left Hand of Darkness* (137–38).

The practical consequences of such doctrine are wide-ranging. Here are two instances. On Anarres, the great "socialist disease" described in *The Cat Who Walks Through Walls* is indeed rampant, even pandemic. Medical care is free—so too are all necessities: food, housing, shelter, clothing, and employment. Any "mathematical impossibilities" are shared by all, as a fact no more unfamiliar than the fact that one must eat in order to live. When Anarres experiences famine, all citizens share the risk (*The Dispossessed* 199–217). Where all share the same risk, all stand to gain: Shevek will argue that human solidarity comes precisely from this "shared pain" (50, cf. 241).

A second clear consequence is that knowledge (scientific, philosophical, technological) should be freely disseminated rather than licensed for private profit, what Lyotard calls "the mercantilization of knowledge" (5). With Lyotard, Shevek would "give the public free access to the memory and data banks" (67). And he does, sharing his discoveries first with Sabul, head of Abbenay's institute in physics, and later with the Urrasti, Terrans and Hainish. Shevek cannot see any reason to prohibit the free circulation of knowledge (89), but this is not the case on Urras, where "to be a physicist . . . was to serve not society, not humanity, not the truth, but the State" (219).

Urrasti social and political culture, therefore, is everything the Anarresti repudiate. The direct antithesis of anarchism, A-Io's American-style capitalism (105) is driven by property, profit and privacy. From early childhood, Anarresti children are taught to share, to revile the "propertarian" and "profiteering" Ioti whose appalling excess makes life (for a minority) so luxurious that Shevek is repulsed by it as "a kind of ultimate apotheosis of the excremental" (52; cf. 80). Their clothes (104-05), furnishings (51–52), and homes (176) reveal a dedicated eroticism totally absent from Anarresti culture, something Shevek notices as soon as he boards the space shuttle for Urras (15). He calls this phenomenon "the woman in the table," which resonates as a leitmotif in Shevek's analysis.

The sensuality first observed in objects extends to the objectification of women. The sister of an Ioti physicist (158), Vea is "the woman in the table" who "incarnate[s] all the sexuality the Ioti repress . . ." into dreams, art, and material goods (172). Vea is a "body profiteer" (171)—someone who recognizes (and subsequently exploits [173]) the fact that within capitalism everything is commodified; in A-Io, as in America today, some women actually profit from sexism. Men, however, maintain their bigotry because of a pervasive sense of "propriety" (20)—of the proper and natural positioning of people and things that extends far back into Urrasti history.

Every bit as patriarchal as Prof, Ioti men think beautiful women can't perform abstract analytic operations and smart women suffer "vaginal atrophy" (59). Himself the metonym for a wizened, atrophied ethos, Atro is the venerable professor given by Le Guin the sorry task of justifying Ioti sexism, arguing that "A beautiful, virtuous woman is an inspiration to us—the most precious thing on" the planet (60). Urrasti women, Shevek notes to himself, are "suppressed, silenced, bestialized." Atro's argument bears remarkable similarity to Prof's; Atro also invokes an evolutionary analogy to legitimate this archist bias as natural and just (115). Appalled by the confusion of physical and social law (164) Shevek, like any Odonian, acknowledges essential differences of sex (biology) but thinks gender the product of cultural codes: "A person chooses work according to interest, talent, strength—what has sex to do with that?" (13).

Urras and Anarres are indeed dialectical, binary opposites: "A psychopathy on Anarres was rational behavior on Urras" (223). Their ideological opposition is also represented by imagery. Where Urras is an oasis (105) of water and forest, Anarres is an arid desert. Where Urras hides the truth behind taboo and law (120, 228–30), on Anarres "nothing is hidden" (80). Where Urrasti live behind walls (107), on Anarres "no doors were locked, few were shut" (80). Throughout *The Dispossessed*, the narrative emplotment of utopian discourse traces a dialectical ambiguity between alternatives—between utopia and dystopia, self and other, us and them, natural and pathological—and these dialectics are first and foremost suggested by matters of style. Beginning in Shevek's present, the chapters toggle between present and past, juxtaposing the present on Urras with scenes from Shevek's psychological and political development on Anarres. The novel's central conceit is its reliance on several organizing metaphors, three of which I'll consider here: the wall, the circle, and empty hands.

Shevek's science mirrors his politics: just as he seeks to unify the two cultures, he seeks a grand unified field theory to unite sequency (linearity) and simultaneity (circularity). But Shevek is also caught in the dialectical ambiguities of ironic reversal and metonymic substitution. Once on A-Io, his altruism, his proselytizing for Odonian anarchism undergoes trials. Never having experienced the tantalizing charms of privacy or profit, Shevek finds leisure and riches seductive; so alluring, that having his "social conscience" sedated by alcohol (unavailable on Anarres), he experiences a "moral stammer" (211), assaults Vea (185), and comes close to rape, ejaculating on her dress.

So while Urras and Anarres are opposites, their precise status turns out to be far more ambivalent and reversible than Shevek had been taught to believe. Anarres has its propertarians, characters who double Urrasti models—Sabul mirrors Dearri (180, 192), Rulag behaves like Atro. Shevek would transcend such essential ambivalence: "I want my people to come out of exile" (111); "The Odonians who left Urras had been wrong, wrong in their desperate courage, to deny their history, to forgo the possibility of return" (72). Odo's epitaph had been "To be whole is to be part / True voyage is return" (68), and Shevek hopes to realize the second half of Odo's ideology, which the Anarresti have forgotten.

Anarres's error can only be overcome by Shevek's journey. As Odo had been "an exile" (82) in her own land, he now plays her role in reverse (72). An outcast (86), ironically both inside and outside Odonian ideology, Shevek is the ambivalent Christ figure whose suffering will redeem his people. Thinking they have resolved the problem of Authority, the Anarresti cannot see the archism reinscribed within their anarchism; they have "forgotten" the fact that "Everybody does business with Authority for the same reason everybody does business with Law of Gravitation." Anarres's immediate danger is that its logistics clearinghouse—the bureau of Production and Distribution Coordination (the PDC) (61)—has become "an archistic bureaucracy" (134). In the 170 years since the first settlers arrived, Anarres's institutions have ossified, its people becoming progressively more dogmatic (264). As Bedap so passionately argues, Anarres is now more like Urras than any anarchist should tolerate (just as Luna Free State now seems more restricted than under Warden). For some Anarresti, the options are few: playwrights (Tirin) go into exile (137) or madness (262); musicians are denied the resources to do innovative work. Nozick notes that the most significant problem within an anarchy is that an individual may "lack the power to enforce his rights; he may be unable to punish or exact compensation from a stronger adversary who has violated them" (Nozick 1974, 12). Particularly powerless are Anarresti children, programmed by skewed propaganda that doesn't reflect the factual conditions on either world. This final outrage, Bedap argues, is intolerable: "education, the most important of the social organism, has become rigid, moralistic, authoritarian. Kids learn to parrot Odo's words as if they were laws—the ultimate blasphemy" (136). What the Anarresti fear most is change and difference—mirroring precisely the Urrasti conservatism Odo sought to raze.

Shevek tries to bridge the gap—or to follow the novel's fundamental trope, to dismantle the wall separating the several binary pairs that structure the narrative's theme and action. The image-metaphor of the wall opens each of the first two chapters, allowing Le Guin to show it is the product of Anarresti as much as Urrasti culture (1, 21). The trope's source is Bedap, who identifies Shevek's frustration with Sabul as "you've come up against the wall" (133); Bedap initially configures "the wall" as a general rubric for any limit, any senseless or destructive frustration, the sort of cliched topos found from poetry (Frost's "Mending Wall") to pop music (Pink Floyd's "The Wall"), where the wall is usually little more than a metonym for some psychic obstacle (101). Shevek similarly encounters "walls around [others'] thought" (13, 35, 184, 224, 265, et al.). Faced with such difficulty, Shevek takes the "natural initiative" (66), first declaring he will go to Abbenay (7) and then to Urras (267) "to unbuild walls." Yet, as we are warned on the opening page, walls themselves "are ambiguous, two-faced," and so the wall serves both as emblem and as icon of the novel's dialectical play. The wall is, after all, a hypertropic representation of the virgule, the very emblem of binary opposition. Where Heinlein envisions rigid, ineluctable impediments between "us" and "them," Shevek would bridge, surpass, embrace, transgress difference(s), suggesting the second of the novel's central metaphors: the circle. Like the wall, this one also has a specific source—Odo. Her Circle of Life literally inscribes everything the Anarresti produce (26), including Shevek's book on simultaneity physics, bound in green to signify rebirth. As a political metonym, the matriarchal circle represents a specific, centrifugal resistance to the linear and hierarchal thought of Urras, which in contrast is marked by the phallic emblems of lines and arrows (179). As Shevek takes on Odo's role, so too he assumes her signet in the attempt to unify linear with circular time, sequency with simultaneity physics (178–82). Bedap's insights again prove valuable, for it is he who notes that the circle ironizes centripetal, authoritarian reinscription: conditions on Anarres are such that "the circle has come right back round to the most vile kind of profiteering" (142).

The oxymoronic resolution of the arrow's chaotic dynamism and the circle's rejuvenating stasis (180) must incorporate both progress and preservation. The resolution of these competing theses must find its full articulation in another image, one proffered by Shevek and identified solely with him: empty hands. As the opening chapters begin with descriptions of the wall, which they subsequently juxtapose to the circle, the chapters typically close with a gloss on Shevek's state, such as the novel's final line: "His hands were empty, as they had always been" (311). These empty hands announce Shevek's return, his Odonian epitaph, the gesture of the circular journey that affects making the part whole (cf. 68). *The Dispossessed*'s rhetorical dialectics are perhaps most obvious in this set of images. His two dreams of the wall offer only ambiguous promises about the unification of opposites (27, 124), but the third dream provides the synthesis, and tears down the wall (225–26).

Such romanticized synthesis is offered up as spiritual, almost religious, transcendence. Indeed, the topoi of apocalyptic religious legend continually mark how others understand Shevek. A-Io's popular press sees him as "the 'Forerunner' . . . the one who comes before the millennium—'a stranger, outcast, exile, bearing in empty hands the time to come'" (186). When Shevek finally meets the Ioti underground, they gloss him as the Christian Logos: Shevek is the word, "the idea of anarchism, made flesh. Walking amongst us" (237). The third-person narrator also imbues Shevek with such mystery, for what he brings in empty hands is the light of his world (cf. John 8:12): "The shadows moved about him, but he sat unmoving as Anarres rose above the alien hills, at her full and

59

mottled dun, lambent. The light of his world filled his empty hands"
(73). When he later tells Takver, the mother of his child, what powers their star, he says "It's not talk. It's not reason. It's hand's touch.
I touch the wholeness, I hold it. Which is moonlight, which Takver?
How shall I fear death? When I hold it, when I hold it in my hands
the light . . . " (154).

Holding the insight, the illumination of Odonian anarchism,
Shevek's empty hands actually are rather Christ-like; his message (241–
42), like Jesus to the wealthy Ephesian prince (Luke 18:18–30), is that
one must give up all possessions and property, indiscriminately love all
humankind, and keep the bond of fidelity to all others even though it
might cause personal suffering. But you recall that Shevek's position on
suffering is that shared pain, and only shared pain, produces human
solidarity. From self-dispossession, future rewards follow: the human
solidarity of "hand's touch." Atro, because his only "relationship to . . .
things [is] one of possession" (107), thinks that Shevek's contribution to
physics should be held, controlled for profit; "with a great gift in our
hands," he says, misunderstanding Shevek's real gift (116). Asked what
he offers and what he wants, he replies: "I want the walls down. I want
solidarity, human solidarity" (112). The final wall to fall is the most elemental: the one between people.

When we find it, however, Anarres has retreated from the human
circle. Isolated and afraid of difference, Anarres's heterophobia (fear
of "the other") reinscribes certain biases of the culture it rejects. Le
Guin envisions Anarres as she envisions nature, "a ceaseless harmony composed of disharmony" (145), but Anarres's current rigidity actually suppresses dissent, privileging a decayed Odonian
dogma. While the culture manages to deflect the excesses of individual wants—the propertarian, virtually monomaniacal individuality reminiscent of Melville's Ahab, a notion of subjectivity that
would say, as Shevek does as an infant, "mine sun!" (22)—the culture
still remains fundamentally ambivalent, because its heterophobia op-
presses any divergence from group consensus as "egoizing" (24). Hence
it suppresses individuality, innovation, self-critique, ingenuity, the "natural initiative" that Odo's system takes as its given.

While considerably more self-aware, unfortunately this is the same
kind of moral hypocrisy found in *The Moon Is a Harsh Mistress*, where
Mannie's conscience sleeps, allows him to joke that while Prof is both
vegetarian and pacifist it doesn't stop him from eating meat or from

killing; he remains "rational" (*Moon* 139). Anarres's similar dilemma differs slightly, for it contains a feedback mechanism for self-correction. Anarresti political philosophy argues that individual conscience must remain vigilant against momentary individual exigency; Odo holds that "only the averted eye" (*The Dispossessed* 206) allows force, authoritarian power moves and violence, and what keeps the eye seeing is "private conscience": "the promise, the pledge, the idea of fidelity, an essential in the complexity of freedom" (187). As Shevek later adapts Odo's position, "The revolution is in the individual spirit or it is nowhere" (289).

Le Guin gives to Bedap the role of Anarres's conscience, Shevek's Jiminy Cricket. When the PDC begins to ossify, to centralize authority and preclude dissent, the culture is still structured to allow corrective feedback loops (264–67); it remains possible for Bedap to create a "Syndicate of Initiative" capable of destabilizing and reversing the PDC's rigidity. In this respect, Le Guin's overly romanticized view of how such a minimal state comes into being is countered by her gritty refusal to romanticize the solutions: only hard work and struggle can solve a society's political differences. Even the apolitical Shevek can be radicalized, take initiative, disrupt the walls Anarres has built around its thought and reinscribe the circle of life.

Anarres, however, has a deeper flaw. In "To Read The Dispossessed," Delany identifies how several blind spots "subvert [Le Guin's] otherwise laudatory enterprise of reversing our modern symbology" (270). He highlights the novel's many omissions—jealousy, female sexuality, homosexuality, the essence/genesis of the Great Theory (234–38)—arguing that it reinscribes the patriarchal sexuality it seeks to critique. Since Takver's sexuality is simply missing, the novel reaffirms the Urrasti code: women cannot act, or where they do, they are slaves of biology (cf. *The Dispossessed* 266). The novel's heterosexism remains homophobic, excluding and isolating Bedap: why is he alone and separate (268) except if a heterosexist episteme inscribes itself on Le Guin's view of the homosexual? Why can he "never have intimacy" or raise a child? Delany goes on to argue that *The Dispossessed*, like Heinlein's *Moon* (to which he draws no direct comparison), is flawed both because of clumsy writing and because of the overabundance of "didacta," which appear as author's lecture "rather than either characterization or social portraiture" (Delaney 1977, 246). Le Guin's deus ex machina invasion of the narrative, we might go on to point out, creates exactly the sort of Anarresti myopia Le Guin critiques—where like Prof, Bedap's insight has a reciprocal relation to the narrative's blindness. Once we see this blindness, we also see that like Heinlein's novel, *The Dispossessed* contains an authorial metonym, which in this case isn't a composite of the several protagonists but Sabul, the silent editor, the one who failing to appreciate the truly radical paradigms at play mangles and manipulates Shevek's physics text (cf. 246–47).

Nevertheless and despite the novel's defects, its political imagination remains vastly preferable to Heinlein's, whose repulsive antidemocratic desire to purify the breed is countered by Shevek's comment that "We don't want purity, but complexity" (*The Dispossessed* 182). Odo's conception of social amelioration retains several of Prof's economic arguments, but transforms them to public rather than personal use. On Anarres, there are no entitlements; the Loonie Law of Tanstaafl still holds. "Free" means no cash changes hands, but labor always circulates. "Cooperation and function, essential concepts of [Odo's] Analogy, both implied work" (216–17). Indeed, the fundamental right in Anarres's anarchy isn't the right to bargain, to exert economic power, but instead it is plural, ". . . the rights of any citizen in any society: the right to work, to be maintained while working, and to share the product with all who wanted it. The rights of an Odonian and of a human being" (222). To the Anarresti, work is play, and play is work (216).

On Luna, there is one punishment for crime—death. On Anarres, there is no corporal (let alone capital) punishment (150). Those Loonies who reject the "right" of the revolutionary government to "legislate" on their behalf, those who endorse an anarchy rather than Prof's "rational" rule are "spaced." Those Anarresti who don't cooperate are simply left alone; shunning does not kill, it says, take responsibility for yourself. Anarres's pacifism is also authentic. Violence and sexuality, rather than being connected as they are for Heinlein, remain separate: on Anarres no one has orgasms while committing murder. In fact, to the Anarresti, a gun resembles "a deformed penis" (3), suggesting not only just a silly joke but a significant reconceptualization of how individual power is currently modeled by a parallel to macho sexuality. Odo's and Shevek's pacifism is the rejection of hierarchal order, the very structure of the military authority (245). Anarres's free dissemination of knowledge is also presented as a practical alternative rather than an idealist's dreaming.

Except for the fact that a privileged few live in luxury in Heinlein's system, Le Guin's anarchy is superior in every respect. An immature

Shevek might say "Mine sun," miming the Sun King, but it is Prof who would equate self with state, say "c'est moi." At the end of *The Dispossessed*, "things" on Anarres are "a little broken loose . . . dangerous" (309): not social chaos, but not authoritarian tyranny either. Perhaps the perpetual ambiguity, the essentially human risk of an anarchy.

Rhizome

If in Delany's *Triton* the ambiguities of good governance are just as pronounced as in *Moon* and *The Dispossessed*, here they are also explicitly ironized, an effect achieved primarily by positioning anarchic politics as the background, the texture against which personal consequences are mapped. Rather than developing a drama of political doctrine with characters as nugatory analogs of or agents for politically "correct" behavior, as we see in each of the other two novels, *Triton* examines the protagonist's personal failure to adapt to a multiplicity of ethnic, generic, and social codes.

This is not to say that the backdrop against which Bron's trials are displayed is any less edifying than the foregrounded didacta of Heinlein or Le Guin. Delany still investigates the prospects of anarchy as a viable political alternative. But in postmodern fiction generally, and especially Delany's science fiction, the emplotment of utopian discourse is deployed not so much as lecture, manifesto, or allegory as disclosed through the science fiction synecdoche; it is the spatialization of Utopian visions "in which the transformation of social relations and political institutions is projected onto the vision of place and landscape, including the human body" (Jameson 160). Here Jameson paraphrases Foucault's position that the human body is the fundamental site of political struggle—not abstractions, granfalloons like "Loonies" or "Humanity," but always already realized in individuals. Not an altogether atypical position, it is found, for example, forcefully expressed in James Joyce's *Ulysses* when Bloom, whose variegated ethnicity is dispersed across all Europe, maintains that human cruelty and "injustice" (14.1474) are what we must struggle against—"And I belong to a race too, says Bloom, that is hated and persecuted. Also now. At this moment. This very instant" (14.1467–68).

Triton explicitly critiques contemporary conceptions of gender and follows the sort of feminist analysis found in Judith Butler's *Gender Trouble* and *Bodies That Matter*—books that call for the reformation of questions of agency from epistemological or ontological grounds to their function as "a given set of signifying practices" which would amount to a gender "reconfiguration" (*Gender*, 144), "reformulation" or "rearticulation" (*Bodies* passim).[2] Butler addresses gender as a socially coded regulatory practice rather than an essence, which precisely parallels the thematics of Delany's novel. Tethys, the main city of Neptune's Triton, represents a culture where "the mechanism of gender construction implies the contingency of that construction" and "proves useful to the political project" of feminism's desire "to enlarge the scope of possible gender configurations" (*Gender*, 38).

Delany's political imagination differs from the more familiar precedents in that his speculation hinges on a technology capable of erasing the binary oppositions that currently engender many of contemporary society's woes. Not simply gender's social roles, but biology itself: sex-inscriptions are genetically reversible. In Triton's future, every conceivable sexual orientation or kink can be induced in a matter of seconds. Or reprogrammed, as you wish, for there exists "no majority configuration" (*Triton* 276). It is almost as if Delany has extrapolated Derrida's question: "What if we were to approach . . . the area of relationship to the other where the code of sexual marks would no longer be discriminating?" (Derrida 1982, 76), or as if he had extended Butler's comment that "if gender is not tied to sex, either causally or expressively, then gender is a kind of action that can potentially proliferate beyond the binary limits imposed by the apparent binary of sex" (*Gender* 112). Butler argues that "The material irreducibility of sex has seemed to ground and to authorize feminist epistemologies and ethics, as well as gendered analyses of various kinds" (*Bodies* 28); she describes her project as "an effort to displace the terms of this debate" (28), claiming not only that a "coherent subject position" is not desirable, but that "it may be only by risking the incoherence of identity" (113) that a political poststructuralism is possible.

This anarchic incoherence, coupled to our concomitant fears, is what we find in Delany's novel. Tethys contains "forty or fifty sexes, and twice as many religions" (*Triton* 117), "and thirty to thirty-seven" political parties (220) which govern simultaneously—producing a social system that "is both individuating and stabilizing" (221). With neighborhood co-ops catering to every conceivable ideology, every taboo and fetish is simultaneously accommodated and obliterated—depending on where one lives and with whom one associates. Mutually consenting partners can do anything they like, provided that their choice is free.

"What are your social responsibilities when you have a technology like that available?" (269). For a lesson in social responsibility Bron Helstrom is as edifying as any lecture on free markets or shared pain. Shevek's claim that revolution must live within each individual or it will fail is illustrated in Bron, a "metalogician" (58 ff.) who may be able to map the "Universe of Discourse" (61) but who cannot effectively reflect on his own—partly because any "rigorous mapping of the Universe of Discourse" is a "metalogical reduction" (107) that distorts its own semiosis by eliminating inherent conflicts and contradictions.[3] Bron realizes that with another vocabulary (123), he would conceptualize his own problem (122) differently; but he is incapable of the poststructural maneuver, which Rorty would define as changing the question or altering the vocabulary (1989, 44–47). Delany's Bron, to adapt Deleuze's phrase, "is neither axiomatic nor typological, but topological" (*Foucault* 14); Bron is the problem mapped rather than its emblem. Rorty thinks such fictional or ethnographic topologies should constitute "the principal vehicles of moral change and progress" (Rorty 1989, xvi) for contemporary society (192); what Delany's *Triton* offers, then, is similar to what Rorty sees in "the fiction of . . . James or Nabokov [which] gives us details about what sorts of cruelty we ourselves are capable of" (xvi). Prof, Mannie and Mike possess miraculous judgment and moral clarity, and consequently are mere caricatures of human beings. Shevek's purity may be sullied by momentary lapses, but he remains so angular a character that he lacks the psychological complication of a real human being. Bron, on the other hand, is one of us.

Almost an anachronism, Bron is completely unable to adjust to his new social model, for he conceptualizes life's power-relations hierarchically, or perhaps more accurately, unilaterally. But Triton's world will not permit such unidirectional behavior. The practical consequences of Bron's personal failures are several and, finally, predictable; there is no need to rehearse their catalog, already so well indexed by Michelle Masse. Despite an innocuous exterior and vaguely sympathetic self-analysis (he may be "a first class louse" but he's "trying hard" [Masse 83]), Bron remains intolerant, moody, sexist, homophobic, and "rotten with neuroses" (32). Finally, what Bron cannot address is Odo's dicta: "The choices of the social being are never made alone" (217).

Triton also has a rather conventional story line, with a minor kink: Bron meets girl, Bron gets girl, Bron loses girl, Bron becomes girl: Literally. But even though he becomes a woman, he still doesn't get it, in the political idiom of 1992, for he never subverts his dialectical logic. To the very end, he still thinks in binaries—man/woman, owner/owned, client/servant, and so forth. The sexual ambiguity is further developed by the fact that Bron's girl has a phallic professional name (the Spike) and that her profession is "micro-theater" (20), which—as you may expect—clothes the entire novel in theatrical metaphors both expressed and implied (cf. *Bodies* 14–15). (When *Triton* was published, The Spike was a heavy leather New York gay bar.)

Triton's tropology begins with the Spike's (micro)theater of cruelty (19) which enacts, simulates passions, violence, hatred—all in order to elicit an emotional response from the audience. Bron would be a player (and at one point performs), but more importantly, would dominate the simulator, would have the Spike subordinated to his individual desire. These classical motifs embed a metacommentary. The "space" for (micro)theater is Tethys's "un-licensed" sector (9), fully anarchic space of art (75). At a party, the theater company's discussion of what modern audiences can't "relate to" applies especially well to Bron, since their twentieth-century dramas are structured by sexual jealousy and peripeteia (134): indeed, the novel's plot revolves around Bron's jealous reversals, the kind which produce a "nausea" (19) bordering on cognitive dissonance.

One could read most of the novel's imagery and events as self-reflexive or metapoetic tropes. For instance, Tethys is protected from its harsh environment by a dome, within which an Earth-like atmosphere and gravity are artificially maintained; the interior surface of the dome is a "Sensory Shield" (37). Triton, so distant from its antagonist Earth, experiences its revolutionary war not as a direct assault but as sabotage against its artificial environment. The city's "gravity wobble," a phrase which is "just [a] highly physicalized metaphor" (40), operates as a metonym for Bron's condition; immediately after he reads the Spike's brutal analysis of his character, Tethys suffers "decompression" (231), a "gravity deflection" (240) that almost destroys the city. Lawrence, a tenant in Bron's co-op and the only one who might be called Bron's "friend," names his own (clearly also Bron's) fear as "anaurophobia": "fear of losing one's atmosphere" (243), where "atmosphere" suggests worldview, Bron's anachronistic episteme, the artificial environment Bron exists within. A second simple example is the war game "vlet," introduced to Bron by Lawrence—a game Bron always loses. As a synecdoche for the larger plot, Bron's war against himself and others, it is no surprise that the first game leaves Bron, "the scarlet foot soldier" (28) later "trapped between two mirrored screens" (38). Bron simply cannot negotiate the poststructural *mise en abyme*, the abyss of reflection that threatens an anarchy's stability.

The same sort of analysis might be offered for any of the larger motifs or images in the novel, for all are "overdetermined systems" (5) that function metapoetically to point their finger at Bron, isolated and individual within a culture defined by its multiplicity. Typically, Bron is "alone in a conversation niche" (140), one who sees his "reflection in dead glass" (80), or who equates happiness with "edgeless[ness]" (158) but fetishizes himself as a clear and distinct Cartesian subject (see Masse 1983, 50–53). Cartesian subjectivity and hierarchy appeal precisely because they are clear, certain, coherent, stable—and so by the principle of parsimony, preferable. Like Kafka's Joseph K., Bron desires a more determined, "simpler" (*Triton* 302) arrangement of moral and social order. Of course, he is the novel's sole "straight" character, and for him Tethys is too complex, too chaotic, too hetero. Bron wants to be "at the center" (306) within a culture with none; Bron wants to be "the only one" (120, 134) in a place based on multiplicity (122).

Tethys provides not the simplicity and certainty of utopia or isotopia, but the specific complexity of heterotopia. Triton's subtitle, "An Ambiguous Heterotopia," pays homage first to *The Dispossessed,* but more significantly to Foucault, whom Delany quotes in opening his "Appendix B" (345): "Utopias afford consolation" but "Heterotopias are disturbing, probably because they make it impossible to name this and that, because they shatter or tangle common [concepts], because they destroy 'syntax' in advance, and not only the syntax which causes words and things (next to and also opposite one another) to 'hold together'" (Foucault 1966, xviii).

This syntax placed into question is doxa, the social syntax, the epistemic ground, the foundational order that allows us to conceptualize our world. Delany's heterotopia would shatter our episteme, resulting in a new syntax that, in a passage Delany does not cite, Foucault clarifies: the disorder in which fragments of a large number of possible orders glitter separately in the dimension, without law or geometry, of the heteroclite; and that word should be taken in its most literal, etymological sense: in such a state, things are "laid," "placed," "arranged" in sites so very different from one another that it is impossible to find a place of residence for them, to define a common locus beneath them all (Foucault 1966, *xvii-xviii*).

The only thing these various syntaxes hold in common is the contingent, heterotropic framework (the semiotic space that rhetorically structures topoi, places), the way they are situated within (a) space. This revolutionary space, then, constitutes, compels the convoluted, "folded-back-on-itself . . . psychology of the political alien" that Delany argued is missing in Le Guin ("To Read," 254).

The Moon Is a Harsh Mistress's political imagination insists on hierarchical patterns (rigid binaries), *The Dispossessed*'s on the ineluctable confrontation of binary differences (with a neat if incomplete dialectical synthesis), but *Triton* demands the non-resolved play of difference, the deconstructive play that Derrida calls differance. In articulating a single, global political philosophy, utopian discourses (like those of Heinlein and Le Guin) attempt to legitimate the social bond by suppressing difference—subordinating all human beings to a single system.[4] This imperialistic tendency is acutely delineated in the term isotopia, a "same" or "equal" place that would homogenize alterity. Rather than looking for a subordinating rule, and envisioning utopia as a kind of monastic order, *Triton* exemplifies some of the consequences of a socio-political system that refuses to impose a totalizing, global ideology. One could, following Lyotard, call these micronarratives (Lyotard 1979, *xxvi*, 60 ff.) that preserve a general theory of social agonistics (14–17); or abstract from its operations an epistemology of paralogy (60–66). But since Delany investigates the semiotic space prefigured by heterotopia, any mapping of heterotopia's "universe of discourse" must be cross-referenced against the conception of rhizome space developed by Foucault's two friends, the philosopher Deleuze and the psychoanalyst Guattari. More concerned with the real spaces that structure social difference (brothels, prisons, boats, cemeteries) and the institutions that maintained them (repression, the state, the circulation of capital, the church), Foucault never fully explored the consequences of his view. In "Of Other Spaces," a brief essay originally given as an address in 1967 and only published seventeen years later, Foucault takes up the question again. Delany was probably unaware that in this essay Foucault sets out the six "principles" of heterotopia; these six reveal Foucault's intense interest in describing "constant[s] of every human group" (Foucault 1986, 24), "the space in which we live" rather than speculating about change. It is, he says, simply a fact that "we live inside a set of relations that delineates sites which are irreducible to one another and absolutely not superimposable on one another" (23). These hetero-topic and irreducible sites are real, actual places, not the sort of "unreal, virtual space"—those good-nowheres—that constitute utopia (24). Foucault also offered some indirect commentary in texts such as the lectures and interviews collected in *Power/Knowledge* (1980), but he never expressly turned to political speculation. Deleuze and Guattari followed Foucault's lead, his interest in the way that power circulates within the social matrix—but less in what separates the individual sites than in the structure that accounts both for their coexistence and passage between them, that "common locus beneath them all."

In the two massive volumes of capitalism and schizophrenia, *Anti-Oedipus* (1972) and *A Thousand Plateaus* (1980), Deleuze and Guattari attempt to articulate the contradictions of contemporary culture and to project an alternative behavioral (hence political) model, which they name "nomadology." In his preface to the English edition of *Anti-Oedipus*, Foucault introduced their work as a guide to the "art of living counter to all forms of fascism," suggested that *Anti-Oedipus* could be renamed "Introduction to the Non-Fascist Life" (xiii). Antithesis of the tyrant, the anarchist nomad or postmodern hero travels easily between microdiscourses, acknowledges the usefulness of each while privileging none: revels in a sort of schizophrenia. The nomad embodies a version of what Rorty calls the "all-purpose intellectual" or, more romantically, "the strong poet." What this nomad wanders through is the intertextual semiosis of rhizome space (*A Thousand Plateaus* 3–27). As a schema of discourses, rhizome implies an episteme that structures itself as an infinite labyrinth of possibilities rather than an arborescent hierarchy, a unidirectional tree of power: "A rhizome has no beginning or end; it is always in the middle, between things, interbeing, intermezzo. The tree is filiation, but the rhizome is alliance, uniquely alliance" (*A Thousand Plateaus* 25).

Any adequate exposition of the rhizome and its consequences would take far more development than is possible here, so allow me to pursue an analogy. If "the Universe of Discourse" can be conceived of as a matrix, a maze of competing vocabularies and practices, then we can (following Umberto Eco) articulate at least three distinct models of the maze. The first is the Classical: no one gets lost within this "linear labyrinth" (Eco 1986, 80) because going in and out are simple, unproblematic—the maze "itself is an Ariadne thread" (Eco 1986, 80); therefore the

Greeks put a Minotaur in its center. The second, or Mannerist maze, can be unraveled to reveal "a kind of tree, a structure with roots, with many blind alleys . . . you need Ariadne's thread to keep from getting lost"; such "a maze does not need a Minotaur: it is its own Minotaur" (81). Each maze corresponds to the way a universe conceives its episteme; roughly speaking, *Moon*'s problematic is of the first type and *The Dispossessed*'s of the second. The third kind of maze is the Net, or rhizome: "The rhizome is so constructed that every path can be connected with every other one. It has no center, no periphery, no exit, because it is potentially infinite. The space of conjecture is a rhizome space."

We could further adapt Eco's comment: Bron's world already has a rhizome structure: "it can be structured but never structured definitively" (Eco 1984, Postscript 57–58). I invoke the rhizome here to describe several phenomena: the particular semiotic problematic Bron encounters in his future; how the science fiction synecdoche can map the topography of future culture; and as a legitimation of the postmodern claim that human being is above all else a linguistically constructed social being. As Eco argues, "The universe of semiosis, that is, the universe of human culture, must be conceived as structured like a labyrinth of the third type" (Eco 1986, 83).

What happens to the problem of authority in rhizome space, in postmodern culture? Individual agency remains problematic, but the notion that any discourse could legitimate cruelty vanishes. For example in *Moon*, Heinlein's supple casuistry can justify murder as "the prudent course" (*Moon* 257), but in heterotopia (postmodern liberal utopia) nothing can rationalize cruelty. The question of Utopia, for *Moon*, is: as someone who knows what's best, can I (finally) make decisions for everyone else? The question of Utopia, for *The Dispossessed*, is: won't everyone just sit down and talk this out? But the question of Utopia, in *Triton*'s postmodern discourse, is: is a "shit-free Universe" possible (253)? Heterotopia's answer is "no." We are human, and shit happens.

Heterotopia

A "humanist" liberal utopia is an isotopia; a postmodern liberal utopia is an authentic anarchy, a heterotopia. The schema of a heterotopia is the rhizome: a model of rhetorical, semiotic, intertextual, heterotropic space—convoluted, oxymoronic, folded back on itself, distinctly poststructural. Rhizome space cannot be conceptualized using Classical, Enlightenment, Romantic, or Humanist models, all of which presuppose some ineluctable foundation, a certain ground upon which one builds the edifice of a Utopia. Only the anarchist can actualize the rhizome.

Deleuze and Guattari acutely observe that the rhizome is manifest throughout American literature. Americans "know how to move between things, establish a logic of the AND, overthrow ontology, do away with foundations, nullify endings and beginnings. They know how to practice pragmatics" (25). Nowhere are poststructural pragmatics more visible than in the episteme of speculative fiction. In *The Moon Is a Harsh Mistress*, cruelty is a law of nature; in both *The Dispossessed* and *Triton*, cruelty is the worst thing we can do, and their political imagination qualifies as "liberal"; *Triton* provides no explicit foundation for anarchy (and implicitly critiques any attempt to do so), and so therefore is an example of postmodern liberal utopia.

What makes one an anarchist is the philosophical disavowal, the renouncing and debunking of extrahistorical (transhistorical) or extrapolitical ("natural") grounds upon which one might theorize a better state. Like the nominalist or historicist, this anarchist contends that any theorizing must happen within the historical, cultural, and ideological conditions of its being, of its moment in being, its historicity. Anarchists should properly be called "pragmatists," for their arguments concerning ideal polity will be antifoundationalist or antiessentialist. To adapt Rorty's quotable formulation of pragmatism, heterotopia is politics without foundations, without legitimation. This recognition that the real basis or ground of political discourse is always already mediated by universal semiosis leads to the pragmatist notions that "what binds societies are common vocabularies and common hopes" (Rorty 1989 86); that "The social bond is linguistic" (Lyotard 1979, 40); that human "solidarity [is] made rather than found, produced in the course of history rather than . . . an ahistorical fact" (Rorty 1989 195).

The pragmatist's answer to what legitimates our common faith, our hope for heterotopia recalls Kierkegaard's: there is no legitimation for faith. It differs from Kierkegaard by maintaining that faith is also historical. A heterotopia, an ideal liberal society, "recognizes that it is what it is, has the morality it has, speaks the language it does, not because it approximates the will of God or the nature of man but because certain poets and revolutionaries of the past spoke as they did" (60–61). In such a place we hope to be less cruel, more inclusive, more tolerant, more liberal. "Liberals," Rorty writes in an attempt to recuperate this belea-

71

guered, almost exhausted term, "are the people who think that cruelty is the worst thing we do" (xv); they are "people who are more afraid of being cruel than anything else" (192). Since one can only recognize cruelty as happening to "us," to someone with the circle of "we" (192) (which is why Prof is neither liberal nor an anarchist), the ethnocentrism of the postmodern liberal is therefore "dedicated to enlarging itself, to creating an ever larger and more variegated ethnos" (198). This new Utopian thought is "horizontal rather than vertical" (Jameson 166). It does not ask: what are the philosophical foundations for pain?, but are you suffering? (cf. Rorty 1991 198).[5]

Heterotopia is liberal because it is open to radical alterity and attends first to human suffering; libertarian because its minimal state prohibits oppression, prohibits the tyrannical or fascist use of power; postmodern because it refuses to structure its multiple discourses under a single set of principles; and poststructural because it recognizes the inevitable reinscription of the very structures it contests—it never expostulates an epistemological certainty that might conceptualize itself as free of error, or in the possession of some final, definitive truth. Presumably, actualizing this heterotropic space as an intervention in the classical economy of patriarchy is the goal of poststructural thought. It is so in both in Delany and in Butler, whose "enabling disruption[s]" (*Bodies* 23) might recall Irigaray's much earlier call that we "jam the theoretical machinery itself" (Irigaray, *This Sex Which is not One*; quoted in Nye 1989, 81). Heterotropia sees itself as just one of myriad possibilities; it is a system without certainty, without pretension to totality; a system that, following Lyotard, would "wage war on totality; let us be witnesses to the unpresentable; let us activate the differences . . . " (Lyotard 1979, 82).

Notes

1. This notion appears in Malthus's "Essay on Population" (1798). Contemporary economists have increasingly attacked his views. The current famine in sub-Saharan Africa, like those in 1920s China and 1930s USSR, was produced by policy decisions made by centralized tyranny (rather than local anarchies). The Harvard economist Amartya Sen has shown that in each case ". . . their poor never starved because granaries were bare, as Malthus thought, but because they couldn't afford the grain"; "there has never been a famine in any country that's been a democracy with a relatively free press; I know of no exception. It applies to very poor countries with democratic

systems as well as to rich ones . . . my point is that if famine is about to develop, democracy can guarantee it won't" (qtd. Nasar 5). Sen's book is *Poverty and Famines: An Essay on Entitlement and Deprivation* (New York: Oxford University Press, 1981); an accessible summary of his views can be found in his "Freedoms and Needs," *The New Republic* (10–17 January 1994): 31–38.

2. Similar analyses can be found in Wittig and Irigaray.

3. Bron actually misunderstands metalogic, thinking that all conditions, even Boolean or Meinongian conditions, can be reduced to algorithms; but according to Ashima Slade, the discipline's founder, metalogic doesn't map the universe of discourse in algorithms, flow charts, or hierarchic trees (369). As the perceptive Lawrence tells Bron, "Your problem, you see, is that essentially you are a logical pervert" (258).

4. For discussion of the incompleteness of philosophic systems, see my "By indirections find directions out"; Lyotard 1979 55–65; or Barthes's discussion of the "strictly paranoid insanity" of the system ("Fourier" 367). Another useful account can be found in *Against Method*, where Paul Feyerabend sets out his "anarchistic theory of knowledge" (21 n.12, 33 n.4). Feyerabend's project provides for the philosophy of science (17) an analysis consonant with the postmodern critique advanced by Rorty, Lyotard, and Foucault for philosophy, history, and literary theory. See especially his Chapter 16 (181–214), where he establishes an implicit alliance with Rorty's "liberal ironist," arguing that the telos of science should be to relieve human suffering.

5. For a discussion of Rorty that reads him as asking all the correct questions but supplying all the wrong answers, see Bernstein. For fine discussions of poststructural politics which I came across long after completing this essay, see Corlett, Grosz, May, and Vattimo.

Works Cited

Asimov, Isaac. 1969. *Nightfall and Other Stories*. Greenwich: Fawcett.

Barthes, Roland. 1971. "Fourier." Translated by Richard Miller in *A Barthes Reader*, edited by Susan Sontag. New York: Hill & Wang, 1982.

———. *Mythologies*. 1957. Translated by Annette Lavers. New York: Hill & Wang, 1972.

Bernstein, Richard J. 1992. "Rorty's Liberal Utopia." In *The New Constellation: The Ethical-Political Horizons of Modernity/Postmodernity*. Cambridge: Massachusetts Institute of Technology Press. 258–92.

Butler, Judith. 1990. *Gender Trouble: Feminism and the Subversion of Identity*. New York: Routledge.

———. 1993. *Bodies That Matter: On the Discursive Limits of "Sex."* New York: Routledge.

Conrad, Joseph. 1907. *The Secret Agent*. Reprint, Prospect Heights: Waveland, 1990.

Corlett, William. 1989. *Community Without Unity: A Politics of Derridian Extravagance.* Durham: Duke University Press, 1993.

Delany, Samuel R. 1977. "To Read The Dispossessed." In *The Jewel-Hinged Jaw.* New York: Berkley, 1978. 218–83.

———. 1976. *Triton.* New York: Bantam.

Deleuze, Gilles. 1986. *Foucault.* Translated by Sean Hand. Minneapolis: University of Minnesota Press, 1988.

——— and Felix Guattari. 1980. *A Thousand Plateaus: Capitalism and Schizophrenia.* Translated by Brian Massumi. Minneapolis: University of Minnesota Press, 1987.

Derrida, Jacques. 1982. "Choreographies." [Interview.] *Diacritics* 12.2: 66–76.

———. 1980. *The Post Card: From Socrates to Freud and Beyond.* Translated by Alan Bass. Chicago: University of Chicago Press, 1987.

Easterbrook, Neil. 1995. "By indirections find directions out: Kierkegaard's Socratic Attractor." *Philosophy and Rhetoric* 28.2: 89–104.

Eco, Umberto. 1962. *The Aesthetics of Chaosmos: The Middle Ages of James Joyce.* Translated by Ellen Esrock. Cambridge: Harvard University Press, 1989.

———. 1984. Postscript to *The Name of the Rose.* Translated by William Weaver. San Diego: HBJ.

———. 1984. *Semiotics and the Philosophy of Language.* Bloomington: Indiana University Press, 1986.

Feyerabend, Paul. 1975. *Against Method: An Anarchistic Theory of Knowledge.* London: Verso, 1978.

Foner, Eric. 1992. "The Education of Richard Hofstadter." *The Nation* (4 May): 597–603.

Foucault, Michel. 1977. "The Eye of Power." *Power/Knowledge: Selected Interviews and Other Writings. 1972–1977.* Edited by Colin Gordon. New York: Pantheon, 1980. 146–65.

———. 1972. Preface to *Anti-Oedipus: Capitalism and Schizophrenia,* by Gilles Deleuze and Felix Guattari. Translated by Robert Hurley, Mark Seem, and Helen R. Lane. Minneapolis: University of Minnesota Press, 1983. xi–xiv.

———. 1966. *The Order of Things.* Translated by Alan Sheridan-Smith. New York: Vintage, 1970.

———. 1967. "Of Other Spaces." Translated by Jay Miskowiec. *Diacritics* 16.1 (1986): 22–27.

Grosz, Elizabeth. 1994. "A Thousand Tiny Sexes: Feminism and Rhizomatics." In *Gilles Deleuze and the Theater of Philosophy,* edited by Constantine V. Boundras and Dorothea Olkowski. New York: Routledge.

Heinlein, Robert A. 1985. *The Cat Who Walks Through Walls.* New York: Berkley, 1986.

———. 1968. *The Moon Is a Harsh Mistress.* New York: Berkley.

Irigaray, Luce. 1984. *An Ethics of Sexual Difference.* Translated by Carolyn Burke and Gillian C. Gill. Ithaca, N.Y.: Cornell University Press, 1993.

Jameson, Fredric. 1991. "Utopianism after the End of Utopia." In *Postmodernism, or the Cultural Logic of Late Capitalism*. Durham, Duke University Press.

Joyce, James. 1922. *Ulysses*. Edited by Hans Gabler, Wolfhard Steppe, and Claus Melchior. New York: Viking, 1986.

Kadrey, Richard. 1988. *Metrophage*. New York: Ace.

Klein, Arnold. 1982. "Destination: Void (Science Fiction is to Fiction as Christian Science is to Science)." *Harper's* (December): 64–67.

Le Guin, Ursula K. 1974. *The Dispossessed: An Ambiguous Utopia*. Reprint, New York: Avon, 1975.

———. 1969. *The Left Hand of Darkness*. Reprint, New York: Ace, 1976.

Lyotard, Jean-François. 1979. *The Postmodern Condition: A Report on Knowledge*. Translated by Geoff Bennington and Brian Massumi. Minneapolis: University of Minnesota Press, 1984.

Madison, James. *The Enduring Federalist*.

Masse, Michelle. 1983. "'All you have to do is know what you want': Individual Expectations in Triton." In *Coordinates: Placing Science Fiction and Fantasy*, edited by George Slusser, Eric Rabkin, and Robert Scholes. Carbondale: Southern Illinois University Press.

May, Todd. 1985. *The Political Philosophy of Poststructuralist Anarchism*. University Park: Pennsylvania State University Press.

Nasar, Sylvia. 1993. "It's never fair to just blame the weather." *New York Times* 17 January: 4:1+.

Nozick, Robert. 1974. *Anarchy, State, and Utopia*. New York: Basic.

Nye, Andrea. 1989. "Irigaray and Diotima at Plato's Symposium." *Hypatia* 3.3 (Winter): 77–93.

Rorty, Richard. 1989. *Contingency, Irony, Solidarity*. New York: Cambridge University Press.

———. 1991. "Postmodern Bourgeois Liberalism." In *Objectivity, Relativism, and Truth*. New York: Cambridge University Press.

Vattimo, Gianni. 1992 "From Utopia to Heterotopia." In *The Transparent Society*, translated by David Webb. Baltimore: Johns Hopkins University Press.

Vonnegut, Kurt, Jr. 1963. *Cat's Cradle*. Reprint, New York: Dell, 1970.

Wittig, Monique. 1992. *The Straight Mind*. Boston: Beacon.

Chapter 5

The I-We Dilemma and a "Utopian Unconscious" in Wells's *When the Sleeper Wakes* and Le Guin's *The Lathe of Heaven*

Carol S. Franko

In her keynote address at the International Conference on Women, Feminist Identity, and Society in the 1980s (Utrecht, Holland, June 1, 1984), Adrienne Rich meditated on the ongoing need in any political movement to historicize lofty abstractions that ignore the concrete realities of people's lives. Thus Rich examined the "politics" of her own "location" as a white, female, Anglo-American, Jewish feminist. She argued that feminism must recognize that ordinary pronouns like "I" and "we" pose a political problem: "Two thoughts: there is no liberation that only knows how to say 'I.' There is no collective movement that speaks for each of us all the way through" (16). This difficulty of saying both "I" and "we" structures utopian narrative as well as feminist movements; hence it poses an important issue for the political significance of utopian fiction. Utopian novels confront what I will be referring to as the I-we dilemma on at least two levels—at the level of the description of the utopian society and at a "meta level," that of an "I" authoring a vision that is presumably desirable for a "we."

In *The Concept of Utopia*, Ruth Levitas argues that the most essential component of utopia is "desire—the desire for a different way of being" (181). Within this broad understanding of utopia, Levitas identifies three functions of utopian discourse: compensation, critique, and change. The function of compensation reveals how utopia is inseparable from ideology. In contrast, "critique" is synonymous with estrangement—with the disorienting and reorienting of readers. Levitas refers to this function of utopia as the "education of desire" (181). Finally, at its most potent, utopian discourse can play an active role in the transformation of society. Levitas equates this transformative function with hope—hope, she argues, goes beyond the expression and reorienting of desire because it grounds desire in a conviction that changes for the better can and will be made by human agents (191–197).

Levitas argues that contemporary ambiguous or open-ended science-fiction utopias are educating desire without instilling hope. This problem can be reframed usefully as another instance of the political problem of ordinary pronouns—the I-we dilemma. *Who* is/are going to build a more utopian society? Levitas argues both that this question of agency is the key for utopian discourse and that despite their ability to critique our world, contemporary ambiguous utopias are mirroring back a pervasive ideology of fatalism, a lack of faith in human agency (195–97). In contrast, Bulent Somay represents advocates of nontotalized utopias who argue that it is the unfinished, self-critical qualities of recent fictions that open up the "horizon" of utopia, unlike previous utopias that fixed that horizon within the unselfconscious "I" of the author (Somay 1984, 25). While Levitas rightly asks *who* will make utopia, Somay's position implies equally important questions such as *whose* utopia? and who is fit to speak the utopian longing of an age? Also, Somay presents utopian texts "from More['s] to Morris['s]" thus: "The *utopian longing* which arose from the people's collective imagination throughout history was thus enclosed in a fictive *utopian locus* which arose from the individual imagination of the author, who presented it to her or his audience in a finished, unchanging, form" (25). Tom Moylan's important *Demand the Impossible* was the first extensive study of what he terms the critical utopia of the 1970s, a self-reflexive form that remakes the utopian genre. Somay and Moylan do not treat *The Lathe of Heaven*.

This paper examines how two ambiguously utopian novels, one from the turn of the century and one contemporary, engage the I-we dilemma of utopian discourse at the levels of theme, story (what happens) and discourse (the "how" of storytelling). Through patterns of imagery, the theme of perception, and an elaboration of the sleep/dream framing device (the Rip Van Winkle convention), Wells poses the I-we dilemma vividly and ambivalently. Le Guin's wittily intertextual *The Lathe of Heaven* "rewrites" the dilemma embodied in *When the Sleeper Wakes*, offering what might be termed a "textual solution." Neither work solves the question of agency in utopian fictions; both inscribe the question as a "struggle for accountability" (Rich 1984, 7).

When the Sleeper Wakes (1899) and *The Lathe of Heaven* (1971) have been criticized for political murkiness and/or pessimism, and this criticism is typically linked with observations on how the novels do not fit easily into generic categories. Alexandra Aldridge, for example, views *When the Sleeper Wakes* as evidence that Wells "was incapable of writing a pure dystopia" (Aldridge 1984, 32). Conversely, John Huntington seems to consider *Sleeper* an abortive utopia. Pointing to its dearth of economic and political analysis, Huntington concludes that Wells's failure here "to envision a righting of the nightmare his cool ironic intelligence has invented" reveals a weakness in the novel's form, "expos[ing] the limits of the logical and symbolic mode of fantasy in the face of real political issues" (Huntington 1982, 97). The form of Le Guin's novel has also been viewed as evidence of political evasiveness. Levitas sees *The Lathe of Heaven* as typical of the fatalistic quality in contemporary utopian fiction—a trend of disbelief in the possibility of successful, willed social change. For Levitas, such fatalism is exemplified in literary uses of the fantastic, a mode which she defines as that which violates "our knowledge of nature and human nature" (Levitas 1984, 21). Frederic Jameson acknowledges the pessimism in *The Lathe of Heaven* but interprets it somewhat differently than Levitas, as part of a general preoccupation with the problem of writing utopia. He suggests that Le Guin's novel is about the impossibility of writing/realizing utopia—but that in the process of exploring this issue, utopia gets written.

In contrast to such assessments, I argue that it is the fantastic qualities, the generic ambiguity, and the self-conscious intertextuality of these two novels that constitute their engagement with utopian hope, and hence their political significance. They both are "border texts"—"extremely varied" themselves, they struggle "with the rules of genre and with literary tradition," thus "continually implicating other texts" (Humm 1991, 5). Their position on the borders of utopia and dystopia, of fantasy and realism, enables them to negotiate the I-we dilemma.

On the level of theme, of the description of utopian alternatives, the

I-we dilemma asks whether individuality and communality can coexist in the just society. This question echoes twentieth-century *dys*topias' perception of utopia as a fictional genre and/or political orientation that idealizes collectivism at the expense of individuality. Katherine Fishburn argues that this question is fundamental to Doris Lessing's fiction: "the question . . . of how (and if) individuality can co-exist with . . . communality without being totally subsumed within them" (Fishburn 22). On the other side of this I-we debate, from Edward Bellamy and earlier through to the 1970s, utopia counters with descriptions of alienated, "hierarchisized" individuality.

In exploring the "truth" about utopian hope, Wells and Le Guin undercut this either/or of individuality versus community. They reject the liberal humanism that informs both utopia's reliance on the notion of progress and dystopia's defense of the individual. They assert instead that discrete identity is a powerful and usually destructive fiction that masks the underlying fact of communality, or interdependence.

Rip Van Winkle and a "Utopian Unconscious"

Confucius and you are both dreams, and I who say you are dreams am a dream myself. This is a paradox. Tomorrow a wise man may explain it; that tomorrow will not be for ten thousand generations.

(Chuang Tse; quoted in The Lathe of Heaven, *7)*

Utopian fiction is viewed typically as undervaluing individuality because of an excessively rationalistic take on reality, an orientation that produces a "hardness and thinness" in its representations (Wells 1967, 9). Thus Brian Attebery categorizes utopia as a mode that "gazes outward, at social organization and material comfort" and that avoids ambivalence, attempting instead "to arrange the lights so as to eliminate the shadow" (Attebery 1986, 6). Similarly, Northrop Frye's "Varieties of Literary Utopias" closes with a call for a utopia rooted in the body as well as the intellect, and in the unconscious as well as the conscious mind (49).

The idea of a utopian component to the unconscious is crucial to Ernst Bloch's broadening of the notion of utopia away from "novels of an ideal state" and toward a virtually limitless utopian impulse that potentially appears in wishes, fantasy, dreams, art, popular culture, and indeed in all individual and social activities (Bloch 14).[1] For further discussion of how Bloch has transformed the concept of the utopian imagination, see Moylan (20–26), and Jameson (1971, 116–159). For a critical look at the essentialism of Bloch's utopian impulse, see Levitas (1990, 181). Bloch postulates a supplement to the Freudian unconscious: the not-yet-conscious. He asserts that the "threshold of fading" in the unconscious—the activity of forgetting and repression—is countered by the "threshold of dawning," where "something not previously conscious *dawns*" (Bloch 1986, 115). The not-yet-conscious challenges the focus of psychoanalysis on the no-longer-conscious, on the "old [consciousness] which has merely sunk below the threshold and may cross it again by a more or less straightforward process of being remembered" (115). Thus Bloch's concept of the not-yet-conscious asserts that the human psyche is partly constituted by presentiments "not only of the future, but of the good future" (Hudson 94). In Bloch's words: "The Not-Yet-Conscious is thus solely the preconscious of what is to come, the psychological birthplace of the New" (Bloch 116). For Bloch, utopia thus arises from the unconscious; its "foundations" are truly in "dreamland" (Frye 49).

Wells and Le Guin "reform" rationalist utopian fiction by giving it an "unconscious." They thematize a utopian unconscious in two broad ways. First, *When the Sleeper Wakes* and *The Lathe of Heaven* parody the nineteenth-century plot of utopian fictions set in the future—of the Rip Van Winkle protagonist who sleeps his way into a better world. In Bellamy's *Looking Backward* and Morris's *News from Nowhere*, the dream / sleep element is a vehicle for displacing the hero from contemporary reality to the future no-place of a better society. In Wells's and Le Guin's novels, sleeping and dreaming are much more central to the plot; their "sleeper" protagonists spend a great deal of their time sleeping and/or dreaming, as well as thinking about sleeping and dreaming. However, these works do not emphasize the protagonist's unconscious in order to add psychological verisimilitude; rather, their interest in unfamiliar mental states, in unusual dreams, constitutes the extravagant "adventures of an idea" (Bakhtin 115)—the multi-accented idea of utopian hope.

The second way that Wells and Le Guin correct the rationalist bias of utopian fiction is by intensifying the analogy, explored for example in Bellamy's *Looking Backward*, between the mental state of the visitor to utopia and the state of the author's world—a world whose faults contrast with the virtues of the utopian society.[2] In a novel such as Bellamy's, the protagonist's (and presumably the reader's) conversion to the utopian society resolves the I-we dilemma by analogy, through the implied harmony between psychic and social transformation. *When the Sleeper*

Wakes and *The Lathe of Heaven* replace the relative ease of Bellamy's transformations with a more pessimistic and searching look at utopian dreaming. Wells and Le Guin use the analogy between psychic and social
transformation not only to present optimistically a utopian unconscious,
but also to explore what could be termed the solipsism of utopian
authoring. This meta-theme of solipsism expresses distrust in the writing or imagining of utopia: it implies that such an activity involves the
mere repetition of generic conventions and/or the closed system of a
powerful "I"/eye inscribing his/her reflection onto an objectified "we."

"The Darkness of the Lived Instant":
Wells's Enactment of Utopian Solipsism

*The perversity of his experience came to him vividly. In actual fact he had made
such a leap in time as romancers have imagined . . . . And that fact realised, . . . his
mind had . . . seated itself for a spectacle. And no spectacle, but a great vague
danger, unsympathetic shadows and veils of darkness. Somewhere through the
labyrinthine obscurity his death sought him. Would he, after all, be lulled before
he saw? It might be that even at the next shadowy corner his destruction
ambushed. A great desire to see, a great longing to know, arose in him.*

(Sleeper 68)

*The darkness of the lived instant represents one pole of conscious anticipation
and of the anticipatory disposition of the world as well.*

(Ernst Bloch, quoted in Jameson 122)

I do not wish to claim that *When the Sleeper Wakes* is an unambigu-
ous success. Huntington's point about the absence in it of lucid economic and political analysis is a serious and fair criticism. However, his
assumption that the best justification for this narrative would be an economic and political "solution" for the society of 2100 neglects the effects
of the generic mix that Wells here concocted.

Two generic plots clash in this novel: the Wellsian scientific romance
plot of a voyage into the unknown—of facing danger—and the utopian
"plot" of minimal action in which an unknown—the utopian alternative—is fully explained. The plots of Wells's scientific romances typically feature three elements: an unexpected change in environment, the
forming of conflictual relationships between the protagonist and his new
environment, and the frequency of violence in these conflicts (Vernier
1977, 75). In *When the Sleeper Wakes* the potential for violence (typical of

Wells's scientific romances) is confined to social causes—to political intrigue and economic and social injustice. This emphasis on social critique indicates the novel's affinity with utopian literature. And yet, the plot of *When the Sleeper Wakes* also differs greatly from Bellamy's *Looking Backward* and Morris's *News from Nowhere*, the two utopias Wells plays off of. Unlike Bellamy's and Morris's visitors, who see the problems of their present solved in the future no-place, Wells's protagonist, "the man from the nineteenth century" (*Sleeper* 86), must strive to right the wrongs of a future that is much like his nineteenth-century world.

In addition to adulterating the detailed exposition of generic utopia with the violence and uncertainty of scientific romance, Wells also makes intensified use of the Rip Van Winkle convention, only relinquishing the sleep/dream frame with the protagonist's death, which ends the novel. And upon his death Graham is depicted as posing once again the questions that have recurred throughout: what is the ontological status of his journey into the future? is it dream or reality? and what is the relation between dream and reality? Wells's utopian satire fails to explain how to "fix" the world of 2100, but this very failure is part of a larger success: Wells's "exposure" of, or meditation on, the solipsism of utopian model-building. In order to explain this thesis it is necessary to consider the shape of Wells's plot.

Graham, who has been contemplating suicide, falls into a trance in 1897, sleeps for 203 years, and wakes to the tumult of rioting workers. He tries desperately, and for half the novel unsuccessfully, to learn about the society of this future world. He eventually learns that his waking was induced by the political opportunist, Ostrog (the Boss). Thus the rioting he heard upon awakening was part of Ostrog's phony revolution, which overthrew the oligarchy (the Council). In the second half of the novel, Graham learns three crucial things. First, to his great joy, he learns to fly an "aeropile." Secondly, he learns that the rich (a decadent minority) and the poor (the vast majority) are so stratified as to bear traces of becoming separate species.[3] Finally, he discovers his own grotesque relation to the England of 2100: because of a bizarrely managed inheritance, he *owns* more than half of it—hence his political importance. Graham, inspired by Ostrog's niece (Helen), throws in his lot with a "real" but seemingly doomed revolution of the poor. In the conclusion, Graham perhaps gains a decisive victory through his heroic maneuvers in an airplane before crashing to his death: "he was suddenly aware that the earth was very near" (187).

Such a summary fails to convey the peculiar feel of this work. Although it is strongest in the first half (chapters 1–12), the whole novel is dominated both by Graham's frustrated desire to know, to grasp this world, and by his concurrent sense of the thinness, the insubstantiality of this world, this dream. And Graham's responses represent those of the reader, with the difference that the reader contemplates Graham's function in the uncertain status of this narrative.

Critics often comment on Graham's unusual relationship to the world of 2100. Huntington, for example, gives an apt summary of part of Graham's symbolic function: "[He] is an outsider in the future age, but he is at the center; he is a common man of no special distinction who is also "the Master"; he is economically most powerful, but also most moral; he rules, but he is powerless; he despairs at the beginning and he ends up an optimistic idealist" (Huntington 145). Huntington claims that Graham's symbolic function is an obfuscation covering up the absence of economic and political analysis. However, Graham's symbolic importance has even more drastic implications for the fabric of this narrative. Simply this: whether Wells fully intended to or not, he provides numerous clues suggesting that the world of 2100 is literally Graham's dream—that he is not a Rip Van Winkle miraculously transported to the future but a man having a confusing dream, a dreamer exploring the disturbing images in his unconscious.

Several factors contribute to this reading: Graham's turbulent mental state, which is duplicated in the turmoil of 2100; the nightmarish quality of Graham's attempt to *see* and to grasp this future; Graham's repeated thought that it is all a dream; and finally, the fact that when knowledge does come it is largely self-referential: Graham is the all-purpose icon of this world—he sees his image and hears his titles (Sleeper, Master) everywhere. One can even speculate that 2100 "is" the instantaneous vision of a man falling to his death. When we first meet Graham he is thinking of leaping off a cliff. In the conclusion his aeropile falls to earth; moreover, there are images of vertigo throughout. However, this is a suggestive repetition of images and not a "proof." Though what follows emphasizes the inscription of solipsism in *When the Sleeper Wakes*, I am suggesting that this novel is radically ambivalent, double—that it asks to be read as both straight satirical-adventure and as self-reflexive, self-unraveling dream.

When the Sleeper Wakes parodies the analogy between the rehabilitation of the hero and the reconstruction of society established in Bellamy's

Looking Backward. Graham's troubles are mirrored in—not healed by—the future society. Our first encounter with Graham (before he falls into his sleep/trance) is marked by the extremity of his mental torment, a condition insufficiently motivated, though admittedly aggravated by insomnia. He is lonely: "I am a lone wolf. . . . I am wifeless—childless" (*Sleeper*, 5). We do learn later that he is also a frustrated worker for social justice (14). However such nods to "psychology" do not explain away either Graham's peculiar mental state nor the melodramatic language he uses to describe it: "[M]y mind has been a whirlpool, swift, unprogressive and incessant, a torrent of thoughts leading nowhere, spinning round swift and steady. . . . towards the vortex" (5). "My head is not like what it was. . . . There is a sort of oppression. . . . No—not drowsiness, would God it were! It is like a shadow, a deep shadow falling suddenly and swiftly across something busy. Spin, spin into the darkness. The tumult of thought, the confusion, the eddy" (7).

The tumult in Graham's mind is echoed by the tumult in the future world. 2100 is a world of political unrest and ubiquitous machinery: perpetual noise is its keynote. Graham wakens to the "beat" and the "steady, sweeping shadow" of machinery (17) and to the "undeviating droning note," the "subdued tumult" (17) which he eventually realizes is a "tumult of shouting" people (23). Similarly the sense of vertigo that Graham reports in chapter one is suggestively mirrored in the gigantism of 2100, in its "vast and vague architectural forms" (17). Graham's first look at the city is from a high balcony, where he becomes the focus of the people's shouting (28–29). At climactic moments throughout the novel the emphasis on tumult and vertigo recurs, right up to the throb of his plane before it begins its fall.

The noise and vertigo that are the hallmarks of Graham's mind and of the future society belong to the dangerous world of scientific romance, not to generic utopia. Indeed, Wells's juxtaposition of scientific romance and utopia places his protagonist in one ambivalent position after another until he is finally killed off. In contrast, Morris's socialist hero is allowed a hopeful, rejuvenating dream, while Bellamy's West is happily integrated into the just society of 2000. Although they make contrasting use of the Rip Van Winkle device,[4] Bellamy and Morris both allow their protagonists to *learn* about the utopian society in great detail. To do so both rely on the convention of one or more citizens of utopia serving as guides for the visitor-protagonist. *When the Sleeper Wakes* repeatedly satirizes the availability, loquacity, and reliability of such guides. The result is an odd blend of satiric deflation and a sort of visionary bathos.

As a threat to the Council and a tool of Ostrog, Graham is kept ignorant of all the layers of political intrigue. Moreover as Howard, Graham's initial guide-jailor, remarks—*no one* really understands this world: "Our social order will probably seem very complex to you. To tell you the truth, I don't understand it myself very clearly. Nobody does" (32). Howard's remark is representative of Wells's satire on the omniscient guides of utopia, which reaches a climax nearly halfway through the novel. Fleeing through the darkened city (police have turned out the lights as a curb to rioters), Graham finally encounters a garrulous inhabitant, "The Old Man Who Knew Everything" (chapter 11), who parodies the guides in *Looking Backward* and *News from Nowhere*. Although Graham's old man does impart some useful information about Ostrog's machinations, his reliability is undercut by his conviction that the real Sleeper is dead—that Ostrog has set up a fake one (70, 75).

Just before he meets the Old Man Who Knew Everything, Graham's frustration reaches a peak: "A great desire to see, a great longing to know, arose in him" (68). If Graham's mental vertigo seems to be repeated in the city's vertiginous architecture, his inability to gain knowledge is mirrored in repeated images of veils, shadows, mazes, slender bridges that seem to go nowhere, myriad windows onto unnamed views, and darkness. It is as though the city hides its nature from Graham, or rather, as though it has nothing but insubstantiality, false knowledge, mere onionskin layers of political intrigue to offer him: "And no spectacle, but a great vague danger, unsympathetic shadows and veils of darkness" (68). As to what would constitute "real knowledge" of this vividly but mysteriously rendered world—I think there is a double answer. On the explicitly didactic level the reality behind the veils is this society's cynical institution of slave labor, which Graham encounters in his descent into the underworld of the Labour Company (chapter 21). On the epistemological level, however, the "reality" of 2100 is that it is a dream world imperfectly separated from Graham's troubled, turn-of-the-century unconscious.

Graham's desperate search for knowledge of 2100 continually leads him back to distorted images of himself. He is at the center of all political intrigues. His title, "Sleeper," is both a symbol of hope and a byword of cynics. His signature is on the money. His bizarre wealth and longevity is the inspiration for crazed speculation (for example, life insurance on the Master). These correspondences go beyond indicating that Graham is a latter-day King Arthur—they also thematize the solipsism of utopian dreaming and thus undercut Graham's messianic status. A final example of the self-reflexive aspect of this novel supports this reading.

While imprisoned in an apartment equipped with various gadgets, Graham finds rows of "cylinders" labeled with phonetic lettering—the future's library. Three titles attract his attention: "The Man Who Would Be King," "The Heart of Darkness," and "The Madonna of the Future" (the respective authors are Rudyard Kipling, Joseph Conrad and Henry James—the title of James's story is perhaps a sideways allusion to Helen, Ostrog's niece). Graham remembers "The Man Who Would Be King" as "one of the best stories in the world" but decides that the other two must be "by post Victorian authors" since he has no knowledge of them (39). These titles that Graham doesn't know reassert 2100 as a "real" future, but the resonance of the stories also contributes to the metafictional "unreality" of the future. He doesn't play these cylinders, turning instead to some contemporary melodramas. Thus, the titles appear for the reader's information; I think they serve three functions. Kipling's story, like Wells's novel, combines adventure, pathos and satire. The allusion to it is a case of foreshadowing: Graham acts out a similar tale, including the tragic conclusion. Even by itself Kipling's title raises doubts about the wisdom of Graham's embracing the role of "Master," just as it raises the specter of "white man's burden." The addition of Conrad's and James's works—both ambiguous stories of failed idealism—reinforce the satire. In particular, the combination of Kipling and Conrad in this early allusion serves a second function—it foreshadows a passage which deflates the importance of the people's uprising. Hardly more than ten pages before the end, Graham suggests that the workers' struggle is part of the "older sin" of imperialism (175). Huntington cites this passage as evidence of thematic confusion in *When the Sleeper Wakes*. In contrast, I think Graham's sense that his interest in the workers is overshadowed by a larger, older "race quarrel" (175) is of a piece with his ambivalent status as the "man who would be king." Just as Graham's symbolic unity with the people is rendered at least partly ironic by Wells's wry satire of insane capitalism—with Graham its bizarre icon—similarly Graham's awareness of the sins of imperialism undermines his acceptance of a monarchical role.

Thus the third function of the allusion to Kipling, Conrad, and James is to add to the "double" status of the narrative. The didactic strand of

When the Sleeper Wakes affirms Graham's role as spiritual leader of the revolution. This "representational" aspect of the novel presumably asks readers to reevaluate their real-world political commitments. The self-reflexive strand suggests that 2100 is Graham's dream. This aspect of the novel is also didactic, but its "message" explores the difficulty of imagining a future that is not implicated in the sins of the past and present. The utopian element in Graham's psyche is plagued by all the detritus of turn-of-the-century civilization: progress, imperialism, laissez-faire capitalism. Yet what he projects is not all bad: he dreams the people's song of revolt as well as his own grandiose status; his final thoughts are that Helen, who represents the utopian hopes of the people, is at least real (187).

Thus, in *When the Sleeper Wakes*, Wells suggests that the utopian dreams of an individual unconscious recapitulate the horrors as well as the viable hopes of its age. By making his protagonist act out *both sides* of his unconscious—the grandiose dreams of kingship as well as the dreams of mutuality—Wells is uncompromising in his portrayal of utopian solipsism. He also puts a nearly intolerable strain on his narrative. *When the Sleeper Wakes* replaces the seemingly full knowledge of the future that generic utopia offers with a troubling mirror of the cultural unconscious.

The Lathe of Heaven:
The Utopian Unconscious and the Desire for History

> *Dreams, daydreams, insanity, destroy the epic and tragic wholeness of a person and his fate: the possibilities of another life are revealed in him, he loses his finalized quality and ceases to mean only one thing; he ceases to coincide with himself.*
>
> (Bakhtin 117)

> *Once again: who is* we?
>
> (Rich 21)

In *The Lathe of Heaven* Le Guin writes her way out of utopia and dystopia through intertextuality—through parodic reworkings of familiar elements from utopian, dystopian, and science fictions. Her novel ends with unanswered questions, the chief one being, how can a utopian impulse that is not restricted to rationalism, and that chooses to act with people rather than on them, join up with a vision of present social reality, a reality that contains all the mess and evil of modern history? As we have seen, Wells's *When the Sleeper Wakes* is informed by two structural paradoxes that place a great strain on the narrative. First, the protagonist is placed on the border between two genres—the scientific romance which typically involves a confrontation with a dangerous unknown, and the utopia, which places talkative guides at the disposal of a visitor. Secondly, with more drastic implications, a covert tension exists in *When the Sleeper Wakes,* due to the possibility (inscribed through patterns of imagery, for example) that Graham is not traveling to the future but dreaming. This would mean that his de facto status as Master of an imperialist nation, as well as his willed sympathetic relations with the striking workers, are products of his unconscious. Through this ambiguity, Wells casts doubt on the project of giving utopia an "unconscious"—of relating social, collective planning to individual experience comprised of nonrational as well as rational elements.

Crucial for understanding the tensions of Wells's novel is the fact that all the burden of "epistemological uncertainty" (is the setting a dream or a "reality"?) as well as the ambiguous moral status of a utopian unconscious (is dominance or mutuality its keynote?) is placed on Graham's character. Mark Hillegas has noted the importance of Graham's adversarial relationship with Ostrog—how this pair may have influenced other polemical pairs like Huxley's John Savage and Mustapha Mond, for example. Within the present discussion, however, Ostrog is not as thoroughly developed an antagonist as Haber, because he does not impinge on the epistemological question of "utopian solipsism." Graham himself must be several things at once: the visitor to "utopia," desperately seeking for the guides who normally appear in such romantic adventures; the hero of the people who leads a revolution against the oppressive oligarchy; the dreamer of utopia/dystopia who creates a future that seems a trap—an extravagantly enlarged version of his nineteenth-century world. Graham's death at the end of the novel preserves the ambiguous status of 2100 (is it Graham's dream? is it "real"?), but it is also arguably Wells's acknowledgment of frustration with a work that lacks narrative strategies to render its ambivalent themes fully intelligible.

There is no need to uncover the problem of utopian solipsism in Le Guin's novel: the protagonist in *The Lathe of Heaven* is "literally" a dreamer of utopia. As the novel opens, George Orr has nearly killed himself with a drug overdose trying to block a power he regards as immoral: his capacity to dream "effectively," to change reality with some of his dreams (the "effective" ones). Sentenced to mandatory therapy (called "voluntary" therapy in Orwellian fashion) by the bureaucracy of a near-future Portland, Oregon, Orr is assigned to a "mad scientist": William Haber, dream specialist and egomaniac. Under the guise of hypnosis therapy, Haber starts using Orr's dreams to solve the world's problems and create utopia. With each new reality that he programs Orr to create, Haber's dream machine (the Augmentor) gets bigger, his powers and influence more extensive, until finally he is the director of a massive global agency. George, meanwhile, engages a lawyer (Heather Lelache) to extract him from Haber's legally sanctioned clutches. Though this attempt fails, George and Heather become allies and lovers. Ultimately, with the help of Aliens (the Aldebaranians, apparently born of an effective dream), George confronts his power and the real fear behind it: apocalypse, annihilation.

Since he has the power to change reality with his dreams, George Orr would seem to symbolize the collapse of the I-we dilemma into solipsism. However, in the allegorical way that I'm arguing Le Guin's novel may be read, her protagonist represents a captive utopian unconscious that is masquerading as dystopian pessimism. Gerard Klein refers to the unconscious in *Lathe* as "the place where history inscribes itself," and he makes the somewhat puzzling suggestion that this novel is the converse of Le Guin's other works, in which the unconscious "only appears by its absence" (Klein 1977, 292). Bernard Selinger's interesting recent study of Le Guin takes "the psychoanalytic route to the mysterious heart" of her fiction (Selinger 1988, 10). Selinger argues that on one level *The Lathe of Heaven* dramatizes the infant's passage from an undifferentiated, omnipotent and oceanic sense of self to a differentiated identity that recognizes the (shifting) boundaries between self and other (87–88).

George Orr's name surely is meant to evoke not only either/or but also George Orwell, and hence Orwell's dystopian novel, *1984*. This allusion is reinforced by others: for example, late in the novel we learn that several oppressive amendments to the constitution were made in at least one version of the year 1984. There are several levels of irony to the novel's implication that Orr is a latter-day Orwell. The future Portland that George inhabits as the novel opens is certainly a nightmare of centralization (like *1984*), but this "real" dystopia is more the result of overpopulation, destruction of the environment, and bureaucratic inefficiency than of totalitarianism. As Haber begins using his client's dreams to change the world, George Orr becomes an "author" of serial realities, most of which resemble the utopian satires and dystopias of Samuel Butler (*Erewhon*), Zamyatin, and Aldous Huxley, as well as Orwell. For example, in one of the serial realities (a post-carcinomic plague world "cured" of overpopulation), having cancer is a crime—a probable allusion to *Erewhon*, where illness is criminal and crime is a disease. With each successive "utopia" that Haber manipulates George into authoring, the world gets grimmer—more oppressive, a hybrid of *1984* and Huxley's *Brave New World*—and "reality" gets thinner, acquiring the unsatisfying texture of a bad novel. *The Lathe of Heaven* thus suggests the poverty of both the utopian and dystopian literary traditions. A final irony is that Le Guin's latter-day Orwell becomes a figure of hope—of a renewed utopian impulse.

The ultimate twist to the treatment of utopian dreaming in this novel—the double loop of solipsism—is that the future Portland setting in which George Orr disapproves his power of effective dreaming is itself the product of an effective dream. Several years before the novel begins, in an ordinary bad world of food shortages and several wars, nuclear war makes an end of things. Except that George Orr, fleeing the city while dying from radiation, falls asleep and has an "effective" dream—wakes up at "home" in a different reality. The memory of apocalypse returns occasionally in his dreams. So on one level, with a dizzying circularity, *The Lathe of Heaven* explains Orr's problem with effective dreaming by reference to this initial, save-the-world one. As Orr rather contradictorily tells his lover: "There is nothing left. Nothing but dreams" and "It isn't evolution. It's just self- preservation" (104, 105).

The Lathe of Heaven rewrites the problem of utopian solipsism implicit in Wells's *When the Sleeper Wakes* in two main ways, which in turn undo the clear-cut ideological positions of utopia and dystopia. First, Le Guin's novel makes literal and central to the plot what is only hinted at in Wells's novel: the trope of the narrative as dream of the protagonist. *The Lathe of Heaven* thus brings the problem of utopian solipsism "into consciousness," retrieves it from the "unconscious" if powerful place it occupies in *When the Sleeper Wakes*. Secondly, in contrast to the lone, burdened figure of Wells's Graham, Le Guin fashions a dialogic narrative structure that opposes two styles of experience, two ways of dreaming the world: Haber's emphatic abstract instrumentalism versus Orr's tentative literal holism. This debate between two versions of the self's relation to world rewrites the struggle between hierarchy and mutuality embodied in Wells's protagonist. One of the ambiguities in Graham's character is the conflict between his passion for social justice and his attraction to the role of Master, or King, of the future world. Haber is roughly equivalent to this aspect of Graham. Haber uses the rhetoric of progress and social change, he fantasizes about himself as a hands-on leader ("Relevance was his touchstone" [54], as the narrator ironically imitates his daydreams), and yet he is shown to be suffering from a kind of moral and emotional autism. As Orr ponders it: "the doctor was not . . . really sure that anyone else existed, and wanted to prove that they did by helping them" (32). George Orr, who seems to be a "literal" solipsist in his ability to change reality with his dreams, here diagnoses the novel's "real" solipsist.

If Haber resembles the part of Graham who "would be king," Orr resembles Graham's intuitive side that has spontaneous sympathy for the labor class. George Orr's character, of course, continually acts in contrast with Haber's. Where Haber is glib and snappy, Orr is tentative yet plainspoken. Where Haber is instrumental and abstract, Orr emphasizes the tangible and the intuitive. (Thomas Remington also discusses the importance of touch in the contrasting portraits of Orr and Haber—see 168–70.)

The narrator represents Orr as a slow thinker: "He did not see connections, which is said to be the hallmark of intellect. He *felt* connections—like a plumber" (*Lathe*, 42). In this passage Orr's slow process of feeling connections between ideas is linked to his emotional and physical presence, which communicates connection between people. During a subway ride it slowly dawns on Orr that Haber does know about the reality of his client's effective dreaming. This realization affirms Orr's sanity, and the pleasure that gives him is communicated to the other subway riders (42). Thus the man who can dream the world into successive continuums of reality is nonetheless *in* the world and *with* the world in properly Taoist fashion. Such representations of Orr's connection with other people reinforce the novel's transferring of "real" solipsism from Orr to Haber. And like Graham, Orr's unconscious is full of monsters, but also something else—something like an awareness of mutuality. In terms of the Taoist tradition that informs the novel, George Orr represents a consciousness in harmony with the "unnameable," the Tao or "Way," which can be defined tentatively as a law of the dynamic relatedness of all things and beings (Spivack 6–7). Orr embraces two principles of Taoism that grow out of the notion of the Way: the relativity of opposites and the law of "letting alone." The latter principle can be misunderstood as a kind of quietism or defeatism, but it is better described as a willingness to wait for the appropriate time to act—the appropriateness a function of respect for the multiplicity of cause and effect in a world of interrelations.

The Tao stands for interdependence through its shifting, paradoxical status as being and nonbeing, or nonexistence. Orr's character embodies this paradox. He is sometimes explicitly associated with the Taoist symbol of the uncut block of wood, which presumably stands for completeness or wholeness of being. On the other hand, the no-place/no-time of Orr's effective dreams implicitly connects them with the image of the Tao as a primordial nonexistence which, using a background-foreground analogy, enables being and relations between beings to appear. The epigraph to Chapter Two remarks cryptically that "The portal of God is non-existence" (Chuang Tse, quoted p. 11). This image of nonexistence as the threshold to some unknown state of being ("God") is a fitting one for Orr and Haber's contest over the power to change reality through effective dreaming. Near the end of the novel, Haber learns how to transfer the power of effective dreaming from George to himself. He will now be able to change the world without an intermediary; science/technology (for example, the speed with which nuclear war has already and could again destroy the world) will be indistinguishable from magic (magic as the instantaneous materializing of a thought, a dream). Haber's version of nonexistence—that of the "real" solipsist who disbelieves in the existence of others—threatens to annihilate Orr's Taoist version of nonexistence, which enables (dreams) the existence of others.

Orr is not completely passive. He discovers part of his "utopian unconscious" that Haber apparently cannot access; this repressed utopian unconscious is presumably the power that enabled Orr to effectively dream off apocalypse. This power is also personified in the Aliens. Appropriately, since they have seemingly been born from his unconscious, the Aliens (Aldebaranians) confirm for Orr what he has long suspected: that he is not alone in his effective dreaming, that in fact the fabric of reality is perpetually shifting (71). According to the Aldebaranians, the safeguard of this process is that effective dreaming is properly a communal or interdependent activity (148). It is with such tenuous information that Orr saves the world once more, this time from Haber's own apocalyptic effective dream.

In its dynamic of Haber and Orr as ontological and ethical villain and hero, *The Lathe of Heaven* has a didactic clarity lacking in *When the*

Sleeper Wakes. While Orr's character equals the affirmation of human mutuality and utopian hope as the potential for survival, Haber's character equals instrumental rationalist progressivism, the danger of moral and emotional solipsism, and finally apocalypse. Haber's name in German connotes both being full of one's oats and bogey, or specter. These two meanings sum up the two angles that the novel assumes toward his character. On the one hand he is darkly humorous, an excessively genial and talky egotist, a "phony leveller" (Elgin 10), a pompous speechmaker—hence full of his oats. The other connotation of specter or bogey, however, becomes the final emblem of his character: ultimately, he is represented as a frightening zero, an isolated individual with an insatiable appetite for self-aggrandizement who hides behind a mask of utilitarian, rationalist utopia. At the end of the novel he is in a mental institution and he makes the other inmates uncomfortable.

Haber and Orr's relationship parodies all the male couples—the sort of father-son relationships of both the utopian and dystopian tradition—in utopian novels, the lengthy conversations between the utopian guide and the visitor about to be converted as well as the ironic debates between the apologist for utopia and the rebellious individualist in dystopian novels. But there is also a third main character in *The Lathe of Heaven,* a black woman who in at least one of the dream realities of the novel is an acerbic lawyer who tries to help Orr extricate himself from the mandatory therapy sessions with Haber. In another incarnation this character, Heather Lelache, is George Orr's loving wife.

In utopian novels, the love interest is used to affirm the value of the utopian society (Le Moine and Bogstad 115) and to cement the visitor's conversion to its new ways, and female characters represent sentiment, feeling. In contrast, dystopian novels use thwarted romantic love to symbolize the individuality and freedom denied by the totalitarian state, and female characters represent sexuality. The love interest in *The Lathe of Heaven* fits neither category. Instead, Heather Lelache represents the recent history that Haber's and Orr's contrasting world views contend for. After Haber begins tinkering with reality, Lelache remembers at least two pasts, but in both of them she is the child of a so-called mixed marriage that quickly broke up under the strain of diverse backgrounds. Her black father's family were once slaves in Louisiana: Lelache, which means "the coward," would have been the slaveowner's name (102). Her mother was white—a corporation lawyer's daughter. Heather mentions at one point that she isn't sure what color she is, black or white, or which parent she should identify with. Her mixed parentage, and the painful past of slavery, racism, and of attempts to eradicate racism are too messy for Haber's conception of doing good to the world. In a later effective dream, he hypnotizes Orr to dream away racial problems. The result is a world where, genetically, there has never been more than one race. Everyone is gray. The symbolism is clear, as is the link with the dystopian disapproval of utopia's intolerance of diversity in constructing perfect worlds. Heather does not exist in this world—could not have existed as Orr figures it: "Her anger, timidity, brashness, gentleness, all were elements of her mixed being, her mixed nature, dark and clear right through, like Baltic amber. She could not exist in the gray people's world. She had not been born" (127).

When Orr has saved the world again at the novel's conclusion, even making it more ecologically sound, he also manages to dream Heather Lelache back into existence. However, in this version of reality, Lelache has no memory of a previous relationship with Orr. The woman who symbolizes contemporary reality is described as a "fierce, recalcitrant, and fragile stranger, forever to be won again" (175). Such an ending, taking place as it does on the borders of fantasy and allegory, may seem politically evasive. Certainly the novel remains within the limits of fiction; its solutions are "textual." Nonetheless, in *The Lathe of Heaven* Le Guin resurrects a renewed utopian impulse—George Orr's unconscious—and suggests that its continued vitality depends on a desire to merge with history.

In *A Modern Utopia*, Wells has his narrator declare that there is always a certain "hardness and thinness about Utopian speculations" (9). Utopias lack the "blood and warmth and reality of life"—they possess "no individualities, but only generalised people" (9). One can take this criticism as a regret about the status of utopia both as literature (the genre lacks the vivid characterization of "real" novels) and as heuristic device: how can the genre inspire readers to change their world views if it does not engage their emotions as well as their intellects? While a critic like Levitas understandably regrets contemporary apathy about the possibility of willed social change, Wells and Le Guin suggest that consciousness must be transformed on an individual as well as a social scale. Virginia Woolf once claimed memorably that didactic fiction made her want to join a society or write a check (Woolf 105). In contrast, *When the Sleeper Wakes* and *The Lathe of Heaven* invite readers to reflect on the imaginative and ethical process of constructing alternative worlds. In particular, they encourage meditation on the difficulty of merging subjectivity (the "I") and utopia (the "we").

The theme of the psychically troubled visitor to/author of utopia that is variously inscribed in these novels calls attention to the inherent solipsism of the utopian imagination, even while it gives an "inner life" to the rationalist utopian genre. *When the Sleeper Wakes* contains the prototypical solipsistic hero, whose socialistic idealism and imperialistic urges are equally reflected upon the future society, which may be "real," or may be Graham's dream. Readers are torn between sympathizing with Graham's participation in the workers' revolt and looking askance at his acting out of Kipling's "The Man Who Would Be King." Wells's novel thus asks us to share a troubling dream that is never actually "exposed" as being a dream; thus, we are asked to participate in the unconscious solipsism of the utopian imagination. *The Lathe of Heaven* is more optimistic in its stance toward a utopian unconscious. Early in the novel Orr explains effective dreams to Lelache thus: "chang[ing] reality by dreaming that it's different" (48). By the conclusion this phrase has taken on hopeful connotations.

When the Sleeper Wakes and *The Lathe of Heaven* both inscribe an expectation of the discovery of a utopian mode of relations. These works thematize a utopian unconscious in order to explore and perhaps recover a lost mutuality—a recovery, however, which at best is portrayed as always-about-to-happen. They "novelize" philosophic positions, testing the hope principle that Ernst Bloch asserts and affirms: is the mind dreaming the world an appropriate figure for communal aspirations? Can we proclaim the unconscious as both challenging utopian rationalism and containing the traces of a utopian alternative? These "border texts" pose such questions in ways that enjoin the reader to participate in Mikhail Bakhtin's notion that "Truth . . . is born *between people* collectively searching for [it]" (Bakhtin 110). The lack of final answers is fatalistic, lacking hope, only if one accepts that a utopian novel cannot express ambivalence toward the tradition of utopian thought and still be utopian.

Notes

1. For further discussion of how Bloch has transformed the concept of the utopian imagination, see Moylan (20–26), and Jameson (*Marxism and Form* 116–

159). For a critical look at the essentialism of Bloch's utopian impulse, see Levitas (*The Concept of Utopia* 181).
2. For a discussion of how Bellamy's utopia enacts *"The construction of a social system for the reader [as] . . . the reconstruction of the hero,"* see Suvin (174).
3. For a discussion of the Darwinian thread in Wells's plot, see Mullen. Mullen's article also usefully counters negative evaluations of *When the Sleeper Wakes,* especially Bergonzi's.
4. Morris's protagonist merely *dreams* he has awakened in the epoch of rest after a future revolution, while Bellamy's Julian West really *sleeps* for over a hundred years and wakes in a transformed America.

Works Cited

Aldridge, Alexandra. 1984. *The Scientific World View in Dystopia.* Ann Arbor: University of Michigan Research Press.

Attebery, Brian. 1986. "Fantasy as an Anti-Utopian Mode." In *Reflections on the Fantastic: Selected Essays from the Fourth International Conference on the Fantastic in the Arts,* edited by Michael R. Collins. New York: Greenwood.

Bakhtin, Mikhail M. 1984. *Problems of Dostoevsky's Poetics.* Edited and translated by Caryl Emerson. Introduction by Wayne C. Booth. Minneapolis: University of Minnesota Press.

Barbour, Douglas. 1973. *"The Lathe of Heaven:* Taoist Dream." *Algol* 21: 22–24.

Bellamy, Edward. 1888. *Looking Backward: 2000–1887.* Harmondsworth, U.K.: Penguin.

Bergonzi, Bernard. 1961. *The Early H. G. Wells: A Study of the Scientific Romances.* Manchester, U.K.: The University Press.

Bloch, Ernst. 1986. *The Principle of Hope.* 3 vols. Translated by Neville Plaice, Stephen Plaice, and Paul Knight. Cambridge: Massachusetts Institute of Technology Press.

Elgin, Suzette Haden. 1980. *The Gentle Art of Verbal Self Defense.* N.p.: Prentice & Dorset.

Fishburn, Katherine. 1985. *The Unexpected Universe of Doris Lessing: A Study in Narrative Technique.* New York: Greenwood.

Frye, Northrop. 1966. "Varieties of Literary Utopia." In *Utopias and Utopian Thought,* edited by Frank E. Manuel. Boston: Houghton.

Hillegas, Mark R. 1967. *The Future as Nightmare: H. G. Wells and the Anti-Utopians.* New York: Oxford University Press.

Hudson, Wayne. 1982. *The Marxist Philosophy of Ernst Bloch.* New York: St. Martin's.

Humm, Maggie. 1991. *Border Traffic: Strategies of Contemporary Women Writers.* Manchester and New York: Manchester University Press.

Huntington, John. 1982. *The Logic of Fantasy: H. G. Wells and Science Fiction.* New York: Columbia University Press.

Jameson, Frederic. 1971. "Marxism and Form." In *Twentieth-Century Dialectical Theories of Literature.* Princeton: Princeton University Press.

———. 1982. "Progress Versus Utopia; or, Can We Imagine the Future?" *Science-Fiction Studies* 9: 147–58.

Klein, Gerard. 1977. "Le Guin's 'Aberrant' Opus: Escaping the Trap of Discontent." *Science-Fiction Studies* 4: 287–295.

Le Guin, Ursula K. 1973. *The Lathe of Heaven.* (First published in *Amazing Stories* in 1971.) New York: Avon.

LeMoine, Fannie and Janice Bogstad. 1985. *Comparative Literature 357: Fantasy and Science Fiction.* N.p.: Regents of the University of Wisconsin System.

Levitas, Ruth. 1984. "Need, Nature and Nowhere." In *Utopias,* edited by Peter Alexander and Roger Gill. London: Duckworth.

———. 1990. *The Concept of Utopia.* Syracuse: Syracuse University Press.

Morris, William. 1984. *News From Nowhere and Selected Writings and Designs.* New York: Penguin.

Moylan, Tom. 1986. *Demand the Impossible: Science Fiction and the Utopian Imagination.* New York and London: Methuen.

Mullen, Richard D. 1967. "H. G. Wells and Victor Rousseau: When the *Sleeper Wakes* and *The Messiah of the Cylinder.*" *Extrapolation* 8: 31–63.

Orwell, George. 1949. *Nineteen Eighty-Four: A Novel.* Reprint, New York: New American Library, 1961.

Remington, Thomas J. 1979. "The Other Side of Suffering: Touch as Theme and Metaphor in Le Guin's Science Fiction Novels." In *Ursula K. Le Guin,* edited by Joseph D. Olander and Martin Harry Greenberg. New York: Taplinger.

Rich, Adrienne. 1985. "Notes Toward a Politics of Location." In *Women Feminist, Identity and Society in the 1980's: Selected Papers,* edited by Myriam Diaz-Diocaretz and Iris M. Zavala. Amsterdam/Philadelphia: John Benjamins.

Selinger, Bernard. 1988. *Le Guin and Identity in Contemporary Fiction.* Ann Arbor: University of Michigan Research Press.

Somay, Bulent. 1984. "Towards an Open-ended Utopia." *Science-Fiction Studies* 11: 25–38.

Spivack, Charlotte. 1984. *Ursula K. Le Guin.* Boston: Twayne.

Suvin, Darko. 1979. *Metamorphoses of Science Fiction: On the Poetics and History of a Literary Genre.* New Haven and London: Yale University Press.

Vernier, J. P. 1977. "Evolution as a Literary Theme in H. G. Wells's Science Fiction." In *H. G. Wells and Modern Science Fiction,* edited by Darko Suvin and Robert M. Philmus. Lewisbury, Penn.: Bucknell University Press; London: Associated University Presses.

Wells, H. G. 1905. *A Modern Utopia.* Reprint, Lincoln and London: University of Nebraska Press, 1967.

———. 1960. *When the Sleeper Wakes.* In *Three Prophetic Novels of H. G. Wells,* edited by E. F. Bleiler. New York: Dover.

Woolf, Virginia. 1924. "Mr. Bennett and Mrs. Brown." In *The Captain's Death Bed and Other Essays.* New York: Harcourt, 1978.

Chapter 6

No Future! Cyberpunk, Industrial Music, and the Aesthetics of Postmodern Disintegration

Patrick Novotny

The sky above the port was the color
of television, tuned to a dead channel.
William Gibson, Neuromancer *(1984)*

Much of late twentieth-century artistic work has been based on a postmodern sensibility of cultural eclecticism, fragmentation, indeterminacy, and parody. Postmodernism, according to Stephen Tyler, most properly ought to be named the age of parody. The postmodernist sense of parody is represented by artists, literary theorists and creative writers (Hutcheon 1985). This parody transgresses aesthetic styles and representational norms, and celebrates the fragmented, indeterminate, and unpredictable subject.

A similar sense of irony, disillusionment, and pessimism has preoccupied much of twentieth-century aesthetic representation and culture. Despite the parallels with modernist irony, however, postmodern representation has been *parodic* rather than *ironic*. Postmodern parody revels in the problematization and disruption of aesthetic forms and representations. Parody in the postmodernist aesthetic is the transgression of aesthetic and representational norms. The postmodernist parody of aesthetic representation has been frequently carried to an extreme of self-negation, the playful celebration of the fragmentation and decomposition of the subject. With the collapse of the modern aesthetic tradition and the "implosion of metanarratives," postmodernist discourse transgresses and disrupts the received assurances of traditional aesthetic forms and problematizes the boundaries and limits of representation.

Further, an appropriation of earlier aesthetic styles and forms is one of the most prominent postmodernist textual practices. The collage technique, with its reliance on antecedent works, is the representational form of postmodernism's appropriate aesthetic. Postmodernism is characterized by experimentation with literary form and representation, through the use of styles and conventions from popular culture, music, art and literature. Postmodern collage extracts "found" materials out of their original context and juxtapositions them in other representational settings. Postmodernism's collage of appropriated images and styles undermines and subverts traditional representational forms, and thereby furthers the collapse of distinctions between aesthetic genres.

The works of the postmodern aesthetic have often relied on the technique of detournement, a representational form most fully formulated by the Situationist International. Detournement is the appropriation of existing cultural fragments in such a way as to alter and invert their meaning. The Situationist International, a collection of avant-garde artists and cultural theorists, gained its notoriety during the French student revolt of May 1968, "when the premises of its critique were distilled into crudely poetic slogans and spray-painted across the walls of Paris" (Marcus 1989, 18). The Situationist International experimented with counter-language and detournement. Detournement was characterized by the Situationist International in terms of a collage aesthetic that involved the appropriation and recombination of cultural fragments that transformed their original meaning. Detournement, the politics of subversive quotation, is the "theft of aesthetic artifacts from their contexts and their diversion into contexts of one's own devise" (Marcus 1989, 168). Detournement, as formulated by the Situationist International, constitutes the process of cultural representations and significations becoming subverted into their opposite.

The modernist separation of life and art have given way to an aestheticization of politics and everyday life in postmodern society

(Berman; Harvey). Sophisticated computer, communications, electronic, and media technologies have produced decentering and fragmentation of representational forms and blurred images (Poster; Lash and Urry). Everyday life in postmodern culture is pervaded by a sense of cultural discontinuity and fragmentation not unlike that of the aesthetic tradition of surrealism. For postmodernism, according to Iain Chambers, "whatever form its intellectualizing might take has been fundamentally anticipated in the metropolitan cultures of the last twenty years: among the electronic signifiers of cinema, television and video, in recording studios and record players, in fashion and youth styles, in all those sounds, images and diverse histories that are daily mixed, recycled and 'scratched' together on that giant screen which is the contemporary city" (quoted in Harvey 60–61). Postmodern culture is increasingly oriented toward cultural complexity rather than a homogeneous and monologic cultural dominant. "In a world with too many voices speaking all at once, a world where syncretism and parodic invention are becoming the rule, not the exception, an urban multinational world of industrial transience, where American clothes made in Korea are worn by young people in Russia, where everyone's 'roots' are in some degree cut, in such a world it becomes increasingly difficult to attach human identity and meaning to a coherent 'culture' or 'language'" (Clifford 95).

The dispersion of cultural voices and the blurring of representational genres is a characteristic of everyday life in postmodernist culture. Eclecticism, according to Jean-François Lyotard's *The Postmodern Condition,* "is the degree zero of contemporary culture: one listens to reggae, watches a western, eats McDonald's food for lunch and local cuisine for dinner, wears Paris perfume in Tokyo and `retro' clothes in Hong Kong" (Lyotard 1984, 76). This infusion of different cultural genres and representations is a major theme in the literature, music and culture that has come to define the cyberpunk aesthetic. Cultural eclecticism is reflected in the decentering in everyday life. Postmodern eclecticism has emerged as the contestation of cultural cohesion and homogeneity, and thus embodies the fragmentary nature of contemporary experience.

As postmodern society and culture have been characterized by an aestheticization of everyday life, the critical spaces of cultural resistance emerge in the application of the avant-garde's appropriative practice of detournement and bricolage in everyday life. In his study *Subculture,* Dick Hebdige utilizes the term bricolage to describe "how individuals manipulate disparate cultural phenomena in order to explain their world to themselves in satisfactory ways" (Collins 145). Bricolage is the transgressive activity of individuals who are able to appropriate cultural styles and images for their own ends. It is the manipulation of cultural forms and aesthetic representations in sites of resistance, the forging of a discursive space where alternative forms of cultural expression may emerge. Jim Collins has written that "within media-saturated cultures where no overarching, pan-cultural distinctions between official and unofficial, mainstream and avant-garde are in effect, bricolage becomes the inevitable response to semiotic overload" (Collins 145). Graffiti, scratch music, hip-hop, and other cultural activities all constitute bricolage, sharing a penchant for the eclecticism and juxtaposition from earlier avant-garde traditions, and combining music, fashion, dance, graphics and performance. Parallel with the emergence of the hip-hop scene during the past decade, a contemporary genre of science fiction has explored forms of bricolage and cultural resistance in an immanent dystopian society.

Cyberpunk science fiction has come to fruition in the past decade during a period of cultural upheaval and the crisis of representation in aesthetic and cultural formations. Cyberpunk science fiction is the literary incarnation of postmodernism's eclecticism and decentering, reflecting the shifting contours and disintegration of postmodern culture. The work of cyberpunk science fiction, summarizes Bruce Sterling, "is paralleled throughout Eighties pop culture: in rock video, in the hacker underground; in the jarring street tech of hip-hop and scratch music; in the synthesizer rock of London and Tokyo. This phenomenon, this has a global range; cyberpunk is its literary 'incarnation'" (Sterling 1986, ix-x). The experience of social fragmentation and cultural eclecticism, and aesthetic blurring of the postmodern condition is represented in cyberpunk's novels and short stories. Postmodern eclecticism, aptly described by Lyotard as the "degree zero of contemporary culture," has found its expression in cyberpunk science fiction.

Cyberpunk is one of the most significant efforts in contemporary science fiction and popular culture. Cyberpunk is a wide-ranging representation style, ranging from the sampling techniques of industrial music groups such as Ministry and Front 242 to the magazine *Mondo 2000* to the hallucinogenic energies of techno-music and raves and the eclectic humor of Mark Leyner's short stories. A number of significant works of contemporary popular film have been influential in the development of a cyberpunk aesthetic, especially Ridley Scott's *Blade Runner* and David Cronenberg's *Videodrome*. Cyberpunk is even characterized as having its own philosophers in the works of Jean Baudrillard and Arthur Kroker and David Cook (Fekete; Kroker and Cook). The term cyberpunk, however, is almost synonymous with the works of a group of young science fiction authors, in particular William Gibson and Bruce Sterling. Gibson's *Neuromancer*, the most formidable literary work in cyberpunk, has been called "one of the most interesting books of the postmodern age" (Csicsery-Ronay 1988, 269). Cyberpunk, according to Istvan Csicsery-Ronay, is not a literary movement in science fiction as much as an encompassing aesthetic.

Gibson and other authors have denied that cyberpunk represents a "genuine literary movement" (Dorsey 12). Cyberpunk is, however, "a legitimate international artistic style, with profound philosophical and aesthetic premises" (Csicsery-Ronay 269). Cyberpunk's main themes and literary techniques have represented the apotheosis of postmodernism in science fiction, a "subversive realism" in contemporary science fiction.

Cyberpunk is a genre of science fiction set in an immanent, computerized and information-governed world. Cyberpunk centers around "an alternative post-industrial culture predicated on the interface of biotechnologically enhanced human bodies, interactive information technology, and omniscient corporate power" (Tomas 113). Cyberpunk's main themes focus on the forces of cultural integration, such as media and communications technologies, massive computer and satellite networks, and multinational corporations. Contrasted with the images of immensely powerful multinational corporations and vast computerized networks are the street worlds of the punk underground and urban subcultures. Cyberpunk's settings are reminiscent of the amorphous and decaying urban wastelands of the postindustrial and deindustrialized present, with pervasive images of immanent collapse. Its imaginative themes reflect the dystopian context of postindustrial, technological culture.

Cyberpunk is synonymous with the confrontation between an earlier, expansive science fiction and postmodern science fiction. Cyberpunk represents a postmodern response to the earlier science fiction tradition of technological utopianism. Earlier forms of science fiction, such as the future history of Isaac Asimov or the world building of Hal Clement, were embedded in the modernist confidence that scientific humanism would exert a degree of moral and ethical control over technology. While classic science fiction has been centered around technological break-throughs and progress, the works of Gibson, Sterling, and others have largely abandoned the technological optimism of the earlier tradition and embraced a more nihilistic and dystopian ethos, an "anti-aesthetic" of environmental destruction and social breakdown that has a lineage with the "no future" anticipated in the punk aesthetic of groups such as the Sex Pistols. Cyberpunk represents the implosion of classical science fiction, undermining its ideology of technological utopianism.

The works of Gibson and other cyberpunk authors depart from the dominant utopian and futuristic themes in the early science fiction tra-dition, although surely dystopian and disjunctive ideas have not been absent from early science fiction, going back, at least, to Wells. Never-theless, cyberpunk is particularly ambivalent toward the prospects of an immanent social and cultural system. Gibson's "The Gernsback Con-tinuum" (1986) is emblematic of cyberpunk's rejection of the authoritar-ian themes in earlier technologically utopian science fiction. A fetishization and reverence for technology were important themes in the works of Hugo Gernsback and other early science fiction visionaries (Ross 1991). Cyberpunk has posed a tough, grimly technological dysto-pia against naive celebration of technological innovation and utopianism within much of futurist science fiction.

Cyberpunk's postclassical themes are centered in a decaying, postindustrial world dominated by multinational corporations and in-habited by underground subcultures. Cyberpunk's settings, as within most postmodernist futures, are "grim utopias" (McHale 67). Gibson's *Neuromancer,* the catalyst of the cyberpunk aesthetic, presents a unique literary collage of social stratification, vast multinational corporations, advanced computer technologies, punk underworlds, designer drugs, and dilapidated urban sprawls. Cyberpunk projects the image of artifi-cial intelligence and orbiting space colonies, interspersed with the de-piction of decrepit urban sprawl and social disintegration. Thus, in more than one respect, cyberpunk might be referred to as the first postmodernist *noir* fiction.

Cyberpunk is a gritty, hard-edged science fiction of back alleys and trash dumpsters, littered with discarded computer chips and the detri-tus of the information society. The smokestacks with the fumes from an earlier era of industrial production yield to a world in environmental breakdown, a perpetual haze of smoke and filth with constant rain streaking the concrete on a landscape of abandoned industrial factories. According to Csicsery-Ronay, "the one thing that Cyberpunk is fascinated with above all else, its ruling deity, is sleaze" (Csicsery-Ronay 1988, 277). Cyberpunk fiction is at the forefront of a dystopian aesthetic of social disintegration in which "empty warehouses and abandoned industrial plants drip with leaking rain" (Harvey 310). Cyperpunk, like the contemporary punk movement from which it has drawn its inspiration, signifies the fragmentation of social life, the chaos and disorder at every level of society, particularly in the street's endless cultures and countercultures. Cyberpunk intersperses the style, rhythms and characters of the street with advanced computer and biotechnologies. The novels of Gibson capture the nightlife and street ethos of computer hackers and underworld hired mercenaries, where neurotechnology and designer drugs form the basis of youth rebellion and urban subculture. The images of urban decay and disintegration reinforce the sense of social fragmentation and bleakness which has been central to cyberpunk.

Cyberpunk is the emergence of a postmodern hybridization and bricolage in science fiction. Cyberpunk authors, according to Sterling, "are fascinated by interzones: the areas where, in the words of William Gibson, 'the street finds its own uses for things'" (Sterling xi). Interzones are amorphous and decaying urban wastelands, the decrepit landscape of deindustrialization. Cyperpunk interzones, such as *Neuromancer*'s Night City, are the scenes of violent conflict, amorphous and shifting milieus where the marginalized underworld of the criminal subculture collides with huge multinational corporations for the mutual interest of business. Interzones, often in the shadow of multinational corporations such as "Maas" or "Hosaka," are crowded, seething locales of foggy, rubbish-strewn streets, and shabby hotels and tenement warehouses inhabited by an assortment of criminals, mercenaries, drug addicts, prostitutes, hustlers, smugglers, "data pirates" and thieves. Streets and nightclubs are filled with a diverse mixture of persons, creolized languages, and hybrid subcultures. A crowded matrix of espionage precariously rests on the fringes of the multinational economy, where criminal subcultures exist in a delicate symbiosis with the multinational corporations. Case, the main character in *Neuromancer*, "saw a certain sense in the notion that burgeoning technologies require outlaw zones, that Night City wasn't there for its inhabitants, but as a deliberate unsupervised playground for technology itself" (11). The interzones are tolerated areas of illicit activity, from which the vast multinational corporations draw the marginalized computer hackers and hired mercenaries to carry out illicit activities in their confrontations with one another. Industrial espionage and corporate defections are regular occurrences among the multinational corporations. More importantly, interzones are a useful metaphor for cyberpunk's merging of technologically sophisticated cultures with the instincts of underworld subcultures and marginalized groups.

Cyberpunk is a new sensibility in science fiction, a hard-edged dystopian realism in its depiction of the collapse of technological, postindustrial utopias. Reacting against the antiseptic, relentlessly sanitized vision of much earlier science fiction, such as that of Asimov and Clement mentioned above, the authors associated with cyberpunk fiction have been fascinated by the image of a decrepit postindustrial world governed by huge multinationals and inhabited by rampant subcultures. Cyperpunk, writes Pam Rosenthal, "is interested in a world shaped by transnational corporate hegemony, new forms of core-periphery economic relationships, world beat culture and identity subcultures" (Rosenthal 81). Gibson's themes of urban disintegration are "recognizably and painstakingly drawn from the modern condition" (Sterling x). The intensely detailed prose of Gibson and other cyberpunk authors captures images of urbanization and environmental decay. The classic opening line from *Neuromancer* embodies the cyberpunk aesthetic: "The sky above the port was the color of television, tuned to a dead channel" (Gibson 1984, 3). Gibson's postindustrial landscapes are permeated by physical refuse and ecological decay: Tokyo Bay is a "black expanse where gulls wheel above drifting shoals of white styrofoam," urban areas in Japan and the United States coalesce into massive "sprawls," pouring rains and fog blanketing trash-strewn alleyways, punk subcultures and scavengers roaming endlessly amidst the streets. Cyberpunk's future is an industrial landscape of empty warehouses and abandoned industrial plants, of dead grass in the cracks of broken freeway concrete alongside the broken slag and rusting shells of refineries. Inspired by the extrapolation of present social and technological systems, cyberpunk presents strikingly realistic images of the decay and disintegration of postindustrial civilization. It depicts an often rain-soaked, desolate and empty world set against the background noise of desperation and constant struggle.

Cyberpunk science fiction's representation of technology marks a departure from that in early science fiction, with its nihilism and diminished sense of optimism in technology. Cyberpunk science fiction is particularly concerned with the breakthrough in biotechnologies and the interfaces of humans and computer technologies through prosthetic limbs, implanted circuitry and genetic alterations. Cyberpunk's "most common emblems are the implants which allow people to jack into computer nets directly, or to plug in modules that give them additional memories, skills, or even personalities" (Pierce 186). It is the latest genre of science fiction to represent the innovations and possibilities of biotechnologies, genetic engineering, computer technologies and cybernetics. Through cyberpunk science fiction, according to Darko Suvin, "technology is inside, not outside, the personal body and mind itself" (Suvin 42). In stark contrast to earlier science fiction, technology is visceral in the cyberpunk aesthetic. Technology sticks to the skin, often responding to the touch. Within cyberpunk, technology "is pervasive, utterly intimate. Not outside of us, but next to us. Under our skin; often, inside our minds" (Sterling xi). The oppositions between human and machine, self and other, are broken down and dissolved in cyberpunk. Gibson's works resonate a visceral conception of technology as his "central concerns are cybernetic: human memory and personality, considered as information. People as systems" (Grant 1990, 41). Cyberpunk reflects the pervasiveness of biotechnologies and computer implants in cyberpunk's postindustrial culture, as with *Neuromancer*'s cyberpunk mercenary Molly's implanted blades and mirrored lenses. Cyberpunk is the first genre of science fiction works to grapple with the reality of prosthetic limbs and biotechnological implants as well as the potential of virtual technology and computer networks to create spaces and terrain for social, political and cultural struggle.

Cyberpunk is a radical disjuncture with traditional science fiction imagery, projecting dystopian images of decrepit and corrupted technology. Subverted and detourned technology scavenged from industrial wastelands and corporate data coffers are a prominent image within cyberpunk. Gibson's works resonate with street level incidents of bricolage. Most of the techno-subcultures in Gibson's novels center around cyberspace, a *consensual* visual representation of computerized data and information networks of unimaginable proportions, which has taken more resonance with contemporary society through virtual reality and the expanding presence of the Internet in public discourse. "Cyberspace. A consensual hallucination experienced daily by billions of legitimate operators, in every nation, by children being taught mathematical concepts" (Gibson 1984, 51). Cyberspace is produced by the interaction of massive computer systems and iconographic representations of huge configurations of data and information. "A graphic representation of data abstracted from the banks of every computer in the human system. Unthinkable complexity, lines of light ranged in the nonspace of the mind, clusters and constellations of data. Like city lights, receding" (Gibson 1984, 51). The idea of cyberspace breaks down the dichotomy between the cybernetic technology and the realm of humans, as "every computer in the human system" becomes a consensual system which is as likely to exist in the heads of computer users as in any real space. Cyberspace, according to Glenn Grant, "intended as a convenience for legitimate business purposes, becomes a playground for criminal hackers. Almost anything can be retrofitted, turned into a tool of the subculture" (Grant 43). Cyberpunk hackers subvert the computer technologies of huge multinational corporations, deftly avoiding sophisticated intrusion and monitoring devices. Biotechnology and computer experts are "extracted" from multinational corporate "arcologies" with the aid of computer hackers and underworld mercenaries.

Cyberpunk projects dystopian visions of a vast underclass and rampant subcultures, "speed tribes" whose inhabitants are continually engaged in acts of bricolage and theft against the multinational corporations. Theft, piracy and corruption recur as important themes in cyberpunk, particularly in the poaching of "data pirates" and "computer cowboys" in the computerized universe of cyberspace. Gibson's novels are pervaded by detournement in which social and technological structures are negated and turned against themselves. Gibson's main characters, writes David Tomas, "are human 'gomi' whose economic activities are parasitic on omniscient military and multinational corporate or aristocratic formations" (Tomas 114).

Neuromancer centers around the techno-criminal subcultures which inhabit cyberspace. The main character, Case, is a young computer hacker, a data thief who "worked for other, wealthier thieves, employers who provided the exotic software required to penetrate the bright walls of corporate systems, opening windows into rich fields of data" (Gibson 1984, 5). Once the corporate data formations have been accessed, the cyberpunk hackers steal or manipulate the information. Multinational corporations attempt to regulate and control the circulation of data and information within cyberspace. The criminal hacker underground, however, continually steals such data and uses it to further "penetrate" the corporate computer data banks. The economically disruptive activities of the hacker underground are the main focus for much of the action in Gibson's novels. The subcultures and hackers utilize the computer technologies of the multinational conglomerates for their own ends. The impossibility of transacting legitimate business in currency results in the flourishing of black markets and criminal subcultures at the margins of Gibson's world: Night City.

Cyberpunk projects a distinct view of space colonization without massive settlements and vast orbiting housing developments, drifting unconcerned above an ecologically and socially ravaged world. Cyberpunk challenges traditional science fiction's "collective vision of bright, clean, ecologically, economically, and socially self-contained technocratic, middle-class suburbs in space, with no poor people, no street gangs, no cockroaches, and no dogshit on the streets" (Spinrad 129). Cyberpunk extends the multinational corporate and cyberspace culture into outer space, along with its streetwise, techno-subcultures. Decaying space stations and abandoned orbiting habitats are taken over by marginalized subcultures. Prior to cyberpunk's emergence as a recognized aesthetic, Gibson and Sterling collaborated on the short story "Red Star, Winter Orbit" (1986) which set an important direction for their later works. In the story, the United States has abandoned its space colonization efforts and the Soviet Union is poised to follow. A small coterie of Soviet cosmonauts attempts to resist the shutdown of their orbiting space station; however, such resistance appears vain. In the closing moments of the story, a group of American settlers launch themselves on a makeshift spacecraft and take over the station as a means to avoid the bureaucracy of "army brass" and "pen-pushers." Gibson and Sterling's story is emblematic of the themes explored in subsequent cyberpunk literature as it breaks with traditional science fiction's well-ordered vision of space, and instead presents an image of cultural disintegration and chaotic disarray.

Cyberpunk science fiction abounds with references to creolized ethnic and subcultural groups. The punk underworld and Rastafarian subcultures are important themes in cyberpunk science fiction. The punk movement parodied the alienation and emptiness of modern society through a strategy of interference with dominant cultural representations. Punk's subversive currents merge with modern computerized technologies and myriad underground subcultures to create the cyberpunk aesthetic. Gibson's prose includes references to the youth subculture's urban environments, such as his Panther Moderns. The settings in *Neuromancer* include Zion, a space colony retrofitted into a Rastafarian community. The scent of ganja and the dub of reggae which resonate throughout Zion serve as a reminder of the resiliency of creolized subcultures and their capacity to resist cultural homogenization. The alterations of the derelict and abandoned space colonies by the subcultures makes them far more strange and varied than intended. Gibson's work seeks to introduce the untidiness of subcultures and a punk aesthetic into the orderly world of science fiction.

Cyberpunk recognizes the limits of technological and social systems to eliminate cultural heterogeneity and fragmentation. Multinational corporations attempt to regulate the circulation of data and information in cyberspace, where image and information flows merge to form an oppressively stratified culture. The incursions of the subcultures, however, make cyberspace a chaotic and discordant realm. "What was once an apparently homogenizing virtual reality," according to Tomas, "begins to reflect a chaotic urban existence" (Tomas 125). Technology in cyberpunk science fiction does not "eliminate the sensibility of the street, of underclasses, ghettoes, countercultures, and class struggle" (Spinrad 134). Instead, the subcultures permeate the computer technologies. Cyberpunk reveals the axiom that the street finds its own uses for things. Gibson's novels are a world of streets and back alleys, a realm where the figures inhabiting the decrepit urban landscape are constantly involved in skirmishes with the dominant system. Cyberpunk's subcultures and underworld continually struggle to shape their own identities in the face of multinational corporations and pervasive advertising and commercial pressures.

The standardization and mechanization resulting from increasing technological sophistication in science fiction gives way to a world of subcultures and bricolage in cyberpunk. The pervasiveness of globally integrated computer and satellite networks creates an array of potential entry points for cultural resistance: the potential sites of resistance increase with every expansion of computer networks. "Now that technology has reached a fever pitch," according to Sterling, "its influence has slipped control and reached street level" (Sterling x). The dissemination of computer technologies allows marginalized subcultures to express themselves through the bricolage and detournement of those technologies. Endless subcultures continuously appear and dissolve around the detourned technologies within the works of Gibson and other cyberpunk authors. Cyberpunk's subcultures use genetic engineering and cyberspace's virtual information technologies for their own creolized cultures and representations. The underground clinics in the city of Chiba are a black market of biotechnologies, where technologies are appropriated and subverted for the cyberpunk and hacker subcultures. Genetic surgeons and contraband brain implants provide the basis for the techno-subcultures and underground. Through cyberpunk's postmodern semiotic, technologies are appropriated less for control than for bricolage and detournement. Steven Best has written that cyberpunk "fails to theorize important counter tendencies, contradictions and forms of resistance" (Best 218). Cyberpunk science fiction and its representations of bricolage and detournement, however, serve as an important reminder that the cultural hegemony of standardization and commodification does not entirely eliminate oppositional spaces and cultural heterogeneity. The bricolage and disfiguration of the cultural dominant is a potential site of resistance in an oppressively stratified society dominated by globally televised images and a multinational information and computerized economy.

Cyberpunk science fiction reflects many of the major themes in postmodern aesthetic practice, in particular the sense of cultural fragmentation, disintegration, discontinuity, indeterminacy and heterogeneity. Cyberpunk embodies a dystopian, nihilistic postmodernism similar to that theoretically represented by Jean Baudrillard. Cyberpunk science fiction's metaphor of implosion, according to Csicsery-Ronay, "comes up often in theoretical writings on the crisis of representation and politics in the postmodern condition, especially in the work of Jean Baudrillard and Arthur Kroker, who might be taken as the central theorists of cyberpunk philosophy" (Csicsery-Ronay 271). Postmodern social theorists, according to Best, have discussed the deterioration of the social and "the annihilation of the human subject within technological and cybernetic systems" (Best 214). The fragmentation and disintegration amidst the streets and subculture of cyberpunk's dystopian landscape mirrors much of the postmodern aesthetic of nihilism, implosion and decay. Cyberpunk moreover represents the collision of postmodern literary and "extrapolative" science fiction techniques. Cyberpunk is based upon the simultaneous presence of layered aesthetic forms and representations. In many instances, cyberpunk appropriates the earlier themes and literary forms in traditional science fiction, and thereby emblematizes the dialogic interaction among the styles of discourse within the postmodern imagination.

Cyberpunk science fiction, as exemplified in the works of Gibson, shows that any representational style and form can be appropriated to any end. Gibson's basic technique of juxtaposition is similar to the collage of the avant-garde literary forms and visual aesthetic. Gibson's juxtapositions are the careful, purposeful representation of cultural and aesthetic alternatives, rather than the pastiche of superficial plundering of art history and popular culture. Gibson's juxtaposition technique combines images and cultural fragments from different periods not unlike the film *Blade Runner*. The shift toward postmodernist representation in cyberpunk has been accompanied by a renewed interest in the science fiction tradition that preceded it (Ross 1991). Cyberpunk's aesthetic and representational techniques are often parodically juxtaposed with early science fiction, as in Gibson's satirical references to the Fuller domes. The complex layering of forms and styles through the use of collage-representational technique shows a postmodern influence in cyberpunk. Interzones exemplify cyberpunk's representational technique, juxtaposing the primitive and the sophisticated, combining them with a humor and parody that contrasts with the intellectual solemnity of much early science fiction themes although the important book by Hassler (1982) on traditional science fiction anticipates much of this cyber-joking.

Gibson's novels employ a prose-collage literary technique to capture the fragmented spaces and divergent street cultures of the dystopian city. Gibson makes use of a full range of popular cultural sources, including the news media, advertising and even early science fiction. The vocabulary, idioms, and rhythms of popular slang form much of the basis of Gibson's prose. Gibson has discussed the prose-collage technique as an attempt to make sense of contemporary social and cultural reality: "There are so many cultures and subcultures around today that if you're willing to listen, you start picking up different phrases, inflections, metaphors everywhere you go. A lot of the stuff in *Neuromancer* and *Count Zero* that people think is so futuristic is probably just 1969 Toronto dope-dealer's slang, or bikers' talk" (Gibson 1989, 81). Like one of his own characters, Gibson acknowledges, "I borrow a lot." Cyberpunk science fiction continues the avant-garde's literary technique through postmodernism's appropriation and combination of disparate cultural forms. It is the literary collage of the disintegration and recombination of eclectic, cultural fragments.

Cyberpunk science fiction has drawn upon a wide range of popular cultural materials and literary styles. The cut-up literary technique of William S. Burroughs figures prominently in cyberpunk, making eclecticism and juxtaposition an important textual method within cyberpunk science fiction. Cyberpunk's imaginary realm of the interzone draws its chief inspiration from William Burroughs's depiction of Tangiers in his classic *Naked Lunch*. The setting of the novel was an imaginary dystopia described by Burroughs as "Composite City." Burrough's interzone is a composite scene of the marginalized world of drug addicts, criminals, sexual deviants and other subcultures, "a vast, ramshackle structure in which all the world's architectural styles are fused and all its races and cultures mingle, the apotheosis of the Third World shanty-town" (McHale 1987, 44). Frequently acknowledging Burroughs as a central precursor of cyberpunk through interviews and textual references, Gibson and other cyberpunk authors have explicitly drawn from successive traditions of aesthetic representation in forging the cyberpunk aesthetic. Cyberpunk's interzones thus show the important influence of Burroughs, and provide the setting for the collision of technologically sophisticated culture with the streets of underworld subcultures.

Cyberpunk mixes the elements of popular culture with a postmodern prose-collage technique inspired by Burroughs's cut-up method and literary techniques. Gibson's collage composition, according to Glenn Grant, is part of an avant-garde and twentieth-century "counter-cultural tradition which he acknowledges by including Marcel Duchamp's assemblage sculpture, "the Large Glass," in the Tessier-Ashpool's gallery" (Grant 43). Cyberpunk literature and the literary method of prose-collage and appropriation, according to Sterling, "captures something crucial to the work of these writers, something crucial to the decade as a whole: a new kind of integration" (Sterling 1986, ix). In this way, cyberpunk depicts an eclectic and anarchic landscape familiar in postmodern fiction. Cyberpunk's collage makes possible the representation of the decentering, fragmentation and dissolution in the postmodern aesthetic.

Cyberpunk incorporates a wide range of popular culture forms and literary styles. Cyberpunk's works are infused with references to popular culture, paintings, sculpture, architecture, science fiction films, computer and technical journals, and popular music ranging from reggae to punk, industrial and techno music (Grant 1990, 43–44). The flourishing of rave and techno youth culture, with its hallucinogenic drugs, techno music, infusion of psychedelic culture, and its hip-hop aesthetic and sensibility, and hand-held cameras and electronic mail and computer discussion lists to record the all-night energies of raves, could have easily have sprung forth from the pages of a cyberpunk novel. Raves, with their colorful graphic flyers often inspired by fractal geometry and chaos graphics, and with the reemergence of hallucinogenic drugs and "smart drinks," have a free-floating sensibility of mock secrecy and all-night energy, sometimes held in large warehouses, or on beaches and farms, that reflects the energy of cyberpunk's blending of cultures. Indeed, the cybernetic influence of the rave and techno music culture is unmistakable, as reflected in recent work such as Douglas Rushkoff's *Cyberia: Life in the Trenches of Hyperspace* (1994). Entire mixed sequences from the warehouse raves of San Francisco, London and Chicago can be accessed over computer networks through an ordinary computer modem, bringing a global edge and sensibility to the techno and rave culture. Photographs of raves and the fractal-inspired graphic invitations of the raves have infused the "virtual community" of the techno culture, yielding the kind of "cyberspace" that is an aesthetic theme in cyberpunk science function.

Cyberpunk is engaged in an inventive bricolage and detournement similar to the energy of the punk movement and the explosive technoculture of the early 1990s. The fast-paced and hectic energy of techno music and its industrial music predecessor is the kind of music one expects to hear from the settings of cyberpunk, interspersed with the world-beat ethos of reggae from cyberpunk's Rastafarians. The techno and rave culture and its industrial music culture predecessor share in the resonance of themes from cyberpunk science fiction, in particular the aesthetic of laughter and parody which layers otherwise discordant aesthetic forms.

Cyberpunk is infused with a sense of fragmentation, social detritus and cultural disintegration, and, according to Sterling, is "the overlapping of worlds that were formally separate: the realm of high tech, and the modern pop underground" (Sterling ix). The dinginess, squalor and filth of everyday life are fused with the sophistication of advanced genetic and computer technologies. Cyberpunk's collage and literary eclecticism collide with "scratch music, whose ghetto innovators turn the phonograph itself into an instrument, producing an archetypal Eighties music where funk meets the Burroughs cut-up method" (Sterling xii). Scratch music is the appropriation of existing sounds and records which are mixed together to produce a "layered" collage of synthesized, electronic dance music. The "street tech" of hip-hop music represent points of bricolage in postmodern everyday life. Cyberpunk is the manifestation of the postmodern collusion between street subcultures and advanced technology. "'It's all in the mix'—this is true of much Eighties art," according to Sterling, "and is applicable to cyberpunk as it is to punk, mix-and-match retro fashion and multitrack digital recording" (Sterling 1986, xii). The detournement of the situationist movement has found its heir apparent in cyberpunk literature and the blaring, synthesized fusion of industrial music. Industrial and postindustrial music share an aesthetic moment with the writings of Gibson and other cyberpunk authors (see Devy). Like cyberpunk, the industrial music scene is a street-level cultural intervention, the extension of detournement to everyday noises and sounds.

The detachment in industrial music reflects the ironies and absurdities of postmodern culture. Industrial music is impressed with parody, pessimism, and detachment, providing the dystopian background music with which to survey the postmodern cultural landscape. Like cyberpunk science fiction, industrial music is situated in the context of postmodern urban detritus and decay, the environmental breakdown and skies "the color of television turned to a dead channel." The hard sounds of industrial music inspire images of decrepit modernism: Nitzer Ebb's music punctuated by the sound of airport announcements, Ministry's "Halloween" confronting the banalities of conformism, Skinny Puppy's "Testure" with its chilling images of animal vivisection. Industrial music's brittle and mechanized sounds of detachment reflect the brutality and despair of dystopian, postmodern life, as well as the refusal to passively accept this life.

Like cyberpunk fiction, industrial music is based on the eclecticism of detournement and postmodern appropriative collage technique, although such music has been conspicuously absent from much of the critical discourse on postmodernist culture. Industrial music is infused with the social sarcasm and laughter of postmodernism's parody, in recognition that musical bricolage and parody "are becoming the order of the day" (Kearney 1988, 357). Industrial music's digital sampling appropriates sounds to produce a variety of effects. Sounds are pasted together from disparate sources through sampling techniques, and then juxtaposed with rhythmic electronic music. Sampling and recording technology, according to Front 242's Patric Codenys, provides "the ability to

115

take anything we want from anywhere we want" (Doerschuk 1989, 55). Like Marcel Duchamp's ready-made sculptures, any sound or noises can be brought within the province of industrial music. The availability of synthesizer and multitrack recording techniques facilitates the process of musical bricolage, the recombination of musical and aesthetic forms. Front 242, Nine Inch Nails, Ministry, Consolidated, Skinny Puppy and other industrial groups utilize sampling technology to draw sounds from television and popular music. Industrial music utilizes dialogue fragments from political speeches, television advertisements, and propaganda and military films. Most industrial music, according to Mary Rose and Daniel Warner, "incorporates found musical objects, 'automatic' mechanical, and electronic systems for generating music" (Rose and Warner 1987, 71). Industrial music's style is defined principally through its juxtaposition technique in a way that is strikingly similar to the cyberpunk aesthetic. Front 242's sampling "captures the grotesquerie of American television, the turbulence behind bland media imagery, and the violence of alienation in a body of songs that can make listeners laugh, scream, and dance all at once" (Doerschuk 1989, 52). Synthesizers and multitrack recorders are used to appropriate and reassemble music drawn from a variety of musical forms and sources. Industrial music's "scavenging" and sampling aesthetic have generated an entirely new mode of music, the social recontextualization of music amidst the hum of postmodern everyday life. The recorded materials and sounds are assembled in industrial music similar to an earlier avant-garde collage aesthetic.

Industrial music's hard edge is an anti-aesthetic discordance and counter production to popular music culture. Incorporating the rough, harsh edge of the punk sound, industrial music "is an even noisier resistance to mainstream pop culture" (Rose and Warner 71). Industrial music disrupts the dominant mode of musical production through an unarticulated discordance similar to the punk and hardcore music scenes. Industrial music is an energetic and subversive response to an implosive and stifling culture, providing the critical space for a vigorous, negational subculture. Subverted and "detourned" sounds, scavenged and sampled from the background hum of everyday life, are an important aspect of the counter-production of industrial music.

Sampling and multitrack recording provide groups such as Front 242 and Nine Inch Nails with a device to transform electronic music into a reflection of everyday life. Industrial music's eclectic and creative use of digital recording and synthesizer technologies, the bricolage of everyday noise and sounds, and the *layering* of words over a dance beat suggest that "momentarily, at least, new social textualizations of music are possible in pop music, an industry which has been moving increasingly towards over-produced, empty musical surfaces" (Rose and Warner 71). Industrial music has opened the possibility for a return to the connection between music and street-level forms of appropriation of urban space from the early punk movement. In drafty warehouse clubs and decaying urban centers, industrial music appropriates the social spaces abandoned by an earlier stage of capital and subverts its more recent cultural formations with industrial music's brittle, hard-edged rhythms.

Cyberpunk's vision of a dystopian future has been echoed in the music and multimedia performance of industrial groups. Front 242's "Welcome to Paradise" is an example of industrial music's postmodern appropriative and collage aesthetic. Throughout the song, the words of television evangelists are interspersed and mixed with jarring synthesizers. The phrases "Jesus is here" and "In the name of Jesus" are mixed with synthesized electronic music. Televangelist Jerry Falwell's moral exhortation "Oh God I'm a sinner, I deserve to go to Hell" is subverted and turned against itself, reflected against a backdrops of laughter. The superimposition and layering of the synthesized music over the monologue of the televangelists inverts their exhortations, revealing at once the parody and laughter within industrial music's detournement. The detournement of Falwell and other televangelists' moral exhortations—"No sex until marriage"—in Front 242's "Welcome to Paradise" is similar to the bricolage in *Neuromancer*: "'To hear is to obey.' The Moderns were using some kind of chickenwire dish in New Jersey to bounce the link man's scrambled signal off a Sons of Christ the King satellite in geosynchronous orbit above Manhattan. They chose to regard the entire operation as an elaborate private joke, and their choice of comsats seemed to have been deliberate" (60). The Panther Moderns, one of the numerous techno-subcultures in *Neuromancer*, utilize the communications satellite of a global televangelical consortium and mislead authorities into believing that an obscure Christian fundamentalist group is responsible for the theft of computer data from a multinational conglomerate. Front 242's "Welcome to Paradise" and Gibson's techno-subcultures show the manner in which detournement "would turn the words of its enemies back on themselves, forcing new speech even out of the mouths of the guardians of good and right" (Marcus 1989, 178). In both instances, television evangelists and religious leaders are parodied as part of a cultural elite which manipulates the public. Industrial music's detournement, its politics of subversive quotation, revels in a carnivalesque laughter with the susceptibility of turning everyday speech and sounds into their opposite.

An important theme throughout this discussion is postmodernism's aesthetic of parody and symbolic inversion, particularly in the notions of detournement and bricolage. Both detournement and bricolage can be seen as representative of Mikhail Bakhtin's concept of laughter and the carnivalesque (Bakhtin 1989). Laughter, writes Dominick LaCapra, "is the sole force in life that cannot be entirely coopted by official powers and made hypocritical" (LaCapra 1983, 302). Writing during the social and cultural monologism of the Stalinist period, Bakhtin posed "the popular utopia of 'laughter' and 'carnival,' dialogism that has taken to the streets" (Pechey 1990, 24). Bakhtin emphasizes laughter and the carnivalesque against the prohibitions and repressions of everyday life. Laughter, particularly during carnivals and other festive occasions, is "the social consciousness of the people" (Bakhtin 1989, 305). "In a riot of semiosis," according to Terry Eagleton, "power structures are estranged through grotesque parody, 'necessity' thrown into satirical questions and objects displaced or negated into their opposite" (Eagleton 145). Laughter is the symbolic inversion of authority and the popular transgressions which parody and ridicule power. "Absolutely nothing escapes this great spasms of satire: no signifier is too solemn to be blasphemously invaded, dismantled and turned against itself" (Eagleton 145). Bakhtin's notion of laughter and the carnivalesque reappear in the spray-painted slogans of the Situationist International throughout Paris during the May 1968 revolt. The concept of laughter and the carnivalesque is linked to the aesthetic of transgression and symbolic inversion in postmodern culture. The social sarcasm and parody of Bakhtin's laughter are continued in cyberpunk fiction and the industrial musical scene.

The postmodern aesthetic celebrates the carnivalesque notion of laughter in its playful satire and parody. Bakhtin's ideas of laughter and symbolic inversion in cyberpunk science fiction and industrial music represent instances of the parodic discourse in postmodern culture. Postmodernism does not yield coherent representation or any system of concepts in the wake of its parody, instead dissolving into fragmentary formations and the transgression of aesthetic genres.

Through the postmodern condition, the search for cultural cohesion and unitary signification is discredited. Postmodernism has instead cultivated parody, dislocation, decentering, multiplicity, indeterminacy, and fragmentation. Postmodernism is therefore conceived of as an aesthetic of the fragments. Culture increasingly appears as a social construct which suppresses cultural fragmentation and heteroglossia. The deluge of cultural images and aesthetic styles precludes the possibility of cultural cohesion. "Culture is no longer a unitary, fixed category," Collins has written, "but a decentered, fragmentary assemblage of conflicting voices and institutions" (Collins 1989, 2). Postmodernism has thus signaled the demise of a cultural center; instead, fragmentation and cultural disintegration has been the prevailing ethos and cultural dominant.

Postmodern culture provides political spaces and possibilities for the appropriation of communication and representational technologies, as seen in both cyberpunk science fiction and industrial music. "From the technofunk street rhythms generated by the master D. J.s of scratching, mixing, and matching to the neurochemical sublime of body / machine interfaces," writes Andrew Ross, "the new appropriation culture everywhere feeds off the 'leaky' hegemony of information technology" (Ross 1989, 212). Cyberpunk is the fiction of a subculture where the oppressively rationalizing regime of computer, information and neurotechnologies are constantly being outsmarted and contested by marginalized groups. Social and cultural theorists must acknowledge the subversion of dominant cultural representations by marginalized and subcultural groups to construct their own aesthetic representations and withstand the assimilative constraints of late capitalist hegemony. As anticipated in the aesthetic of bricolage and detournement, postmodernism celebrates the axiom that any cultural fragment can be juxtaposed to anything else. The fragmentation of a unitary cultural and aesthetic monologic identities into diverse, dialogic forms of narrative has clearly signaled the emergence of new forms of critical aesthetic representation.

Aesthetics and art often prefigure politics and everyday life. The cyberpunk fiction of Gibson offers unique insights concerning the detournement and bricolage in postmodern life. Cyberpunk, according to Csicsery-Ronay, is "the increasingly pervasive influence of a particular moment of science fiction on postmodern culture" (Csicsery-Ronay 270). The discussion here has argued that the themes of cyberpunk science fiction and industrial music are an energetic and dynamic reflection of larger developments in the postmodern social and cultural milieu. The so-called "speed tribes" and youth cultures that have flourished in contemporary Japan, for instance, might have stepped directly from the pipes of Gibson or other cyberpunk writers (Greenfeld 1994). The industrial and techno music that is part of the cyberpunk aesthetic has its lineage in the acid house scene in Chicago and later in Manchester and Liverpool, England. The drugs, music and fashion of the acid house scene had even longer connections with the youth culture of the 1960s (Smith 1991). Cyberpunk and industrial music exemplify postmodern cultural indeterminacy, decenteredness and heterogeneity. The vitality of the hacker underground, "zine" subcultures, acid and industrial music scenes, and other contemporary areas of cultural contention have been crucial for the cyberpunk aesthetic.

Cyberpunk is both a reflection of and a precursor to the aesthetic and cultural transformations in advanced capitalist societies. A close reading of the cyberpunk aesthetic is a useful way of anticipating the direction of social, cultural and technological developments in the coming decades. The importance of cyberpunk, according to Rosenthal, is its "ability to talk, sometimes painfully, about a world we are only beginning to know how to describe" (Rosenthal 100). Cyberpunk's contestation of the technological utopianism in much earlier science fiction is exemplary of the complexities and contours of the postmodernist crisis of representation and aesthetics of disintegration. Cyberpunk upholds many of the experiences and aesthetics of the postmodern condition and explores its themes of disintegration, fragmentation, heteroglossia, implosion and dissolution. Cyberpunk is the collapse of a genre of science fiction and in its place the forging of a new aesthetic of discordance and virtual reality whose themes have resonated widely throughout music, culture and society.

Works Cited

Bakhtin, Mikhail. 1989. "Laughter and Freedom." In *Contemporary Critical Theory*, edited by Dan Latimer. San Diego: Harcourt Brace Jovanovich.

Berman, Russell A. 1989. *Modern Culture and Critical Theory: Art, Politics, and the Legacy of the Frankfurt School*. Madison: University of Wisconsin Press.

Best, Steven. 1991. "Chaos and Entropy: Metaphors in Postmodern Sciences and Social Theory." *Science as Culture* 2, no. 2 (Summer): 188–226.

Chambers, Iain. 1985. *Urban Rhythms: Pop Music and Popular Culture*. New York: St. Martin's Press.

Clifford, James. 1988. *The Predicament of Culture: Twentieth-Century Ethnography, Literature and Art.* Cambridge: Harvard University Press.

Collins, Jim. 1989. *Uncommon Cultures: Popular Culture and Postmodernism.* New York: Routledge.

Csicsery-Ronay, Istvan. 1988. "Cyberpunk and Neuromanticism." *Mississippi Review* 47/48 (Summer): 266–278.

Devy, Mark. 1989. "Cyberpunk: Riding the Shockwaves with the Toxic Underground." *Keyboard* 15, no. 3 (May): 74–89.

Doerschuk, Robert L. 1989. "Front 242: The Aggressive Edge of Rhythm and the Power of Recycled Culture." *Keyboard* 15, no. 9 (September): 50–57.

Dorsey, Candas Jane. 1988. "Beyond Cyberspace." *Books in Canada* 17, no. 5 (June/July): 11–13.

Eagleton, Terry. 1981. "Carnival and Comedy: Bakhtin and Brecht." In *Walter Benjamin, or Towards a Revolutionary Criticism.* London: Verso.

Fekete, John, ed. 1987. *Life After Postmodernism: Essays on Value and Culture.* New York: St. Martin's Press.

Gibson, William. 1984. *Neuromancer.* New York: Ace Books.

———. 1986. "The Gernsback Continuum." In *Burning Chrome.* New York: Ace Books.

———. 1989. "Cyberpunk Era." *Whole Earth Review* 61 (Summer): 79–83.

Grant, Glenn. 1990. "Transcendence Through Detournement in William Gibson's *Neuromancer.*" *Science Fiction Studies* 17, no. 1 (March): 41–49.

Greenfeld, Karl Taro. 1994. *Speed Tribes: Days and Nights with Japan's Next Generation.* New York: Harper Collins.

Harvey, David. 1989. *The Condition of Postmodernity: An Enquiry Into the Origins of Cultural Change.* Oxford: Basil Blackwell.

Hassler, Donald, M. 1982. *Comic Tones in Science Fiction.* Westport, Conn.: Greenwood.

Hutcheon, Linda. 1985. *A Theory of Parody: The Teachings of Twentieth-Century Art Forms.* New York: Methuen.

Jameson, Fredric. 1984. "Postmodernism, or the Cultural Logic of Late Capitalism." *New Left Review* 146 (July/August): 53–92.

———. 1991. *Postmodernism, or the Cultural Logic of Late Capitalism.* Durham: Duke University Press.

Kearney, Richard. 1988. *The Wake of Imagination: Ideas of Creativity in Western Culture.* London: Hutchinson.

Kroker, Arthur and David Cook. 1986. *The Postmodern Scene: Excremental Culture and Hyper-Aesthetics.* Montreal: New World Perspectives.

LaCapra, Dominick. 1983. "Bakhtin, Marxism and the Carnivalelsque." In *Rethinking Intellectual History: Texts, Contexts, Language.* Ithaca, N.Y.: Cornell University Press.

Lash, Scott and John Urry. 1987. *The End of Organized Capitalism.* Madison: University of Wisconsin Press.

Lyotard, Jean-François. 1984. *The Postmodern Condition: A Report on Knowledge*, translated by Geoff Bennington and Brian Massumi. Manchester, U.K.: Manchester University Press.

Marcus, Greil. 1989. *Lipstick Traces: A Secret History of the Twentieth Century*. Cambridge: Harvard University Press.

McHale, Brian. 1987. *Postmodernist Fiction*. New York: Methuen.

Pechey, Graham. 1990. "Boundaries Versus Binaries: Bakhtin In/Against the History of Ideas." *Radical Philosophy* 54 (Spring).

Pfeil, Fred. 1988. *Another Tale to Tell: Politics and Narrative in Postmodern Culture*. London: Verso.

Pierce, John J. 1989. *When World Views Collide: A Study in Imagination and Evolution*. New York: Greenwood Press.

Poster, Mark. 1990. *The Mode of Information: Poststructuralism and Context*. Chicago: University of Chicago Press.

Rose, Mary and Daniel Warner. 1987. "Rough Music, Futurism, and Postpunk Industrial Noise Bands." *Discourse* 10, no. 1 (Fall/Winter): 55–76.

Rosenthal, Pam. 1991. "Jacked In: Fordism, Cyberpunk, Marxism." *Socialist Review* 21, 1 (January/March): 79–103.

Ross, Andrew. 1989. *No Respect: Intellectuals and Popular Culture*. New York: Routledge.

———. 1991. "Getting out of the Gernsback Continuum." *Critical Inquiry* 17, no. 2 (Winter): 411–433.

Rushkoff, Douglas. 1994. *Cyberia: Life in the Trenches of Hyperspace*. San Francisco: HarperSanFrancisco.

Silverstone, Roger. 1989. "Let Us Return to the Murmuring of Everyday Practices: A Note on Michel de Certeau, Television, and Everyday Life." *Theory, Culture, and Society* 6 (May): 77–94.

Sirius, R. U. 1992. *Mondo 2000: A User's Guide to the New Edge*. New York: HarperCollins.

Smith, Paul. 1991. "Playing for England." *South Atlantic Quarterly* 90, no. 4 (Fall): 736–752.

Spinrad, Norman. 1990. *Science Fiction in the Real World*. Carbondale: Southern Illinois University Press.

Stam, Robert. 1988. "Mikhail Bakhtin and Left Cultural Critique." In *Postmodernism and Its Discontents: Theories, Practices*, edited by E. Ann Kaplan. London: Verso.

Sterling, Bruce, ed. 1986. Preface to *Mirrorshades: The Cyberpunk Anthology*. New York: Arbor House.

Sterling, Bruce and William Gibson. 1986. "Red Star, Winter Orbit." In *Burning Chrome*. New York: Ace Books.

Sussman, Elizabeth, ed. 1989. *On the Passage of a Few People Through a Rather Brief Moment in Time: The Situationist International, 1957–1972*. Boston: Institute of Contemporary Art.

Suvin, Darko. 1989. "On Gibson and Cyberpunk SF." *Foundation* 46 (Autumn).

Tomas, David. 1989. "The Technophilic Body: On Technicity in William Gibson's Cybord Culture." *New Formations* 8 (Summer).

Tyler, Stephen A. 1987. *The Unspeakable: Discourse, Dialogue and Rhetoric in the Postmodern World.* Madison: University of Wisconsin Press.

Wollen, Peter. 1989. "The Situationist International." *New Left Review* 174 (March / April): 67–95.

Chapter 7

Prince versus Prophet
Machiavellianism in
Frank Herbert's *Dune* Epic
Peter Minowitz

*To attempt an understanding of Muad'Dib without understanding his mortal
enemies, the Harkonnens, is to attempt seeing Truth without knowing
Falsehood. It is the attempt to see the Light without knowing Darkness. It
cannot be.*   (Dune, 13)

*Didn't you learn the difference between Harkonnen and Atreides so that you
could smell a Harkonnen trick by the stink they left on it? Didn't you learn
that Atreides loyalty is bought with love while the Harkonnen coin is hate?*
                                                              (Dune, 433)

   Readers of Frank Herbert's *Dune* are invited to identify with the
main protagonist, Paul Atreides/Muad'Dib, and to favor his family in
its struggle against the wicked Harkonnens. We encounter numerous
examples of Atreides courage, nobility, loyalty, graciousness, and compassion, while there is seemingly no moral taboo that the Harkonnens
hesitate to violate in their all-consuming quest for wealth and power.
Given the eventual defeat of the Harkonnens by the Atreides, *Dune* is a
kind of morality play that might inspire citizens and prospective leaders to select lofty goals and to pursue such goals in an honorable manner.
   Careful inspection, however, reveals that the contrast between the

two families is not as extreme as it first appears: even the Atreides are touched by falsehood, darkness, and hate. For this and other reasons, Machiavelli might hesitate before placing Frank Herbert among the chorus of political writers who allow "imagination" to supplant the effectual truth (*verita effettuale*) [*The Prince*, ch. XV]. Whether or not Machiavelli would conclude that Herbert succumbs to utopianism, the *Dune* series provides a plethora of fictional detail to stimulate the reader's reflections about the virtues and vices of political leaders—and about the various challenges that political "necessities" pose to moral excellence.

By painting a vivid but plausible picture of the ruthlessness, cruelty, and manipulativeness of the Harkonnens, Herbert calls to mind the notorious usurpers, tyrants, and conquerors whom Machiavelli is infamous for praising, including Alexander the Great and Julius Caesar, both "excellent men" (*The Prince*, ch. XIV); Cesare Borgia, whose "great spirit and high intention" contribute to his status as a role-model for the "prudent and virtuous man" (ch. VII); Hannibal, whose "infinite virtues" include "inhuman cruelty" (ch. XVII); and Septimius Severus, the consummate "lion" and "fox" whose brutal and treacherous "*virtú*" is celebrated in chapter XIX as the paradigm for the most impressive type of prince (the "new prince" endeavoring to found a new state). I cannot here recount the scholarly polemics that have raged over Machiavelli's ultimate assessment of such individuals and over a larger puzzle: How can we harmonize the author of *The Prince* with the Machiavelli who loyally served the Florentine republic and who issued such glowing praise, chiefly in the *Discourses*, of the "liberty" that obtains not in monarchies but in thriving republics? There is no dispute, however, that responsibility for Machiavelli's fame—and for the entrance of the term "Machiavellian" into the political vocabulary of the modern world—lies overwhelmingly with *The Prince*. And there is little dispute that his more republican works incorporate pronounced strands of *realpolitik*. Although the *Discourses* clashes with *The Prince* by mentioning conscience and the common good—and by sometimes accommodating the traditional view that aggrandizing, oppressive, and treacherous princes are "tyrants" who must be condemned for the evils they inflict on their subjects and rivals—the book provides tantalizing glimpses into Machiavelli's dark side. To mention just one example: when Machiavelli defends Romulus's infamous fratricide by claiming that the end justifies the means (*accusandolo il fatto, lo effeto lo scusi*), he invites the reader to wonder whether there is any evil beyond the bad precedent (*cattivo esemplo*) that even calls for justification.[1]

The second chapter of *Dune* places us on Giedi Prime, the home world of House Harkonnen, before we have even met Duke Leto Atreides or his chief lieutenants; considering the novel as a whole, indeed, the Baron (Vladimir Harkonnen) is a more prominent character than the Duke. The first image of the Harkonnens intimates their immoderation and love of wealth, as the reader observes a globe "partly in shadows, spinning under the impetus of a fat hand that glittered with rings." A few paragraphs later, Herbert accentuates the costliness of the globe by describing the platinum wire and diamonds that adorn it. Shadows, motion, fat, rings—the attributes of the voracious and the treacherous. (From the vision of a hand spinning a planet, may we also infer the Baron's unmitigated ambition and arrogance?) Only the last words of the chapter, however, complete the sketch of the Baron: "As he emerged from the shadows, his figure took on dimension—grossly and immensely fat," sustained partly by portable "suspensors." He announces his hunger, and sends for food (21).

When the Baron first speaks, we find out that the modeled planet is Arrakis (Dune), which will serve as "the biggest mantrap in history" (13–14). The Harkonnens are plotting to annihilate House Atreides, but they make little attempt to hide the hostility that smolders among themselves. The Baron and his "Mentat," Piter de Vries, spar verbally, and adopt a condescending tone with the sullen-faced Feyd-Rautha, the Baron's nephew and heir-designate; the Baron thinks to himself that Piter has almost outlived his usefulness (15–17). The Baron displays a touch of reluctance about the need to kill Paul (along with Paul's adult relatives)—but only because the lad "has such a sweet young body" (19). Later, we witness the Baron summon a drugged slave boy (186) and hear about Feyd-Rautha's visits to the female slaves of "the pleasure wing" (372). Needless to say, the Harkonnens exhibit no compunction about supplementing their own troops with disguised legions of the Emperor's ferocious Sardaukar for the attack on the Atreides (20), or about torturing the wife of Wellington Yueh, physician to the Atreides, to overcome his "Imperial Conditioning" and suborn his treachery (19, 176).

In the next chapter set on Giedi Prime, the planet receives a more complete portrayal. The chapter begins with the following summary statement: "On his seventeenth birthday, Feyd-Rautha Harkonnen killed his one hundredth slave-gladiator in the family games" (321). The Atreides, of course, employ neither slaves nor gladiatorial contests. The reader has already had ample opportunity to contrast the Baron and the Duke, and now receives a fuller exposure to the Harkonnen counterpart to Paul.

Feyd-Rautha Harkonnen is a formidable fighter who is not devoid of integrity, but he is fundamentally a brute and a cheater. Although Feyd had never been defeated in his hundred contests, he had never prevailed in a fair fight. In every encounter, Feyd could call upon distractors, handlers to implant barbs, "prudence doors" for retreat, a full shield against his opponent's half shield, and a poisoned blade to supplement his regular blade—a poison that caused a slow death, leaving the victim to writhe in pain before a gloating Feyd (333). In every fight but the one we witness, Feyd's opponent was drugged and Feyd's barbs would convey additional drugs. In this fight, the gladiator's skin was altered to mimic the effects of an initial drugging, but he and the barbs were left undrugged as part of an elaborate scheme, partially engineered by Feyd, to reap added glory from victory and to secure the accession of a new slavemaster friendly to Feyd (the old one was framed to take the fall for the drugging improprieties). The gladiator, a courageous and powerful prisoner who was previously an Atreides trooper, almost prevailed, but was defeated by additional treacheries. (Contrary to tradition, Feyd carried the poisoned blade in his white-gloved hand; more importantly, the slave had secretly been conditioned to freeze when Feyd yelled "Scum.") Feyd-Rautha, however, is not totally ignoble. He "prided himself that he never used the pru-door and seldom needed distractors" (331); he admired the gladiator for falling on his own sword before the poison took full effect, and allowed him to be buried with his sword in hand (the crowd clamored for a beheading, to honor Feyd).

Herbert rivets this scene into the book with a variety of subtle devices that can deepen the reader's appreciation of the moral gulf that separates the Atreides from their perversely "Machiavellian" opponents. First, one should juxtapose the chapter with the two preceding chapters (Book II, chaps. 11–12), which describe Paul's initial duel to the death. Needless to say, Paul's conduct is anything but bloodthirsty, arrogant, and treacherous.[2] Second, as David Miller points out (17, 22–23), the setting includes a reference to some Atreides mementos that the Baron had brought back to Giedi Prime: a painting of the Old Duke, Paul's grandfather, and the head of the bull that had killed him. We are thus

invited to contrast the Harkonnen approach—the treacheries and unfair advantages that all but guarantee Feyd's victories in the arena—
with the bullfight "bravura" of Paul's grandfather (*Dune* 329): while the
bull was immobilized and confused, the Duke turned, his "cape thrown
flamboyantly over one arm," to greet the cheers that rained down from
the stands (157). Leto instructs Paul that nothing wins more loyalty for a
leader than an "air of bravura" (105), and practices what he preached by
using the Atreides dining room to display both the painting and the
head—its horns still caked with dried blood (50, 56). In the arena, Feyd
surpasses the Baron by revealing a dollop of courage and two dollops of
"style" or "bravura" (337), but he doesn't approach the Atreides. Turning your back on a bull may be a foolish risk, but Herbert clearly means
us to prefer the risk-taking of the Atreides to the obsession with control
characteristic of the Harkonnens.

It is no surprise that the environment of people who revel in gladiator atrocities is replete with fear, deprivation, and ugliness. A holiday
had been declared to honor Feyd's birthday, so "effort had been spent in
the family city of Harko to create the illusion of gaiety: banners flew
from buildings, new paint had been splashed on the walls along Court
Way." More characteristic, however, were "the rubbish heaps, the sca-
brous brown walls reflected in the dark puddles of the streets, and the
furtive scurrying of the people." There were also ubiquitous checkpoints
and armed guards (322).

The common people of Giedi Prime may have been oppressed, but
only the natives of Arrakis experienced the full nastiness of Harkonnen
leadership. In the words of Duke Leto: "The Harkonnens sneered at the
Fremen, hunted them for sport, never even bothered trying to count
them. We know the Harkonnen policy with planetary populations—
spend as little as possible to maintain them" (45). To recoup the enormous expenditures required by the campaign against the Atreides, the
Harkonnens had to exploit the people of Arrakis even more brutally.
Instructing his nephew Rabban, the new planetary governor, the Baron
exhorted: "You must show no mercy here. Think of these clods as what
they are—slaves envious of their masters and waiting only the opportunity to rebel. Not the slightest vestige of pity or mercy must you show
them. . . . A carnivore never stops. . . . Mercy is a chimera. It can be
defeated by the stomach rumbling its hunger, by the throat crying its
thirst. You must be always hungry and thirsty. . . . Like me" (239–40).

We must not, however, confuse the policy the Baron recommends with genocide, as Rabban does initially (assuming that "new stock" would be brought in to replace the exterminated natives). Such a policy would be wasteful, and the Baron is above all else efficient. The Baron likewise condemns waste when chiding his Guard Captain for suggesting that they torture Thufir Hawat (the Atreides Mentat who was now their captive) for "sport"—instead, the Baron cleverly manipulates Hawat into working for him (232). One may therefore suggest that the Baron is less evil than his sadistic Mentat, Piter, who, like the Sardaukar, seems to revel in "blood and pain."[3] For Machiavelli, of course, people who seek to acquire or even to maintain power must never flinch at the prospect of blood or pain. But nowhere does Machiavelli recommend that injury be inflicted gratuitously, as an end rather than a means. Indeed, the Machiavellian indifference to justice displayed by the Baron may, on rare occasions, remove the impetus for bloodshed: "Never obliterate a man unthinkingly, the way an entire fief might do it through some *due process of law*. Always do it for an overriding purpose—and *know your purpose!*" (*Dune* 236).

There is likewise no guarantee that a passion for justice and due process will never precipitate the kind of inefficient cruelty that Machiavelli critiques in Chapter VIII of *The Prince*: "badly used" cruelties that are "few in the beginning," but increase with the passage of time. As Leo Strauss has argued, moreover, the remark about "pious cruelty" in Chapter XXI points to Machiavelli's condemnation of evils inflicted in the pursuit of exalted but illusory goals (156–57, 167, 187–88).

The Baron sometimes displays a streak of compassion that might detract from his reputation as a Machiavellian (*Dune* 21). Indeed, the Baron is troubled that he has to expose the captive Duke Leto—drugged, dazed, bound, his uniform in tatters—to a group that includes Piter and various Harkonnen underlings. Or is it simply a "bad precedent" for royalty to be displayed before commoners in such straits (180)? (Recall Machiavelli's assessment of the fratricide committed by Romulus.) The Baron hesitates when he threatens to have Piter torture the Duke to extract information, but he overcomes this "reluctance to have a royal person subject to pain" by envisioning himself "as a surgeon exercising endless supple scissors dissections—cutting away the masks from fools, exposing the hell beneath. *Rabbits, all of them!*" (180–82). The Baron's thoughts progress similarly after he feels a spasm of pity for the fine Atreides soldiers being sealed into caves by Harkonnen artillery. He laughs at himself as he reflects upon the meaning of failure: "Failure was, by definition, expendable. The whole universe sat there, open to the man who could make the right decisions. The uncertain rabbits had to be exposed, made to run for their burrows. Else how could you control them and breed them?" (175).

The image of the surgeon suggests the "well-used" cruelties that Machiavelli contrasts with the "badly-used" version: well-used cruelties are "done at a stroke [a uno tratto], out of the necessity to secure oneself." Although Machiavelli adds that such cruelties are not "persisted in but are turned to as much utility for the subjects as one can" (*The Prince*, ch. VIII), one must not forget that his model of well-used cruelty is Agathocles, an inveterately immoral general who seized the throne by slaughtering "all the senators and the richest of the people."

We must conclude that any vestiges of tenderness and pity in the Baron are quickly squelched by the carnivorous ethos that animates him. He is the Machiavellian prince, consumed by ambition, who will perpetrate whatever evils are necessary to acquire and maintain a "state" and whose conscience yields immediately to expediency. The Baron, nevertheless, is aware that a leader may pay a price for treating subjects with unmitigated harshness. Adapting a stratagem immortalized in the seventh chapter of *The Prince*, he installs his brutal but dimwitted nephew Rabban to oppress the Fremen, with the hope of later bringing in Feyd-Rautha as a savior (Piter had been the Baron's first choice as scapegoat) (*Dune* 176, 186, 235, 240–41).

By conducting themselves so perfidiously with their subjects and rivals, the Harkonnens seem to weaken the bonds of loyalty, love, and gratitude that bind a normal family. As described above, Feyd once maneuvered to have his uncle's slavemaster executed. In the first chapter of *Dune*'s third book, set roughly two years after the Baron's recapture of Arrakis, Herbert provides a more detailed picture of the bloody and devious scheming within the Harkonnen camp. Feyd had arranged for a poisoned needle to be hidden in the thigh of a slave boy destined for erotic service with the Baron. Tipped by Hawat, the Baron foiled the plan. While being called to task by the Baron, Feyd unwittingly betrayed several of his agents within the Baron's entourage. These men were executed (and the guard captain chastised for not keeping careful enough tabs upon Feyd). Feyd feared briefly for his own life. Queried about why he hadn't taken advantage of his own opportunities to slay the Baron, Feyd recounted the Baron's lessons about keeping your hands clean. The Baron, mentioning that he doesn't "waste good material," inflicts no corporal punishment on Feyd. He instead reminds Feyd of the utility Feyd still can derive from the Baron, further arousing Feyd's interest by alluding to the possibility that Feyd will ultimately become Emperor. As his punishment, Feyd is forced to kill the female slaves of the pleasure wing, which awakens his festering resentments over previous punishments (365–72).

Although the victim of the henchman scheme described in *The Prince* was not a relative of the prince (Cesare Borgia), Machiavelli belittles familial piety on numerous occasions. Consider Liverotto, a fatherless child who became prince of Fermo by killing all of its "first men," including the uncle who had reared him (*The Prince*, ch. VIII); Romulus, who killed his brother to found the city of Rome (*Discourses* I:9); Giovampagolo Baglioni, who murdered his cousins and nephews to gain the throne of Perugia (I:27); Junius Brutus, who killed his sons to preserve the Roman republic (I:16, III:1, III:3); Tarquin the Proud, who followed his wife's advice by killing her father to become king (III:4); Manlius Torquatus, who killed his son to secure the obedience of his troops (II:16, III:22, III:34). One is reminded also of the vulgar and repulsive callousness displayed by a mother (Caterina Sforza) whose children were being held as hostages (*Discourses* III:6; *Florentine Histories* VIII:34), and of Machiavelli's general thesis that "men forget the death of a father more quickly than the loss of a patrimony" (*The Prince*, ch. XVII).

The Harkonnens, clearly, were second to none in ruthlessness. The reader is provided with comparably persuasive demonstrations of the Baron's keen intelligence. One is therefore entitled to wonder whether the ultimate defeat of the Harkonnens resulted simply from the extraordinary strength of their adversaries, the Fremen under the leadership of Paul Atreides (who for various reasons had developed unprecedented mental powers, including far-reaching prescience). To what degree did the Harkonnens perish because of their moral failings? To what degree is Herbert attempting to teach his readers, implicitly contradicting Machiavelli, that right makes might?[4]

Harkonnen oppression may have augmented the ingenuity and determination of the Fremen, but if the Harkonnens had a fatal flaw, it was their arrogance. First, the Baron had nothing but contempt for the Fremen—"those ragged scum of the desert"—who eventually constituted the army with which Paul Atreides subdued the galactic empire.[5] Second, the Baron underestimated Doctor Yueh. Yueh executed the trea-

131

sonous tasks he was assigned by the Baron, but also exercised a great deal of initiative to thwart him, by facilitating Paul and Jessica's escape, and by providing the Duke with an opportunity to kill the Baron. The Baron despised Yueh, but the importance of Yueh's secret maneuvers is intimated by his dying words ("You . . . think . . . you . . . de . . . feated . . . me") and by the description of his execution: "He toppled. No bending or softening. It was like a tree falling. . . . The Baron looked down at Yueh. From the way he had fallen, you could suspect oak in him instead of bones" (177). The poisoned tooth implanted in the Duke by Yueh in fact succeeded in felling Piter along with others in the Baron's entourage, and the Baron recognized his good fortune in escaping—"Chance and the warning in a dying man's gasp" (183).

When contrasted to the Harkonnens, the Atreides appear as paragons of morality. They utilize no slaves, prostitutes, or gladiators; it is the Baron, not the Duke, who is spurred by greed and ambition—and perhaps also by jealousy and vengeance (63–64, 512)—to unleash an orgy of killing and treachery. The noble orientation of the Atreides is displayed most dramatically in the way they treat their relatives, friends, underlings, and subjects. One presumes that Machiavelli would chastise the Atreides "princes" for their reliance on gratitude, generosity, and self-sacrifice (*The Prince*, chs. XV-XVIII). In *The Prince*, as Paul Rahe observes, when Machiavelli speaks of friends he "nearly always has clients, dependents, and partisans in mind" (Rahe 343, n. 70).

It is obvious that respect, love, loyalty, trust, and courage are integral to the relationships among Paul, Jessica, and Leto. The same qualities infuse the interactions between these three and the chief Atreides officers. Let us begin with their military and espionage lieutenants: Gurney Halleck, Thufir Hawat, and Duncan Idaho. Gurney, who was rescued by Leto from a Harkonnen slave pit, regarded Leto as "the man who gave me freedom, life, and honor . . . gave me friendship, a thing I prized above all else" (*Dune* 431–32); Paul regarded Gurney "more as a friend than as a hired sword" (33). With his quotations from Scripture and his gentle musicianship, Gurney would surely be out of place among the Harkonnens.[6] We witness Gurney providing a deathbed serenade for a wounded soldier, and also note an important Atreides principle: "each wounded man with an Atreides companion. . . . 'We care for our own'" (260–61). Needless to say, both Paul and Gurney are deeply moved when they are reunited years later (412). Shortly thereafter, however, a tragedy almost ensues. Convinced that Jessica was the traitor, Gurney is dissuaded from killing her only by some heartwrenching words from Paul about the love his parents shared (431–33). Gurney in turn begs to be executed: "I've besmirched my name. I've betrayed my own Duke." Jessica's response to Gurney exudes the warmth and graciousness characteristic of the Atreides: "You thought you were doing a thing for Leto . . . and for this I honor you." She requests that Gurney fetch his baliset and prepare to serenade them, a request seconded by Paul as "a thing that brings happiness between friends" (434–35).

Like Gurney, Thufir Hawat regarded the Duke as a "man of honor who deserves every bit of my loyalty" (99), and was persuaded that Jessica had been the traitor. When reunited with the surviving Atreides, however, he apologizes poignantly for his error: "Lady Jessica, I but learned this day how I've wronged you in my thoughts. You needn't forgive" (474). This attractive combination of nobility and humility is likewise displayed when Hawat attempts to resign upon discovering his failure to detect and remove all of the assassination devices concealed in Paul's room (83). Needless to say, things are very different with the Harkonnens and their minions: these men, if suspected of ineptitude or treachery, tremble with anticipation of punishment and do their best to weasel their way out. When finally called to task by the Emperor, the Baron responds in a similar fashion (456–463).

Hawat's subsequent service as the Baron's Mentat, however, raises doubts about the depth of the bonds that unite the Atreides. It is therefore important to understand his motivations. The crucial assumption, of course, was also made by Gurney: that Jessica was the traitor. This assumption had been planted, and subsequently reinforced (in very clever ways) by the Baron, building on widespread distrust of Bene Gesserit "witches." At various times, of course, Jessica had been torn between her family and the Bene Gesserit. By conceiving a boy (Paul) rather than a girl, Jessica defied the Bene Gesserit breeding plan out of her love for the Duke (6, 22–23, 190). In the opening chapter of *Dune*, by contrast, she allows the Bene Gesserit to subject Paul to a potentially lethal test.

Several additional considerations are necessary to explain Hawat's apparent defection: he believed that Paul had been killed along with Idaho and Leto; his work for the Baron was largely directed against the Emperor, whose help had been decisive in defeating the Atreides on Arrakis; he was planning ultimately to strike back at the Baron, and in the interim may have been plotting against Feyd (233, 331–32, 370–71, 379). He certainly remained free of illusions concerning the character of the Baron: "I've sat across from many rulers of Great Houses, but never seen a more gross and dangerous pig than this one" (373). At the end of the book, moreover, Hawat proves that he is Atreides to the core. In response to Paul's generous offer (Paul said he would grant anything Hawat asked, even his life), Hawat stated: "I but wanted to stand before you once more, my Duke." He subsequently displayed the poisoned needle that the Emperor had given him to use against Paul, and implored: "Did you think that I who've given my life to service of the Atreides would give them less now?" These were Hawat's last words (474–75). We may surmise that he perished from the "residual poison" implanted long before by the Baron (233), and that the Emperor had offered the antidote in exchange for Paul's life.

There are many other passages that demonstrate the Atreides ethos. Duncan Idaho offers to transfer his body shield—a force field that deflects all rapidly approaching objects—to Paul, whose shield was removed before he and Jessica engineered their escape from the Harkonnen executioners. Paul responds, "Your right arm is shield enough for me" (220). Shortly thereafter, Duncan is killed buying time for Paul and Jessica to complete their escape (225).

The assassination attempt that precipitated Hawat's offer to resign hinged on the use of a remote controlled needle called a "hunter-seeker." Late one night, as Paul was walking around in his bedroom, he spotted the device. He initially remained motionless, knowing that the operator couldn't see well because of the dim light and would therefore direct the device towards a moving object. Dr. Yueh's bedroom was next door, but Paul refused to call for him because anybody who walked through the door would be killed (67). While Paul was struggling to concoct a response, someone knocked and proceeded to open the door. Rather than save himself by letting the device attack the person who was entering (it turned out to be Mapes, the Fremen housekeeper), Paul put his own life at risk by proceeding to grab the device and smash its nose eye. The reader, impressed by Paul's display of courage, is then treated to a lesson in graciousness as Paul, despite prompting from Mapes, refuses to pat himself on the back for saving her life (67–68).

The irony of Paul saving Yueh's life compounds the irony of the encounter between Jessica and Yueh portrayed in the previous chapter. Possessing the acute observational abilities of a Bene Gesserit, Jessica sensed that Yueh was concealing something during their long conversation. She was momentarily tempted to force it out of him by using her powers of "Voice," but she decided not to because "that would only shame him, frighten him to learn he's so easily read. I should place more trust in my friends" (65).

The loyalty and love that thrive within House Atreides, it seems, spill over into the way they treat their subjects. In a later volume of the series, the "code of House Atreides" is elaborated as follows: "We always paid our way and let the enemy be the pillagers. . . . The Atreides might play a devious game against enemies, but never against friends and allies, and not at all against Family. It was ground into the Atreides manner: support your own populace to the best of your ability; show them how much better they lived" (*Children of Dune* 143–44).

Duke Leto, intending to make Arrakis "a solid and permanent planetary base," refused to adopt "Harkonnen methods" of economic exploitation (*Dune* 89). To save some spice miners threatened by one of the giant sandworms, Leto was even willing to endanger himself (not to mention Paul and Gurney); his concern for the workers' lives dwarfed his concern for their valuable equipment (121–26). Paul showed a still greater respect for his potential subjects during his initial negotiations with the Fremen leader Kynes (who was also the Planetary Ecologist under Imperial appointment). As the coin for Kynes's support, Paul first offers to make Arrakis a paradise. Paul apologizes after Kynes says he's not for sale, which prompts Kynes to observe that "no Harkonnen ever admitted error." Paul then offers his total loyalty—including his life—to Kynes, and states that "No Atreides has ever broken such a bond." Kynes is awed, and casts his lot by helping Paul and Jessica close a thick protective door as Sardaukar suddenly swarm to the attack (223–24). A victorious Paul keeps his promise to expedite the ecological transformation of Arrakis set in motion by Kynes's father, Dune's first Planetologist.

On the basis of the discussion and analysis hitherto provided, one must reject William Touponce's thesis that only people who read *Dune* "for its entertainment value alone" could thoroughly identify with Paul (Touponce 121). O'Reilly's judgment therefore stands: the reader is "caught up in the enthusiasm of the cause; he hates the Harkonnens, he cheers Paul and the Fremen" (189). Both scholars, however, deserve commendation for stressing what Touponce calls the "polyphonic" or "dialogical" character of the series—the tendency for each voice to be "qualified, questioned, even subverted" by other voices (Preface 32, 71, 112). When we read in a later volume of the series that "the best prophets lead you up to the curtain and let you peer through for yourself" (*God Emperor of Dune* 276), we might think of Machiavelli along with other authors of "great books." Herbert not only depicts clever princes and prophets who orchestrate "plans within plans within plans" and nested "feints" (*Dune* 18, 43–44, 332, 485); he also writes in a complex manner that makes it difficult to specify his intentions. But Herbert's illusiveness does not rival Machiavelli's. It suffices here to mention the clash between *The Prince* and the *Discourses,* each of which begins with the claim that Machiavelli is about to convey everything he knows. Indeed, Strauss suggests it would be an "infinite task" to achieve a complete understanding even of the *Discourses* (104; cf. 120–22, 141), where Machiavelli presents himself as a commentator addressing Livy's multivolume history of ancient Rome.

Given Herbert's complexities, we should not be surprised when we realize that the Atreides are far closer to devils than the Harkonnens are to saints—and that *Dune* can be invoked to illustrate Machiavelli's thesis that the acquisition and maintenance of political power are incompatible with devotion to moral virtues such as generosity, charity, justice, mercy, and honesty. First of all, the Atreides are clearly not indifferent to the lure of wealth (42, 311, 489) and luxury (71–72, 126, 130, 133–34). The reader should not be shocked that Leto decides to tolerate smugglers as long as they cough up a ducal tithe (85), but even Paul is troubled by his father's plan to forge certificates of allegiance addressed to the Atreides from the Harkonnen agents on Arrakis who had already been slain in the "war of assassins." (Under the rules of "kanly," the Atreides were allowed to assassinate such agents, but expropriation was permissible only if the agents had falsely pledged themselves to the Atreides.) Leto puts it bluntly: "Confiscate their property, take everything, turn out their families, strip them and make sure the Crown gets its ten percent. It must be entirely legal" (90).

The Atreides defy Machiavelli's nostrum that "a prince should have no other object, nor any other thought, nor take anything else as his art but the art of war" (*The Prince,* ch. XIV; cf. *Discourses* III:31). But the most obvious concession that Herbert makes to Machiavelli may be the emphasis put even by the Atreides on military strength. Without the fear and destruction that only the sword can bring, love, loyalty, and justice are easily defeated. As Leto says to an aide who voices frustration about the way the Spacing Guild had been conducting itself, "We make our own justice. . . . let us not rail about justice as long as we have arms and the freedom to use them" (*Dune* 87). Leto's face was "predatory: thin, full of sharp angles and planes" (49). The Atreides emblem, correspondingly, was not a dove but a bird of prey: "I must rule with eye and claw—as the hawk among lesser birds" (101). Jessica acknowledges that "Where Thufir Hawat goes, death and deceit follow" (63); by forthrightly referring to his position as "Master of Assassins" (4, 28), the Atreides avoid the need for euphemisms such as "secret police" and "intelligence agencies." Befitting his office, Hawat is less trusting— and less troubled by killing—than the other Atreides we have examined (98–100, 153–57, 376–378).

Between them, Gurney and Duncan possess a variety of virtues— courage, loyalty, wit, eloquence, charm, musicality, virility—but they wouldn't have been Atreides officers if they hadn't been superlative fighters and military strategists. A drunk Duncan claims to have killed over three hundred men for the Duke (147). As a ducal heir, Paul may have learned bows, salutes, and forms of address from his dancing master (4, 6, 36, 52–53, 58, 107), but he spent more time being trained in hand-to-hand combat by Gurney and Duncan. We might prefer that youth be spared such an initiation into bloodshed and deceit. During one training bout with Gurney, Paul excuses a potentially deadly mistake by saying, "I guess I'm not in the mood for it today." Gurney's outraged response illuminates the pressures of political responsibility in the universe of *Dune*: "What has *mood* to do with it? You fight when the necessity arises—no matter the mood. Mood's a thing for cattle or making love or playing the baliset" (35). Paul later repeats one of Gurney's observations regarding swordsmanship—that "there's no artistry in killing with the tip, that it should be done with edge"—and we can only sympathize with Leto's disturbance at hearing such brutal talk from his son (45).

Even the admirably intimate relationship between Leto and Jessica is tarnished by Machiavellian necessities. We must first note that the connection between them began with a purchase (from a Bene Gesserit school) rather than courtship (48); in a cynical mood, Jessica once even wonders whether the Duke selected her with a view to her training in business—because "a secretary bound to one by love is so much safer." A sublime love had developed between Leto and Jessica, but she remained a concubine so that other Great Houses could still hope to ally themselves with the Duke via their marriageable daughters (63–65, 104). For the same reason, Jessica herself initially disapproves of Paul's Fremen consort, Chani (310, 383, 396, 430), though she ultimately yields to the imperatives of the heart (396, 433): when Paul proposes to marry Princess Irulan to cement his accession to the throne, it is Jessica who objects ("Don't make the mistake your father made!" [471]). Despite his deep love for Chani, Paul feels he "must obey the forms"; he must marry Irulan as a "political thing," to enlist the cooperation of the Great Houses and to secure the peace (489). Readers of *Dune Messiah* are presumably pleased to find out that Paul makes good on his promise of fidelity (Irulan "shall have no more of me than my name"). The last words of *Dune* conclude a speech made by Jessica as she tries to reassure Chani: "we who carry the name of concubine— history will call us wives." So one might argue that this final thought in the grand epic vindicates the substance over particularized form, love over politics.

One could say that Leto—like most people burdened by responsi- bility—was forced to construct a tough outer shell around a soft human heart. As Jessica puts it, "the Duke is really two men. One of them, I love very much. He's charming, witty, considerate . . . tender—everything a woman could desire. But the other man is . . . cold, callous, demanding, selfish—as harsh and cruel as a winter wind" (65). Just as the move to Arrakis accentuated the harder side of the Duke (49), it accelerated Paul's passage to adulthood, and ultimately, to the almost superhuman capa- bilities—prescience coupled with ancestral memories—of the Kwisatz Haderach that sealed his status as the Fremen messiah (the Lisan-al Gaib).

It is fitting that Paul's transformation is preceded by a long conver- sation (*Dune* I:14) in which Leto reveals his more cynical side. Responding to the suggestion that his father has finally been afflicted by "the melan- choly degeneration of the Great Houses," Paul implores that "you govern well. Men follow you willingly and love you." Leto retorts by describing his propaganda apparatus, and sketching the circumstances on Arrakis that make it impossible to kill large numbers of people with poison (the Atreides are thus compelled to be "moral and ethical"). Leto concludes with a flourish, stating that holding Arrakis requires "decisions that may cost one his self-respect," and identifying power and fear as "the tools of statecraft" (104–5). We hear this specification of the tools of statecraft from Leto even before we hear it from the Baron (231). Indeed, the kinship be- tween Atreides and Harkonnen has a biological component—Jessica even- tually discovers that her father was the Baron, who had once been seduced (for breeding purposes) by a Bene Gesserit (197–98).

Leto Atreides was killed and his army decimated, but Paul Atreides assumed the Imperial throne after leading the Fremen to vanquish the Harkonnens and the Sardaukar. The Fremen were vastly more numerous than the old Atreides army, and probably fiercer. The Atreides home world, Caladan, was a paradise; as a result, "we went soft, we lost our edge" (255). Eons before, when the Fremen inhabited a lush world, they became easy prey for Imperial raiders (358). On the desert world of Arrakis, the extremely harsh environment put a premium on toughness, resourcefulness, and tribal loyalty; the Fremen polished their abilities under the Harkonnen boot, with the finishing touches supplied by Paul's military expertise and superhuman mental abilities. Paul may have persuaded the Fremen to eliminate dueling as the path to leadership (426–29), but the ultimate result of the fusion between Atreides and Fremen was a bloody jihad.

Leto's death constituted a natural threshold in Paul's path toward maturity, wisdom, and the hardening of the heart required by the assumption and discharge of vast responsibilities. During the first explosion of his prescience and heightened awareness, Paul found himself unable to mourn his father and irritated by the slowness of his mother's comprehension (188–92). Finally fathoming the larger forces that were impelling the human universe towards jihad—forces that previously had impinged upon him as a sense of "terrible purpose" (11, 27, 41, 47, 188)—Paul "found that he no longer could hate the Bene Gesserit or the Emperor or even the Harkonnens" (199). (Wisdom, he says later, tempers both love and hate [470].) Only after digesting his terrible purpose, and foreseeing himself finding a new home among the Fremen as Muad'Dib ("The One Who Points the Way"), can Paul finally release the pent-up tears for his father (199). But his heart would be pummeled again, when his infant son is killed during a Sardaukar raid. Upon receiving this news, of which he might have had foreknowledge, "He felt emptied, a shell without emotions. Everything he touched brought death and grief. . . . He could feel the old-man wisdom, the accumulation out of the experiences from countless possible lives. Something seemed to chuckle and rub its hands within him" (455–56).

Paul's initial reunion with Gurney deftly illustrates the change in him wrought by his assimilation to the Fremen. Paul was leading a Fremen ambush on a group of smugglers Gurney had joined after the Atreides defeat. Upon recognizing Gurney, Paul brings the fighting to an end. Gurney observed "a hardness in the expression that reminded

Gurney of the Old Duke," and a "sinewy harshness" that had "never before been seen in an Atreides" (412). When Paul expressed regret that a valuable piece of the smugglers' equipment had been destroyed in the battle, Gurney observed that Leto would have been "more concerned for the men he couldn't save" (414); Paul later comments that the damage caused by a battle (waged with the help of a huge sandstorm) was "nothing money won't repair" (467). The stories Gurney had heard about Muad'Dib taking "the skin of a Harkonnen officer to make his drumheads" (417) seem to have been widely circulated (466).

All of Paul's various roles—Atreides Duke, Bene Gesserit prophet, Fremen leader and messiah; pupil, son, friend, husband, father—are juxtaposed in the final chapter of *Dune*, following the decisive battlefield defeat of the Sardaukar. As we have seen, the old Atreides ethos shines through in Paul's exchanges with Thufir Hawat. The climax of the chapter, however, is the formalized knife fight between Paul and Feyd-Rautha, which invites comparison with several preceding chapters: the encounter between the Leto and the Baron (I:21), the duel between Paul and Jamis (II:11), the duel between Feyd and the Atreides gladiator (II:13). Paul's ultimate triumph incorporates a providential dimension that begins to wash away the Machiavellian aftertastes of *Dune*.

As Duke and Imperial Kinsman, Paul had promised safety to the Emperor's entourage by "word of bond under the Convention" (469). But will Muad'Dib accept the inclusion of Feyd-Rautha Harkonnen in that entourage (480)? Gurney Halleck, who had suffered hideously at the hands of the Harkonnens (36–37, 431–32), pleads for the chance to slay this "Harkonnen animal." Paul responds that "this being has human shape, Gurney, and deserves human doubt"; as an Atreides, furthermore, Paul feels obliged to follow "kanly" by dueling Feyd (480–81).

Paul would appear to be the underdog—a "stringy whipcord of a youth . . . with ribs there to count" opposing Feyd's "heavy shoulders" and "thick muscles" (481). But both young men are superlative fighters, and the real contest is between the Atreides soul and the Harkonnen soul. With Feyd, we encounter first the tincture of nobility: "Excitement kindled in him. This was a fight he had dreamed about—man against man, skill against skill with no shields intervening." We are quickly led, however, to Harkonnen arrogance, treachery, and injustice. In Feyd's eyes, "this yokel duke, this back-world adventurer could not possibly be a match for a Harkonnen trained in every device and every treachery by a thousand arena combats. And the yokel had no way of knowing he faced more weapons than a knife here" (483). Feyd's numerous taunts suggest to Paul that Feyd is overconfident, but Feyd prosecutes the fight with impressive skill and cleverness—"tricks within tricks within tricks," as Paul comes to realize, correcting his own smidgen of overconfidence. On his first pass, Feyd feigns a "shield-conditioned hesitation" that prepares a second pass in which he succeeds in drawing blood from Paul's arm. This blow could have proved decisive, because the blade (provided by the Emperor) conveyed a soporific—something that Paul's poison detectors had missed (the soporific would likewise be undetectable after the fight). With his extraordinary powers of bodily awareness and control, Paul was able to discern and neutralize the threat to his metabolism (484–85). Feyd's second treachery turned out to be more potent. Concealed within a garment was a tiny dart with an immobilizing poison. Paul had observed Feyd "presenting the right hip as though the mailed fighting girdle could protect his entire side," and only at the last minute noticed that a dart had flipped up on Feyd's *left* hip. Squirming to avoid the dart, Paul slipped and was pinned by Feyd.

Before the fight, Jessica had informed Paul that the Bene Gesserit often implant, in dangerous persons, a special word whose utterance would cause the recipient's muscles to go flaccid (481). Would he now use this information to turn the tables on Feyd? Up to this point, Paul's advantages in the contest had been his patience, his acute powers of observation, and a clever counterfeint (Feyd made a rash attack, enabling Paul to draw blood, on the assumption that Paul had been slowed by the soporific). The denouement is one of Herbert's crowning achievements. As Feyd twisted the dart ever closer, Paul heard "the silent screams in his mind, his cell-stamped ancestors demanding that he use the secret word to slow Feyd-Rautha, to save himself." Paul inadvertently blurts out his refusal—"I will not say it!" (486)—which surprises Feyd and causes him to hesitate slightly. This hesitation enables Paul to maneuver a flip that proves decisive when Feyd's dart gets stuck in the floor and traps him as Paul delivers the fatal thrust.[7] When the Emperor capitulates, Paul provides us with a final glimpse of Atreides loyalty and gratitude, insisting upon "titles and attendant power for every surviving Atreides man, not excepting the lowliest trooper" (489).

Machiavelli, in defending evil actions, typically claims that they are necessary: that "human conditions" do not permit a prince to respect the normal precepts of morality. Machiavelli gives conflicting messages, however, about whether the end that justifies the means is the common good—more vividly expressed, the "ennobling of the fatherland"—or merely the prince's good. *Dune* turns crucially on this distinction. The Harkonnens think only of their own wealth, power, and pleasure, while the Atreides labor—and suffer—in the pursuit of nobler goals. Only the Atreides, consequently, attain glory by introducing what Machiavelli calls "new modes and orders." If even the Atreides must sometimes stray from the path that is "wholly good" (*Discourses* I:26), they too can claim that the bad means are necessary to produce a good end.

For Herbert, the ultimate cause of evil lies in biological imperatives. The political and ecological strands of *Dune* are organically linked. The horrifying churning of the jihad is ultimately a manifestation of sexual reproduction, natural selection, scarcity, and the competition between organisms: "The race knows its own mortality and fears stagnation of its heredity. It's in the bloodstream—the urge to mingle genetic strains without plan. The Imperium, the CHOAM Company, all the Great Houses, they are but bits of flotsam in the path of the flood" (*Dune* 23). "The worst potential competition for any young organism can come from its own kind. . . . They are eating from the same bowl. They have the same basic requirements. . . . The struggle between life elements is the struggle for the free energy of a system" (*Dune* 137). "It is possible to see peril in the finding of ultimate perfection. It is clear that the ultimate pattern contains its own fixity. In such perfection, all things move toward death" (*Dune* 380). "The race of humans had felt its own dormancy, sensed itself grown stale and knew now only the need to experience turmoil in which the genes would mingle and the strong new mixtures survive. . . . a kind of sexual heat that could override any barrier" (*Dune* 482; cf. 199). "Beyond a critical point within a finite space, freedom diminishes as numbers increase" (*Dune* 493). "The predator improves the stock" (*God Emperor of Dune* 66). "It has not occurred to you that your ancestor were survivors and that the survival itself sometimes involved savage decisions, a kind of wanton brutality which civilized humankind works very hard to suppress" (*God Emperor* 96). "The urge to conflict went far deeper than consciousness. . . . Mix the genes. Expand Lebensraum for your own breeders. Gather the energies of others: collect slaves, peons, servants, serfs, markets, workers. . . . War is behavior with roots in the single cell of the primeval seas. Eat whatever you touch or it will eat you" (*Chapterhouse: Dune* 306).

The "flotsam in the path of the flood" includes the heroic efforts Paul undertook to prevent a jihad that ultimately claimed sixty-one billion lives (*Dune Messiah* 113)—and the tender human hearts afflicted by the deaths of parents, children, spouses, and friends. Full understanding of the flood is the "old-man wisdom" that tempers love, puts "a new shape on hate" (*Dune* 456, 470), and infuses the detached perspective of the Machiavellian prince from which the good end justifies frightful means.

O'Reilly provides an overview of the biological issues that is particularly suggestive of Machiavelli. An ecosystem derives stability not from security but from the diversity that ensures that some organisms will survive adversities. Those of Paul's enemies who emphasize control at the expense of adaptability can prevail only in "the limited enclaves of civilization, not in the wide open spaces of the desert, or in the terrifying futures Paul opens himself to in his visions." People often deny the power of fate by "creating small islands of light and order" that conceal "the great dark outside" (O'Reilly 4, 51).

For Machiavelli, human beings are adrift in an indifferent if not hostile universe. A people liberated from its prince resembles a captive beast "loosed to rove the countryside at will" in a desperate quest to find food and refuge (*Discourses* I:16). Class conflict is inescapable (I:4–6; *The Prince*, ch. IX; *Florentine Histories* II:12, III:1). So are discontent and ambition, for "nature has so constituted men that, though all things are objects of desire, not all things are attainable; thus desire always exceeds the power of attainment, with the result that men are ill content with what they possess" (*Discourses* I:37). Given the turbulence inherent in human affairs, it behooves a prince to "change his nature with the times"; if you can't achieve such flexibility, you should be "impetuous" and "ferocious" rather than cautious (because "*Fortuna*" is a "woman" who needs to be beaten down) (*The Prince*, ch. XXV). Indeed, periodic executions ("*esecuzioni*") are needed to remind people of the primal terror from which civilization protects them (*Discourses* III:1).

In none of the five sequels to *Dune* does Herbert provide such a detailed and thorough exploration of Machiavellianism, but he continues to wrestle with the themes we have examined: the traits that distinguish good rulers from bad ones, the necessity for fraud and force, the personal sacrifices imposed on people who assume large responsibilities. In *Dune Messiah* and *Children of Dune*, Emperor Paul Atreides defeats some ignoble challengers, Alia marries Duncan Idaho (resuscitated by the miraculous genetic techniques of the Bene Tleilax), and Paul's son Leto II ultimately inherits the throne. But we also witness uglier phenomena: the Fremen pillaging through the Imperium under the green and black banner of the Atreides; the emergence of a stultifying religious bureaucracy; Paul's fall from power, punctuated by bouts of intense frustration and wrenching personal losses; the brutal Regency of Alia, who became possessed by one of the ancestors who lived within her memories (Baron Harkonnen, naturally). *God Emperor of Dune* tells the story of the 3,500-year reign of Leto II, whose physical and mental powers (not to mention his lifespan) were multiplied by his fusion with the "sandtrout vectors" that are gradually transforming him into a giant sandworm with superhuman intelligence. Though Leto II lacks opponents as menacing (or as colorful) as the Baron, he embodies a combination of personae—man and beast, sage and predator, saint and tyrant, God and servant—that forces the reader to reflect about the limits of loyalty and love, the interplay of peace and stagnation, the tension between authority and freedom, and the challenges that wisdom poses to both brutality and gentleness.

The final two novels, set long after the death of Leto II, introduce a new set of characters, although several are Atreides descendants now associated with the Bene Gesserit. These two novels resemble the first insofar as the central characters are struggling courageously on behalf of a "noble purpose." The Bene Gesserits find themselves grappling with a variety of potential enemies (listed in ascending order of potency): the Church of the Divided God, dominated by superstitions and bureaucratic rigidity; the Bene Tleilax, pursuing political and religious hegemony through their mastery of the biological sciences (cloning, "Face Dancer" mimics, etc.); and the Honored Matres, an immense horde of conspicuously brutal and immoderate women, whose special assets are lightning-fast reflexes and finely honed techniques of sexual enslavement. In confronting these adversaries—who are not bereft of admirable qualities—the Bene Gesserits are forced to wrestle with their own demons (e.g., a cynical and manipulative posture towards sex, love, religion, friendship, and family) as they confront painful challenges of the sort faced by the Atreides of old. Throughout the last five books, the biological dimension remains: evolution, desert ecology, and the survival of the fittest.

In a characteristically poignant exchange between Paul and Chani, Chani describes them "giving love to each other in a time of quiet between storms" (*Dune* 362). This is the only time that love can blossom in a Machiavellian world. There is likewise a time for morality, but only between the storms of conquest and usurpation during which force and fraud are the primary tools. People who unequivocally oppose Machiavelli may concede that there are storms, but must allege, contra Frank Herbert, that the turbulence merely interrupts the peace that otherwise prevails within a universe ruled by divine justice and divine love.

Notes

1. Machiavelli, *Discourses*, Book I, ch. 9, hereafter designated as I:9. Although students of *The Prince* are typically surprised by the admiration Machiavelli expresses in the *Discourses* for the ancient Roman republic, they should not be surprised by his endorsements of that republic's conquests abroad and "tumults" at home (*Discourses* I:4–6), or by his claim that, even in republics, "the real rulers do not amount to more than forty or fifty citizens" (I:16). On the ambiguities suggested by Machiavelli's evaluations of Alexander, Caesar, Hannibal, and Severus in the *Discourses*, consult the following passages: on Alexander, I:1, I:20, I:58 (253–54, 329), II:27; on Caesar, I:10, I:17 (157–58), I:29 (183), I:52 (238), III:6 (419), and III:24; on Hannibal, II:18 (329), II:27 (366) and III:20–21; on Severus, I:10 (136–37). One should likewise compare *The Prince* and the *Discourses* concerning princes such as Agathocles, Cyrus, Hiero, and Nabis. I have elsewhere made a brief foray into the scholarly debate over Machiavelli, but the reader should consult Dietz, Hulliung, Rahe (30–36, 323–24, 340–44), and Bock et al., to obtain a more complete sketch of the competing interpretations. For a dated but otherwise thorough overview, see Berlin.
2. The duel occurred when a man (Jamis) invoked a ritual associated with the Fremen messiah myth to challenge the admission of Jessica (Paul's mother) into the tribe (Dune 297–98). Paul and Jamis were shieldless and equally equipped, so Paul enjoyed no perfidious advantages. Paul prolonged the fight, but eventually had to overcome his reluctance to kill. Afterwards, Jessica chided him to make sure he derived no pleasure from his victory (301–306). During the funeral ceremony, Paul sheds tears and credits Jamis with teaching him that "you pay for it" when you kill (314); Paul later promises lifelong care of Jamis's widow, Harah (342–44).
3. *Dune* 16, 164, 177, 181, 451. Even in the aftermath of the Harkonnen triumph on Arrakis, a loyal Atreides lieutenant (Gurney Halleck) correctly deduces that the pogrom against the Fremen was being waged by the Sardaukar rather than the Harkonnens: "a pogrom is wasteful" (259; cf. 238, 326). Although Tim O'Reilly is right to condemn the Baron's acquisitiveness as "pathological," he errs by alleging sadism (75). In the fifth novel of the series, Herbert alludes to sadistic Harkonnen practices and artifacts, but he does not mention the Baron (*Heretics of Dune* 222–25, 285, 305; cf. 24, 111, 235–37, 302, 347, 387, 422–23).

4. Lest I be accused of oversimplifying Machiavelli's posture concerning might and right, I offer the following elaboration. By stressing the advantages that accrue to a prince from *appearing* to possess the moral virtues, Machiavelli implies that traditional morality will remain a force among the people (*The Prince,* ch XVIII). Machiavelli adds that the most important virtue to feign is religiosity (cf. *Discourses* I:11), and some contemporary scholars argue that reflections on the use and abuse of religion pervade his corpus (Lukes, Mansfield, Scott and Sullivan). These issues also reverberate in the universe of *Dune:* although the Baron is capable of exploiting the moral sensibilities of subjects and allies (326, 328, 337–38), no Harkonnen can rival Paul Atreides when it comes to using religion as a political tool (105, 382–83, 426).

5. *Dune* 21, 45, 180, 238–40, 325, 374–76, 457–61; on Harkonnen arrogance, also consider 127, 161, 178, 181–82, 185, 224, 234, 236, 482–84.

6. The Harkonnen equivalent to Gurney would be Iakin Nefud, the Guard Captain whose *addiction* to semuta—"the drug-music combination that played itself in the deepest consciousness"— sealed his allegiance to the Baron (*Dune* 184). Cf. 17–18, 164–65, and 176 on the vices and lusts of other Harkonnen officers.

7. We may assume that Feyd, given his vast experience with treacheries in the arena, would *not* have been surprised and distracted if Paul's exclamation had been the fruit of a deliberate ploy. One is reminded of the ironic words spoken by Count Fenring before Feyd's rigged contest with the Atreides gladiator: "There's nothing like the arena to expose the true person from beneath the mask" (*Dune* 330). In any event, it is fitting that the Baron's death was more ignominious than Feyd's. As the Baron prepared to execute Alia (Paul's two-year-old sister, captured during the Sardaukar raid), she pricked him with a poisoned needle; he then "rolled sideways in his suspensors, a sagging mass of flesh supported inches off the floor with head lolling and mouth hanging open" (463).

Works Cited

Berlin, Isaiah. 1980. "The Originality of Machiavelli." In *Against the Current: Essays in the History of Ideas,* edited by Henry Hardy. New York: Viking.

Bock, Gisela, Quentin Skinner, and Maurizio Viroli, eds. 1990. *Machiavelli and Republicanism.* Cambridge: Cambridge University Press.

Dietz, Mary G. 1986. "Trapping the Prince: Machiavelli and the Politics of Deception." *American Political Science Review* 80: 777–99.

Herbert, Frank. 1976. *Children of Dune.* New York: Berkley Books.

———. 1977 (first pub. 1965). *Dune.* New York: Berkley Books.

———. 1983 (first pub. 1981). *God Emperor of Dune*. New York: Berkley Books.

———. 1987 (first pub. 1985). *Chapterhouse: Dune*. New York: Ace Books.

———. 1987 (first pub. 1969). *Dune Messiah*. New York: Ace Books.

———. 1987 (first pub. 1984). *Heretics of Dune*. New York: Ace Books.

Hulliung, Mark. 1983. *Citizen Machiavellie*. Princeton: Princeton University Press.

Lukes, Timothy J. 1984. "To Bamboozle With Goodness: The Political Advantages of Christianity in the Thought of Machiavelli." *Renaissance and Reformation* (new series) 8: 266–277.

Machiavelli, Niccolo. 1960. *Il Principe E Discorsi*. Ed. S. Bertelli. Milan: Giangiacomo Feltrinelli.

———. 1976. *Discourses on the First Ten Books of Titus Livius*, edited by Bernard Crick; translated by L. J. Walker, S. J. Harmondsworth, U.K.: Penguin Books.

———. 1985. *The Prince*. Trans. Harvey C. Mansfield, Jr. Chicago: University of Chicago Press.

———. 1988. *Florentine Histories*. Trans. Laura F. Banfield and Harvey C. Mansfield, Jr. Princeton: Princeton University Press.

Mansfield, Harvey C., Jr. 1979. *Machiavelli's New Modes and Orders*. Ithaca, N.Y.: Cornell University Press.

Miller, David. 1980. *Frank Herbert*. Mercer Island, Wash.: Starmont House.

Minowitz, Peter. 1993. "Machiavellianism Come of Age?" *The Political Science Reviewer* 22: 157–78.

O'Reilly, Tim. 1981. *Frank Herbert*. New York: Frederick Ungar.

Rahe, Paul A. 1994. *Republics Ancient and Modern: New Modes and Orders in Modern Political Thought*. Chapel Hill: University of North Carolina Press.

Scott, John T., and Vickie B. Sullivan. 1994. "Patricide and the Plot of *The Prince*: Cesare Borgia and Machiavelli's Italy." *American Political Science Review* 88: 887–900.

Strauss, Leo. 1958. *Thoughts on Machiavelli*. New York: The Free Press.

Touponce, William F. 1988. *Frank Herbert*. Boston: Twayne.

Chapter 8

Feminist Utopian Fiction and the Possibility of Social Critique

Josephine Carubia Glorie

If we look at the history of utopian and dystopian writing from Sir Thomas More in 1516 to the present day, we can notice a number of conceptual shifts related to political events within the authors' societies. One such shift occurred in the aftermath of the civil rights, antiwar, woman's movement turmoil of the 1960s and early 1970s in the United States, although it is not unrelated to the philosophical questioning of Enlightenment humanism following the mass destructions of Jews and others during the Third Reich.

Tom Moylan, in *Demand the Impossible: Science Fiction and the Utopian Imagination,* coins the term "critical utopia" to describe a generation of utopian fiction beginning in the mid 1970s that "breaks with the limits of the traditional genre and becomes a self-critical and disturbingly open form that articulates the deep tensions within the political unconscious at the present moment" (210). Moylan aptly engages the work of Frederic Jameson, Ernst Bloch, Michel Foucault, Herbert Marcuse, and others in conjunction with the fiction of Joanna Russ, Marge Piercy, Ursula Le Guin, and Samuel Delany to articulate the contributions of utopian fiction to the project of social critique, namely: "multiple strategies, scenarios, and images based on anti-hegemonic principles of the allocation of resources for basic human needs and the expansion of social structures for the nurturing of human emancipation" (204).

The contribution I propose to make in this paper is to use some of the central insights of two social theorists, Hannah Arendt and Seyla Benhabib, to illuminate Piercy's *Woman on the Edge of Time* as social critique. These theorists are especially helpful for shedding light on the way Piercy has contributed to a transformation of the genre, making it a more deeply "self-critical and disturbingly open form." In particular, I will explore how Arendt's and Benhabib's efforts to identify the necessary conditions for social critique help us to discern the significance of the struggles narrated in Piercy's novel. I will highlight what Benhabib takes to be the enabling conditions for social critique, paying especially close attention to technology as it affects these conditions.

One of the many serious issues raised by Arendt in her 1963 *On Revolution* is "the obvious question of how to preserve the revolutionary spirit once the revolution had come to an end" (239). For the purposes of this paper, perhaps we might replace "revolutionary spirit" with "utopian spirit." Arendt finds that those once filled with revolutionary or utopian spirit "had simply forgotten what actually they cherished above everything else, the potentialities of action and the proud privilege of being beginners of something altogether new" (232). Whether we consider actual revolutions in eighteenth-century America and France, as does Arendt, or fictional revolution, the concern with premature closure when a finite victory is celebrated at the cost of the utopian spirit, remains pressing. If all that results is the replacement of one rigid system inured to social critique by another such system, then a revolution has not truly taken place; it is merely a change in seating. If the utopian spirit does not become a dynamic force in the newly instituted order, then the spontaneity, initiative, and unpredictability of living beings will soon be deemed threats to social stability rather than resources for a continuing revolution. Arendt locates the loss of the "revolutionary spirit" in a fear of and an inability to conceive of conditions that are at one time, both stable and variable (223). Over the course of her life's work she discusses a number of conditions for such a dynamic society. I'd like to mention five conditions, according to Arendt, for a society in which ongoing change is possible and likely. First the inseparable thinking and judging, and then natality, action and plurality.

Thinking is the soundless, solitary dialogue of the self with itself in temporary withdrawal from direct engagement with the world, although, even in solitude, it always anticipates communication with others for an ultimate agreement (Arendt 1961, 220). For Arendt, thinking is not identical to knowing, which applies the intellect to a quest for truth. Thinking is rather an endeavor to discern in some finer or fuller way the significance of what we know or even merely suppose. It occurs only in solitude and leisure, it often disrupts systematized beliefs, and it liberates the faculty of judging to operate in the public sphere. Arendt explains the relationship of thinking and judging thus, "the manifestation of the wind of thought is not knowledge, it is the ability to tell right from wrong, beautiful from ugly" (in Bernstein 1986, 232).

Judging, the by-product of thinking, is the activity by which an individual, amidst a plurality of others, forms opinions especially about contested topics of practical importance. It requires a public space in which the full range of conflicting opinions, embodied in diverse individuals, can be heard, considered, weighed, revised, tested, and confirmed. For Arendt, only societies which allow individuals to create private space for thinking, that promote the existence of public fora for judging, and that also nurture the capacities for participation are viable human societies.

Natality is the quality of initiative, of beginning once again anew that characterizes the human condition due to the fact of individual, unique human birth. It is the certainty that "the unexpected can be expected. . .[that one] is able to perform what is infinitely improbable"(HC 178). Without this capacity for spontaneity, for generating new beginnings, political life would be impossible and humans would be vulnerable to totalitarian rule.

Action, according to Arendt, is like a deliberate second birth; it is the free insertion of oneself into the political world through word and deed. Action initiates change, discloses and shapes the character of the actor, reinforces plurality, and brings pleasure. The process of action can be broken down into an initial assertion, interactive debate, persuasion, negotiation, the possibility of concession, cooperation, and the joint carrying out of decisions (Betz 384). Action takes place in the public sphere constituted by "people living together for this purpose—acting and speaking together" (Arendt 1958, 198). Arendt believed that only where men [and women] live so closely together that the potentialities of action are always present can power remain with them, and the foundation of cities. . . .is therefore the most important material prerequisite for power (Arendt 1958, 201).

Proximity will enable action in the form of local councils which, in the past, "sprang up as the spontaneous organs of the people" who found they had "enormous appetite for debate, for instruction, for mutual enlightenment and exchange of opinion" (Arendt 1963, 246, 249).

Human plurality is that paradoxical spark that makes the whole thing run. Predicated on the simultaneous qualities of distinctiveness and equality, plurality is the human condition that expresses what we all have in common, that is being human, "but in such a way that nobody is ever the same as anyone else who ever lived, lives, or will live" (Arendt 1958, 176, 178). Each individual's sense of uniqueness is strengthened in the private sphere, and each is called upon in the public sphere to exercise equality with great courage and imagination among a variety of unique individuals.

These are the most basic conditions set forth by Arendt for establishing and maintaining a political system that is viable and that contains the living spirit of revolution (or utopia).

Contemporary theorist Seyla Benhabib discusses the possibilities of social justice and critique within the tradition of post–World War II critical theory and the work of Theodor Adorno, of Max Horkheimer, and most particularly of Jurgen Habermas. In her book *Critique, Norm, and Utopia* Benhabib defines two aspects of a critical social theory: (1) its "explanatory-diagnostic" aspect, which amounts to an analysis of "the contradictions and dysfunctionalities of the present" and (2) its "anticipatory-utopian" aspect, which "views the present from the perspective of the radical transformation of its basic structure" (Benhabib 1986, 226). Benhabib fundamentally agrees with Habermas that hope for a better society lies in the paradigm shift he initiated from the Marxian work or production model to a new model based on communicative interaction and communicative ethics where the concept of rational truth is replaced by "a discursive, communicative model of argumentation among a community of investigators" (345). In order to illuminate conditions for social critique pertinent to my study, I want to first glance at the conditions proposed by Habermas for an ideal speech situation and then turn to Benhabib's cautions, concerns, and refinements on Habermas's theory.

In "Discourse Ethics: Notes to a Program of Justification," Habermas finds that certain conditions will virtually guarantee the "satisfaction of the interests of every individual . . . [and] can be accepted by all without compulsion" (note, quoted in Ingram 148):

1. Each and every person capable of speech and action may participate in discourses.
2.(a) Each and every person may call into question any proposal.
2.(b) Each and every person may introduce any proposal into the discourse.
2.(c) Each and every person may express his attitudes and needs.
3. No one ought to be prevented from exercising the rights listed under 1 and 2 above by constraints internal or external to discourse.

In his first condition for the ideal speech situation described above, Habermas makes the assumption that all human beings possess the capacity for speech and action. Benhabib examines ability, willingness, and motivation in some detail and finds them "embedded in the contingency of individual life histories and in collective patterns of memory, learning, and experience . . . [which] can be enabled or frustrated in the life of the individual" (319). So, among the preconditions for communicative interaction we must include the nurturing of the very abilities for and interest in participation.

In general, Benhabib's reservations and refinements of the terms for an ideal speech situation revolve around three conditions: a commitment to human plurality, a sensitivity to what constitutes ability and motivation to participate, and "the vision of a community of justice that fosters a community of solidarity" (346). Benhabib objects to a tendency in Habermas to embrace a "politics of collective singularity . . . where one group or organization acts in the name of the whole" (347). In contrast to Habermas, she recognizes the importance of both human plurality and the *process* of coming to consensus, "A common shared perspective is one that we create insofar as in acting with others we discover our difference and identity . . . the emergence of unity-in-difference comes through a process of self-transformation and collective action" (348). In addition, Benhabib recognizes the indeterminacy of collective action due to "the different narrative histories in which selves are embedded" and the interpretive indeterminacy of the life history revealed in the process of action, that is "the past is always reformulated and renarrated in the light of the present and in anticipation of a future" (349). In place of the formal reciprocity stipulated by Habermas ("each is entitled to expect and to assume from us what we can expect and assume from him or her"), Benhabib insists on a complementary reciprocity informed by the work of Carol Gilligan ("each is entitled to expect and to assume from the other forms of behavior through which the other feels recognized and confirmed as a concrete, individual being with specific needs, talents, and capacities" [340–1]).

Benhabib recognizes the tensions between visions of community based on rights and entitlements and those based on needs and solidarity. She supports a participatory rather than a bureaucratic model of decision-making and offers a corrective conceptual frame:

> It is more correct to speak of a "polity" of rights and entitlements and an "association" of needs and solidarity. By a "polity" I understand a democratic, pluralistic unity, composed of many communities, but held together by a common legal, administrative and political organization. Polities may be nation-states, multi-national states, or a federation of distinct national and ethnic groups. An association of needs and solidarity, by contrast, is a community in action, formed by a set of shared values and ideals, which uphold the concreteness of the other on the basis of acknowledging his or her human dignity and equality.

Benhabib maintains that we can "combine the logic of justice with that of friendship. . . . Such utopia is no longer utopian, for it is not a mere beyond. It is the negation of the existent in the name of the future that bursts open the possibilities of the present" (353).

I will summarize by saying that Benhabib and Arendt share at least two concerns: the commitment to human plurality and its accompanying spontaneity and a concern for a variety of conditions that enable active political participation. Benhabib is additionally concerned with negotiations toward a concept of just community.

In *Woman on the Edge of Time*, Piercy clearly does offer readers a fictional view of revolution in progress, for here is reality burst open by the possibilities of present action and future improvement. But is it a revolution that retains as a goal the nurturing of the "revolutionary or utopian spirit" as Arendt calls it? And do we catch a glimpse of a world where a communicative ethics as defined by Benhabib operates?

Woman on the Edge of Time concretizes the utopian dreaming of Connie Ramos, a twentieth-century Hispanic welfare mother, incarcerated in a mental institution for attacking her niece's pimp. Connie's future possible self, Luciente, connects her to Mattapoisett in the year 2137, a genderless, classless community of diverse racial composition, slightly over half darker-skinned, and comfortably bisexual males and females. Connie intersects by accident with an alternate corporate, technological future where she meets the medically altered, "built up contracty," Gildina (299).

Piercy fuses the themes of revolution and technology (or science) throughout her novel, for example, by naming the project for contact between New York in the 1960s and Mattapoisett in 2137 "The Manhattan Project" because "that was a turning point when technology became itself a threat" (56). Later in the book, Luciente explains further "It's that race between technology, in the service of those who control, and insurgency—those who want to change the society in our direction" (223). "Our direction" can be defined as "technological agrarianism," a term used by Lyman Sargent to mean technology used for the benefit of humankind, "science and technology is supposed to save us from science and technology" (30). The revolutionary goals of the opposing parties can be stated as: (1) the transformation of humans into machines in the present reality with decisions and allocations of funds made by "huge corporations and the Pentagon" (278); and (2) the avoidance of intrusive technology in Mattapoisett with "general questions of direction of science" made in town council meetings (277).

I am going to discuss two broad areas of technological practices in the novel in relation to Arendt's and Benhabib's suggestions of conditions for social critique. The two areas are first communication including information, education, interpersonal skills, and political discourse and action, and second, genetics and reproductive technologies.

In order to understand the potential power of communication for the articulation of and movement toward social change, we have to at least acknowledge the deficits imposed by total isolation. Piercy reminds us of this by sealing Gildina within a technological cell in the dystopian chapter, while empowering Luciente and her contemporaries with creative privacy. In Mattapoisett, each individual past the age of puberty has a private living space for thinking, sleeping, study, meditation, and creative activity. Located "among family" (72) this accommodates Arendt's provision of withdrawal from the world in preparation for the public act of political judgment.

A major contribution of this novel to the discussion of technology and critique is, I believe, the "kenner," variously called a "high-tech encyclopedic wristwatch" (Bartwoski 66) and "part personal memory, part telephone, part analytical tool" (Moylan 132). In order to appreciate the value of this technological augmentation of human capacities, it is helpful to review the meanings related to the base word, "ken," through the Indo-European root, "gno," to this range of meanings: to know, to recognize, to make known or declare, to know how to or be able, to name, to narrate, to think and judge; and in noun form: perception, understanding, range of vision, insight, and cunning. As the utopian opposite to the control device implanted in Connie's brain, the "kenner" functions as an enabling device for individual action and for participation in the community. Each person's uniqueness for the full range of kenning activities is fortified and magnified through this device. In addition, it facilitates instantaneous contact with all members of a family and a community. It functions, therefore, to enhance plurality, to nurture capacity for participation, and as a stand-in for proximity.

Education is one of the institutions we maintain to prepare individuals for what we call citizenship, but what Arendt and Benhabib would prefer to call political action or participation. Piercy creates a fictional system of education against a backdrop of a hierarchical system that educates the intellect in isolation from practical application, pits success against failure, and rewards conformity and obedience to authority out of all proportion to creative individuality. No wonder Benhabib questions the capacity and motivation of all individuals to engage in ideal speech situations! In Mattapoisett on the other hand, "We educate the senses, the imagination, the social being, the muscles, the nervous system, the intuitions, the sense of beauty—as well as memory and intellect" (140). The guiding principles of education are to develop the talents of the individual and to "root that forebrain back into a net of connecting" (140). These principles extend into adulthood with all individuals engaged in useful work utilizing their particular talents and also with responsibilities to the community in "family duties, political duties, [and] social duties" (267). Political duties include serving on the councils which perform at various levels from local villages, to townships, to regions. On the councils, individuals "argue till we close to agree. We just continue. Oh, it's disgusting sometimes. . . . There's no final authority" (153). Piercy describes council meetings in more detail in *He, She and It* and concludes, "Here politics was still a participatory rather than a spectator sport. Every last voter expected to voice her or his opinion at some length and to be courted or denounced" (418). An education that decentralizes the authority of the intellect and includes goals of social responsibility and interpersonal connection seems to answer some of the concerns for a community of needs and solidarity raised by Benhabib in her critique of Habermas. The widening circles of councils in the fiction differs, however, from Benhabib's suggested framework of communities of needs and solidarity associated in a polity of rights and entitlements.

Piercy's fictional world would seems also to confirm Benhabib's concern for the need to allow for interpretive indeterminacy in constructing unified positions for action. First of all, Piercy boldly incorporates a predisposition for change into the future society. "We'd change it if we didn't like it, how not? We're always changing things around" (70), reinforced by the "First rule we learn when we study living beings in relation. . . . In biosystems, all factors are not knowable" (97). On a larger scale, Piercy has Luciente correct a misperception of the past concerning "myths that a revolution was inevitable. But nothing is! All things interlock. We are only one possible future" (177). At the level of the text, Moylan points out that Piercy "challenges realism. . . . Piercy can break the rules of the historical situation and posit a future society with the power to reach back in time and help one of our society's victims fight back and thereby ensure the survival of utopia" (150). This is analogous to a fluidity in interpreting our own past experiences to create new narratives of personal and collective history and upon which to predicate future action.

On all of the points I have grouped under the heading of communication: information, education, political discourse and action, I find that Piercy has fictionalized a society in which conditions enabling social critique emphatically do exist.

Connie's home world, similar to our own, is undeniably laced with technological land mines for women, particularly in the forms of psychiatry and medicalized reproduction. In her world, the female body has become a field for experimental science and abuse: forced abortion, hysterectomy, "those bastards . . . had spayed her for practice, for fun" (62), prostitution, and chemical control, "we are not three women . . . we are ups and downs and heavy tranks [tranquilizers] meeting in the all-electric kitchen . . . like shiny pills colliding" (359). In this world, the authority of science, personified in male physicians, is nearly absolute. Women themselves and alternate ways of knowing are denigrated, as when Connie asks a fifty-year-old female nurse for a change of medication and, of course, is referred to the ultimate authority, "I'll mention it to the doctor . . . He'll say in the end" (162). If this deference sounds reasonable, it is only because we, too, are accustomed to this authority.

Piercy transforms the technological prowess of this abusive society in several unexpected directions guided by humanistic principles and a postmodern release from the goal of closure. As Luciente explains to Connie, "Our technology did not develop in a straight line from yours . . . some problems you *solve* only if you stop being human, become metal, plastic, robot computer" (125). Two related areas of scientific transformation in the fictional community are genetics and reproduction, both of which Piercy removes away from the individual as controlled by the medical establishment and relegates to the community directed by local councils. The decision has been made to separate genetic inheritance from culture, so each distinctly "flavored" community, Ashkenazi, Wamponaug Indian, Harlem-Black, is composed of individuals of diverse genetic backgrounds including all races and shades of color. Thus, Piercy makes visible and concrete Arendt's conceptual model that "we are all the same, that is, human, in such a way that nobody is ever the same as anyone else who ever lived" (Arendt 1958, 8). The cultural unity of the community is an imaginative model for our human sameness, while the deliberate differences among the members emphasizes the value of unique individuality. Here the technologies of extrauterine conception and gestation have been employed to facilitate a dramatic plurality, which for Arendt is the sine qua non condition for political action.

Piercy reinforces a living utopian spirit by including an ongoing debate between the "Shapers" and the "Mixers" in the local council: "Shapers want to breed for selected traits" while "Mixers don't think that people can know objectively how people should become" (226). This seems an effort to reject the impulse toward absolute truth and possible totalitarianism on two levels: on the issue of genetic manipulation itself, and on the larger issue of the right of one group to impose its principles on another. The guiding motive on both levels seems to be to preserve "diversity, for strangeness breeds richness" (104), and to this end, the goal of science in this society is to treasure "every patch of woods as a bank of wild genes" (274). This principle allows for a future that includes the unexpected, or in Arendt's words, a respect for the human condition of natality.

Piercy employs science one step further in the interests of a viably active political community. She releases females from the exclusive capacity for childbearing, releases males from the onus of being the "father," and enables all members of the community to nurture infants with breast milk. The members of the community "signal the intent to begin a baby . . . [and] discuss into which family the child should be born and who are to be mothers" (162). Three co-mothers are selected from volunteers and at least two agree to breast feed the baby with the help of hormones if necessary. The community never relinquishes the responsibility for the child to these individuals; "The children are everyone's heirs, everyone's business, everyone's future" (183).

Piercy completely dismantles the hegemony of the medical profession over mental health and illness by granting to the individual the power to name her or himself as "mad" and in need of "retreat . . . to collapse, carry on, see visions, hear voices of prophecy, bang on the walls . . . How can another person decide that it is time for me to disintegrate, to reintegrate myself?" (66). Another blow to medical authority by this fiction is the validation of many forms of "folk medicine," but the most significant deconstruction attempted and accomplished by Piercy is that of the genre of utopian fiction itself. "She makes sure to express the limits and problems that continue within the utopian system and utopian discourse" (Moylan 151). This is the mature utopian spirit at its best.

Works Cited

Arendt, Hannah. 1958. *The Human Condition*. Chicago: University of Chicago Press.

———. 1961. *Between Past and Future*. New York: Viking Press.

———. 1963. *On Revolution*. New York: Penguin Books.

Bartowski, Frances. 1989. *Feminist Utopias*. Lincoln: University of Nebraska Press.

Benhabib, Seyla. 1986. *Critique, Norm, and Utopia: A Study of the Foundations of Critical Theory*. New York: Columbia University Press.

———. 1990. "Hannah Arendt and the Redemptive Power of Narrative." *Social Research* 57.1 (Spring): 167–196.

Bernstein, Richard. 1978. "Thinking on Thought." *The New York Times Book Review* (28 May): 1–2.

———. 1986. *Philosophical Profiles: Essays in a Pragmatic Mode*. Philadelphia: University of Pennsylvania Press.

Betz, Joseph. 1992. "An Introduction to the Thought of Hannah Arendt" *Transactions of the Charles S. Peirce Society* 28.3 (Summer): 379–422.

Cutting-Gray, Joanne. 1993. "Hannah Arendt, Feminism, and the Politics of Alterity: 'What Will We Lose If We Win?'" *Hypatia: A Journal of Feminist Philosophy* 8.1 (Winter): 35–54.

Kristol, Elizabeth. 1993. "Picture Perfect: The Politics of Prenatal Testing," *First*

Things: A Monthly Journal of Religion and Public Life 32 (April): 17–24.

Maciunas, Billie. 1992. "Feminist Epistemology in Piercy's Woman on the Edge of Time" *Woman's Studies* 20: 249–258.

Moylan, Tom. 1987. *Demand the Impossible: Science Fiction and the Utopian Imagination.* New York: Routledge.

Piercy, Marge. 1976. *Woman on the Edge of Time.* New York: Ballantine Books.

———. 1991. *He, She and It.* New York: Alfred A. Knopf.

Romans, Robin. 1992. "Private and Public in a Social World: Gender and Modernity in Hannah Arendt's Political Thought." Ph.D. diss., University of Southern California.

Sargent, Lyman. 1983. "A New Anarchism: Social and Political Ideas in Some Recent Feminist Eutopias." In *Women and Utopia: Critical Interpretations,* edited by Marleen Barr and Nicholas Smith. Lanham, Md.: University Press of America.

Chapter 9

Governing the Alien Nation
The Comparative Politics of Extraterrestrials

Clyde Wilcox

Human societies are governed in myriad ways. Among democratic societies, there are presidential and parliamentary systems, and single-party, two-party and multiparty systems. Some party systems reflect religious cleavages, some economic, and some ethnic or tribal. Among nondemocratic nations, there are military dictatorships, party dictatorships, and monarchies, among others. Political scientists have spent much time attempting to understand and explain this often confusing plethora of political systems.

Some political scientists have focused their attention in developing typologies of human governments. This project is an ancient one: Aristotle compared the constitutional and political arrangements of the various Greek city-states, and attempted to explain the diversity by focusing on socio-economic and political-cultural factors. Plato and Cicero also count among the earliest comparativists, and Niccolò Machiavelli, Thomas Hobbes, Baron Montesquieu, and Karl Marx all compared political and economic systems (Wiarda 1991). Yet typologies offer little explanation, so political scientists have attempted to build broader theories.

During the late 1950s and 1960s, many theorists sought to integrate all extant political systems into a comprehensive developmental theory.

These political scientists posited that nations go through a relatively invariant set of stages on the route to political development, and that the nation-states of Latin America, Africa, and Asia were simply transitional forms en route to Western-style democracy (Almond 1970; Rostow 1960; Lipset 1959.)

Other political scientists rejected the developmental paradigm, and instead rooted their theories in structural-functionalism, which suggested that all societies must perform the same basic functions, and that one useful way to compare nations would be to focus on the way they set about to socialize their members, allocate resources among competing groups, or mobilize resources (see Hempel 1968 for a discussion and critique). If all societies must aggregate and articulate interests, then it is useful to focus on parties, interest groups, and other mechanisms to perform these functions. Although functionalism never explained why a particular society performed a given function in a particular way, it at least allowed comparisons across radically different governmental forms.

Functionalists, developmentalists, and others generally believe that it is possible to compare across a wide variety of political systems (see Almond and Powell 1992 for a review). Such studies make simplifying assumptions that may be more or less useful. Studies of comparative public policy, for example, frequently investigate the impact of the strength of leftist parties on social welfare spending. Such research assumes that in some way the British Labor Party is similar to the Swedish Social Democratic Party or the French Socialist Party. Frequently, these cross-national studies take into account the most obvious structural or cultural differences (e.g. Powell 1980).

Some political scientists, however, are more skeptical about the utility of comparing multiple political systems. They argue that comparisons should be limited to systems that share a number of characteristics in common—comparing the emerging democracies in Latin America, for example, or the capitalist systems in the Pacific Rim. Comparisons should be limited because political institutions have different meaning in different cultures, and blind comparisons across countries obscure as much as they reveal. Generally political scientists who adopt this approach center their work on nations that share a common political and social culture, in part because such comparisons hold constant these important factors, allowing the researcher to focus on the role of political parties, interest groups, or governmental structures.

Still other political scientists believe that it is seldom helpful directly to compare political systems, because the meaning of political institutions and behavior is deeply embedded in the culture of each country. Conover and Searing (1994) have argued, for example, that it is not possible even to compare the attitudes of citizens of different countries on abortion, because the issue involves different symbols and life circumstances in a poor Catholic country than in a more affluent, Protestant one or in a rapidly industrializing Asian nation. Scholars who adopt this viewpoint generally study a single political system, and attempt to gain an insider's perspective on not only the structure and functioning of governmental and quasi-governmental institutions, but also the meaning of these institutions and various political processes to the citizenry. Most political scientists in this tradition do not reject altogether the possibility of comparisons, but rather believe that they should be made very cautiously, and be narrowly focused.

These various views of comparative politics have implications for the study of extraterrestrial governments. Those who accept a developmental model might expect that all species sufficiently developed to achieve interstellar flight will have developed democratic forms of government—perhaps far more efficient ones than currently in existence. Indeed, such species may be far wiser than humans, and may have developed ways to aggregate citizen preferences that are more efficient and less coercive than contemporary human democracies.

Functionalists would predict that we can understand the basic operations of governments of alien species, even if they are radically different from any on Earth. If all species must find some way to allow divergent points of view to be aggregated and then expressed in the political system, then we should be able to eventually identify the way that any species performs this function. This suggests that we should be able to understand alien governments, even of fundamentally different species. The strong form of this assumption might even suggest that there is a relatively finite range of possible governmental forms that efficiently perform these functions, so that any species encountered in the void between star systems must have one of these basic forms of government.

In contrast, those who believe in more limited comparisons might find it useful to focus on humanoid species, especially those linked by some common cultural heritage. Only these kinds of comparisons are viable, for some aliens would be far too strange to compare directly with human society. Finally, those who are the most skeptical of comparisons would focus on the difficulties of understanding alien species, and what their governmental forms mean to them. They would caution that political processes and forms that initially appear to be similar may in fact have very different meanings to species with radically different biological forms and functions. A detailed account of a single extraterrestrial species would fit this approach.

In this chapter, I will examine the depiction of the politics of other planets, both of extraterrestrial species and of human societies on other worlds. Because a large, diverse genre of science fiction stories and novels depict politics in some form, I will not attempt to create a comprehensive survey of governmental forms that are directly or indirectly depicted, but rather use specific examples to illustrate the basic divisions within the field of political science. Similarly, at the far edges of political theory are those theorists, descended most directly from writers such as William Godwin and Henry David Thoreau, who prefer to imagine, perhaps nostalgically, social structures organized with a minimum of government. So the following survey will touch briefly, also, the importance of images for philosophic, even pastoral, anarchy among science fiction writers. Not surprisingly in the Western world, a number of science fiction writers imagine that space is populated by nonviolent, democratic species. Since the history of Earth is filled with cultures and nations that were (and often remain) violent and dictatorial, these writers need a mechanism that would prevent more hostile, dictatorial species from dominating the galaxy, or even of achieving space flight. Most commonly, writers suggest that all species undergo a critical period when their technology enables them to develop weapons that could destroy the planet. Either they evolve social systems that allow for better conflict management and resolution, or they destroy themselves.

In Carl Sagan's *Contact*, humans are tested for admission to a galactic civilization. Clearly not all species are invited to join, and humans are judged not yet ready. This coalition of democratic species engages in public works projects of a massive scale, such as repairing a sort of subway system between the stars. The coalition occasionally steps in to stop violent species from entering space, but "In the long run, aggressive civilizations destroy themselves, almost always. . . . In such a case, our job would be to leave them alone. . . . To let them work out their destiny." Humans are judged to have a short-term perspective, and "after a while, the civilizations with only short-term perspectives just aren't around. They work out their destinies also." In *Beyond Heaven's Gate*,

Greg Bear imagines a universe in which 4,000 sentient species have destroyed themselves. Nancy Rampe has noted that this logic depends on species reaching spaceflight without outside aid. When species are given assistance, then they may achieve spaceflight long before they would have the opportunity to "mature," or to destroy themselves. In David Brin's work, species are genetically altered by patron species to become more intelligent, and the technology of the galactic encyclopedia made available to allow them to reach the stars. In the stories in the various volumes of Isaac's Universe, less advanced species are contacted by starfaring ones and aided or hindered in their development. In these and other works, only those species that are basically nonviolent, or those who evolve governmental forms that allow for conflict resolution, survive and reach the stars.

If the developmental model is correct, then species more advanced than contemporary humans should have even more democratic forms of government. The most common tack in depicting such advanced democracies centers on the role of consensus. Many writers imagine town meetings writ large, in which all members of government, and perhaps even all members of the species, agree on policy. In this way, the writers depict a government that is in an important sense "above politics." In Jeffrey Carver's *The Rapture Effect*, five Ell attempt to reach consensus telepathically, with a "binder" to facilitate the discussion. Donald Moffitt in *The Genesis Quest* depicts the Nar, a species of decopods that decide policy by touching each other and letting information ripple through the community through the cilia on each Nar's pods. In some vague, undefined manner the Nar are shown reaching consensus through these large mass meetings.

Consensual politics are also common in feminist futures, perhaps because of the large scholarly literature that suggests that women's decision-making styles differ from those of men. In Joan Slonczewski's *A Door into Ocean*, the exclusively female inhabitants of Shora are shown as sitting naked on their large lily pads, talking until consensus is reached. Sheri S. Tepper's *The Gate to Women's Country* shows a culture of women ruled by an amorphous council with no fixed number of seats and no fixed method for selection. Such an ambiguous governmental structure works because of underlying consensus among the ruling women.

These latter two works do depict disagreement, and in *A Door into Ocean*, political conflict is frequently intense. Yet ultimately most members of the society are persuaded by rational argument and hard data.

164

The need for complicated decision rules and elaborate governmental structures is obviated by the societal consensus on values, but more importantly by the "reasonableness" of the citizenry. When a policy is shown to be in the best interest of the entire society, most (and in some cases all) of the citizens approve it. Such worlds that border on pastoral simplicity offer a nice distinction to a more "hard-nosed" and even more urban philosophic anarchy that can be read in Samuel R. Delany's masterpiece *Dhalgren* (Delaney's is, also, a feminist anarchy as in Ursula K. Le Guin's *The Left Hand of Darkness*). Thus I would suggest that the passive, more "feminine," anarchy with roots back to Thoreau in Slonczewski's ocean world is significantly different from the more georgic-pastoral anarchy with roots, perhaps, to Godwin's *Political Justice* and to the eighteenth-century urban world of *The Beggar's Opera*, as Hassler argues with regard to *Dhalgren* in particular; but in any case many science fiction writers seem drawn to the laissez-faire, anarchic theories that have their deepest origins in the classical genres of pastoral and georgic.

But reasonableness and a reliance on logical laissez-faire are not always obvious in contemporary human societies, especially where economic self-interest is involved. Loggers in the Pacific Northwest oppose restrictions on cutting old-growth timber even when their own research shows that at current rates those forests will disappear in a few years, because the lure of short-term profits trumps the public good. For most humans, when the public good clashes with their private self-interest, the public good is problematic. Science fiction that shows successful consensual governments therefore relies on showing species that are more rational than humans (or, in the case of feminist fables, in the depiction of women as reasonable beings who could reach consensus but for the influences of patriarchy). Often this reasonableness comes from heredity. The "Gentle Giants" of James Hogan's trilogy can govern primarily by consensus because they are a species that evolved on a planet with no large predators, and where predation and even scavenging was prevented by a complicated biochemistry. They are therefore more trusting, guileless, and willing to defer to the public good.

Not all science fiction that fits the developmental paradigm depicts a universe populated by wise, consensual sentients. Some show species developing increasingly sophisticated governments that help their citizens, although they may not all be democracies. In Olaf Stapledon's *Star Maker*, species are clearly shown to develop toward a common political end, although some relied on nondemocratic structures. The nature of the world orders varied "because of the biology of the species" (Stapledon 133), but all were communistic in some loose sense. In some, dictators governed for the common good, though "under the constant supervision of the popular will expressed through radio" (Stapledon 170). In others, the leaders were elected by the citizens.

Stapledon depicted species with radically different biologies all evolving more complex and humane governmental systems. In Robert Forward's *Dragon's Egg*, a species evolving on a neutron star appears to go through the same political history as humans, despite their radically different physical surroundings and biology. Ultimately they develop a democratic political system as they pass the humans in scientific and social development. Thus the developmental paradigm seems to imply that sentience is sentience, and that all mature species will face the same problems and solve them in very similar ways.

Although the developmental paradigm would suggest a steady evolution to more sophisticated political forms, functionalism merely suggests that the governments of sentient species will be understandable, for they will undertake the same tasks, albeit in radically different ways. Indeed, functionalism is most interesting where the cultures and species are most divergent, since this makes identifying the basic functions of government more complicated.

Many science fiction novels and stories depict a dazzling variety of types of sentient species. In Stapledon's famous *Star Maker*, the narrator visits planets dominated by sentient plants, by collective minds of avians or insects, and by a symbiotic relationship between crustaceans and fish. In Brin's *Startide Rising*, species of sentient trees, insects, and other complex entities seem to coexist in a crowded galaxy. When species have widely divergent biological imperatives, it becomes difficult but interesting to imagine the way that the species performs the basic function of government.

Often the politics of these aliens are recognizable versions of human political systems. In Larry Niven's "Known Space" series, for example, the catlike Kzinti are governed by a Patriarch and appear to be a totalitarian culture. In contrast, the herbivorous Puppeteers are a democracy with an Experimental and a Conservative party. In times of stress, the Experimental party is elected to produce bold new solutions, but since any bold Puppeteer is by definition insane, the Conservative party is elected again as soon as the crisis has passed. Thus two starfaring species have radically different political institutions, yet both are readily recognizable variations on basic human forms.

One basic function of all governments is to resolve disputes in an authoritative manner, preventing the nation or species from fighting a civil war. When environmentalists and loggers disagree about old-growth forests in Oregon and Washington, for example, the United States government can provide a solution that may deeply anger one side (or even both sides). Yet the government's edict will prevail, and this prevents an escalation of the conflict.

To perform this function, the government must consult with experts and with the various involved parties. From these consultations, the government must develop a plan that provides some solution to the problem. In democratic systems, this plan will generally involve some kind of compromise between the various groups, since the legitimacy of the government rests in part on its ability to produce solutions that appear to all sides to be at least somewhat fair.

It would seem that this function must be performed by all governments. Yet the unique biological characteristics of some species may obviate the need to aggregate citizen preferences in any way. The "Buggers" in Orson Scott Card's "Ender" series are an insectoid species in which the mind of the queen inhabits the bodies of all other bodies in the hive. In this way, government need not resolve conflicts or aggregate preferences, because there are no individuals.

For other species, biological imperatives create special governmental processes that aid in settling disputes. The Simiu in A. C. Crispin's *Starbridge* are a species that resemble dog-faced monkeys. Their society is organized around clans, and the political interactions between clans are conducted by debts of honor. It is implied that the evolution of the species has left it with a finely honed sense of outrage and honor, which is now somewhat dysfunctional. When a clan has a dispute with another, representatives of each battle as gladiators to the death, with the winning side also victorious in the political dispute. Presumably this procedure historically involved the leaders of clans, but has now evolved to where the clans hire professional gladiators to do battle.

In sharp contrast, in *Polar City Blues* Katherine Kerr depicts the Carlis, a feline, carnivorous species that evolved detailed rituals of deference to defuse violence in decision-making. The political process is conducted through these elaborate rituals, which prevent the hot-tempered Carlis from killing each other over a political dispute. The function of these rituals in mediating political conflict is readily apparent.

In Larry Niven and Jerry Pournelle's *Footfall*, a species of pachyderms attack the Earth from orbit. These elephant-like creatures have a herd mentality, and need constant social interaction to prevent them from going "rogue." The leader consults with the females before making major decisions, a trait that echoes the dominant female elephants of Earth. Yet the leaders are male, a reflection of the authors' traditional sex role attitudes. Despite the novelty of the species, the politics are recognizable, with a leader (Herdmaster) and his advisors (e.g. the Attack Master).

Brin's *The Uplift War* provides perhaps the most detailed portrait of the politics of another species in recent science fiction. The Gubru are a bird-like species that are invading a human-held planet named Garth. Their language and metaphors reflect their avian heritage—they refer to the "perch" of command, and make statements such as "There are times a nest cannot avoid taking risks."

Gubru politics is divided into three sectors, administration (cost and caution), religion (propriety), and military (force). The heads of these sectors are called Roost Masters. Each Roost Master sent representatives to Garth to represent their special concerns. These representatives were all neuter, and as the invasion unfolds they argue with one another through dances. Whichever Gubru becomes dominant through argument will then molt and emerge as female, and lay the eggs of the species. This sort of politics is quite different from most human interactions, yet the process merely allows governmental elites to resolve disputes, a function that all human societies perform in some other manner.

In Orson Scott Card's *Speaker for the Dead*, the "piggie" species included a non-sentient larval stage, a mammal stage, and "third life" as a sentient tree. The trees are the elders, and provide governance to the entire species. Those "piggies" in the mammal stage communicate with the trees by drumming on their bark, and listening to the nuanced sound. Once again, this seemingly bizarre system performs the basic functions of all human political systems. Thus the functionalist paradigm suggests that there are certain ways to efficiently perform certain functions, and that all sentient species will eventually select one of these strategies.

Although there are many science fiction stories and novels that fit the developmental approach to comparative politics, and a far larger number that are consonant with a functionalist approach, it is more difficult to identify stories and novels that might be classified as limited comparisons. Of course, in all stories of first contact with an alien species, a limited comparison between human and alien societies is implicitly or explicitly made. Yet in political science, the limited comparison approach is reserved for nations that share some common cultural characteristics—usually some combination of racial/ethnic, religious, and economic characteristics. It is also common to compare countries who may be involved in complex interactions, such as the Eastern European nations of the former communist bloc.

Yet such limited comparisons do exist, especially in feminist or quasi-feminist science fiction. In *A Door into Ocean*, Slonczewski compares the societies and politics of an all-female society on a planet's moon with the more traditional and somewhat patriarchical society on the home planet. In Tepper's *The Gate to Women's Country*, the egalitarian and humane women's societies in the cities is contrasted to the aggressive and cruel men's world in the surrounding countryside. Tepper succeeds at creating an interesting and inviting women's society, but her depiction of men's societies is a caricature. Indeed, in one scene her militant men dance around a statue of an erect penis. Le Guin's *The Dispossessed* compares a utopian civilization on a moon with the Earth-like warring nations on the home planet. And her most wide-ranging comparative speculations, of course, are those on the planet Gethen itself as well as across the Ebunen of galactic government in *The Left Hand of Darkness*. Also, Slonczewski, Tepper, and Le Guin delight in blending sexual speculations with political speculations—with Tepper, perhaps, being the least interesting. But the varieties of sexual speculation is another essay.

To a certain extent, science fiction that depicts multiple human societies on various planets or satellites fits this comparative category well, since all share a common human ancestry. Isaac Asimov's comparisons of the Spacer Worlds and Earth in *The Caves of Steel*, for example, assume a minimal common culture. Similarly, the countless comparisons of the politics and culture of Beltway miners vs. those of Earth (e.g in the anthology *Life Among the Asteroids*) or of the politics of other Earth colonies and those of the mother planet (e.g. Kim Stanley Robinson's *Green Mars* and *The Memory of Whiteness*) assume common cultural roots.

The governmental systems of Earth generally diverge from those of its colonies in these works. The most frequent pattern is to depict Earth as mired in the politics of the past, while the courageous colonists forge a new political system that avoids these problems. In some cases, various ethnic and religious groups settle different planets or satellites, creating their own unique political systems in much the same way that the Puritans and Quakers formed their own colonies in America. In some cases, the physical or economic demands of the colonies lead to different politics: the libertarian culture that is most frequently extrapolated for Asteroid-belt society comes from the unique combination of isolation and interdependence that "Belter" prospectors must face.

The works described above assume that sentient species will be able to communicate at some basic level. The scientists in the SETI program frequently argue that mathematics are basic, and that certain scientific truths are inescapable on any planet. Yet exchanging a basic "hello" by listing the first one hundred digits of pi is simple compared to understanding the culture and politics of a society. If humans frequently blunder across cultural divides, how much more difficult to communicate with a species that is not recognizably alive?

Many science fiction novels portray this communication as a difficult process. In Rebecca Ore's fascinating *Alien* series, various sentient species must overcome their initial repulsion by other sentients to form a galactic government. The Rector, a huge birdlike alien who is titular head of galactic society, argues that there is a universal mind, but his arguments do not persuade all. Communication is shown as very difficult, and made with the greatest efforts. Yet Ore's depiction actually describes contemporary human reality, where communication between Asian, Arab, African, and European cultures is quite difficult. It is possible that alien governments would be impossible to understand, as would the aliens themselves. In Stanislaw Lem's novella *Solaris*, the humans cannot decide if the ocean is intelligent, if it is trying to communicate, and if so, what it is trying to say. It is possible that the ocean is a species of individuals, a single individual, or something that is not sentient.

Kerr's *Polar City Blues* imagines a universe in which divergent species can communicate through telepathy. Yet not all species can communicate, because "they conceptualize the universe in such radically novel ways that they share no general categories of thought with any other species, not even, for example, the distinction between general category and specific thought" (97).

Contemporary political scientists face the extremely difficult task of explaining the endless diversity of human political systems. Yet science fiction writers imagine a far more complex galaxy with sentient species that are often exotic in their biology, culture, and politics. In such a galaxy, political scientists would have a far more daunting, but probably more interesting, task. Some writers imagine that all sentients who achieve spaceflight will have very advanced political systems, with democratic decisionmaking structures that are perhaps more advanced than those currently on Earth. Others imagine that all governments will perform recognizable political functions, albeit in quite different ways. Some contrast political systems of two related groups, showing the roots and consequences of political institutions. And some species are so radically different that humans cannot understand their politics, their society, or even their fundamental ways of thought.

Science fiction allows political scientists to expand their thinking about the ways that different cultures develop different politics. Instead of confining their analysis to contemporary human politics, they can imagine politics of a fundamentally different kind that range across the whole spectrum from highly organized structures to the most nostalgically "pastoral" of anarchies. Such thought experiments can stretch the imagination, and help us rethink our theories, categories, and hopes.

Works Cited

Almond, Gabriel A. 1970. *Political Development: Essays in Heuristic Theory.* Boston: Little Brown.

Almond, Gabriel A., and G. Bingham Powell, Jr. 1992. *Comparative Politics Today.* New York: HarperCollins.

Asimov, Isaac. 1983. *The Caves of Steel.* New York: Ballantine.

Bear, Greg. 1980. *Beyond Heaven's River.* London: VGSF.

Brin, David. 1983. *Startide Rising.* New York: Bantam.

———. 1987. *The Uplift War.* New York: Bantam.

Card, Orson Scott. 1986. *Ender's War* (includes *Speaker for the Dead*). New York: Omni.

Carver, Jeffrey. 1987. *The Rapture Effect.* New York: Tor.

Conover, Pamela Johnston, and Donald D. Searing. 1994. "Studying Citizen Identities Contextually: A Cultural Approach to the Explanation of Political Behavior." Paper presented at the annual meeting of the Midwest Political Science Association, Chicago.

Crispin, A. C. 1989. *Starbridge.* New York: Ace.

Delany, Samuel R. 1975. *Dhalgren.* New York: Bantam.

Dogan, Mattei, and Dominque Pelassy. 1990. *How to Compare Nations: Strategies in Comparative Politics.* Chatham, N.J.: Chatham House.

Forward, Robert. 1980. *Dragon's Egg*. New York: Ballantine.

Godwin, William. 1793. *Enquiry Concerning Political Justice*, edited by F. E. L. Priestley. 3 vols. 1946. London: Oxford University Press.

Hassler, Donald M. 1989. "*Dhalgren, The Beggar's Opera*, and Georgic: Implications for the Nature of Genre." *Extrapolation* 30:4 (Winter): 332–338.

Hempel, Carl G. 1968. "The Logic of Functional Analysis." In *Readings in the Philosophy of the Social Sciences*, edited by May Brodbeck. New York: MacMillan.

Holt, Robert T., and John E. Turner. 1970. *The Methodology of Comparative Research*. New York: Free Press.

Kerr, Katherine. 1990. *Polar City Blues*. New York: Bantam.

Le Guin, Ursula K. 1969. *The Left Hand of Darkness*. New York: Ace.

———. 1974. *The Dispossessed*. New York: Avon.

Lem, Stanislaw. 1971. *Solaris*. London: Faber & Faber.

Lipset, Seymour Martin. 1959. *Political Man: The Social Bases of Politics*. New York: Doubleday.

Merritt, Richard L. 1970. *Systematic Approaches to Comparative Politics*. New York: Rand McNally.

Moffitt, Donald. 1986. *The Genesis Quest*. New York: Del Rey.

Niven, Larry, and Jerry Pournelle. 1985. *Footfall*. New York: Ballantine.

Ore, Rebecca. 1988. *Becoming Alien*. New York: Tor.

Pournelle, Jerry. 1994. *Life among the Asteroids*, edited by John F. Carr. New York: Ace.

Powell, G. Bingham, Jr. 1980. "Voting Turnout in Thirty Democracies: Partisan, Legal, and Socio-Economic Influences." In *Electoral Participation: A Comparative Analysis*, edited by Richard Rose. London: Sage.

Rampe, Nancy. 1994. Personal communication.

Robinson, Kim Stanley. 1985. *The Memory of Whiteness*. New York: Tor.

———. 1994. *Green Mars*. New York: Bantam.

Rostow, W. W. 1960. *The Stages of Economic Growth*. New York: Cambridge University Press.

Sagan, Carl. 1985. *Contact*. New York: Pocket Books.

Stapledon, Olaf. 1937. *Star Maker*. Los Angeles: Jeremy Tarcher.

Slonczewski, Joan. 1986. *A Door into Ocean*. New York: Avon.

Tepper, Sheri S. 1988. *The Gate to Women's Country*. New York: Bantam.

Thoreau, Henry David. 1937. *Walden and other Writings*, edited by Brooke Atkinson. New York: Modern Library.

Wiarda, Howard J. 1991. "Comparative Politics Past and Present." In *New Directions in Comparative Politics*, edited by H. Wiarda. Boulder: Westview.

Chapter 10

Reality Transfigured
The Latin American Situation as Reflected in Its Science Fiction

Ingrid Kreksch

Just as in science fiction, environment itself functions much like character. Let us first consider the Latin American region, and then draw some inferences about its science fiction. A favorite overview of mine having to do with Latin American values is the following:

> The world will hardly look to the Latin American for leadership
> in democracy, in organization, in business, in science, in rigid
> moral values. On the other hand, Latin America has something
> to contribute to an industrialized and mechanicist world con-
> cerning the value of the individual, the place of friendship, the
> use of leisure, the art of conversation, the attractions of the
> intellectual [life], the equality of races, the juridical basis of
> international life, the place of suffering and contemplation, the
> value of the impractical, the importance of people over things
> and rules (Inman 10).

Latin American reality is a complex one, since South and Central America is a huge continent, comprising more than twenty different countries with many different languages. Of a great geographical variety, as Peter Nehemkis expresses, "the attitudes are as varied as the geography. Indeed, geography has conditioned the attitudes of the people" (Nehemkis viii). The differences between the peoples of each country are indeed great. But there also exist other differences. "Latin America is an area of dramatic contrasts: The twentieth century and the fifteenth century exist side by side. Factories as modern as any in the United States or Europe can be found in countries whose population are largely outside the cash economy. Nuclear physicists pursue their studies in countries where a majority of the people live under medieval conditions. Renowned writers are native to countries in which illiteracy is widespread. Spectacular cities are surrounded by appalling shanty towns" (Nehemkis x). In the same way, "the Latin American political systems are bewildering in their diversity" (Nehemkis x).

What Nehemkis affirmed in 1964 is still accurate. Latin American reality is complex, although there exist authors who have successfully described it, such as Octavio Paz and Carlos Fuentes. We cannot dig too far into the complexity of this reality but rather will show some traits common to the whole continent, and then see to what extent these are reflected in the science fiction written by Latin American authors.

Even though every region experienced the conquest by the Spaniards in a slightly different way, as they later did when every country declared its independence, two phenomena repeated throughout the whole continent: the quest for El Dorado initiated by the conquerors, and the Caudillismo, or selfish leadership, following independence. Both have marked Latin America until our day.

When they arrived, the Spanish started the quest for the Fountain of Youth, the Amazons and El Dorado (The Golden City). According to Carlos Rangel (1976), "the navigators and conquistadors who came after Columbus sought these fabled Amazons and their country full of gold. We see that the myth of El Dorado is linked to very ancient legends. In this as in other instances, the discovery of America brought nothing to European mythology that was not already there; it only rekindled old dreams of Golden Age and the State of Innocence that preceded the Fall" (Rangel 12). Many claim that Latin America was from the beginning sought for its richness and not as a place to stay and make livable. This is claimed to have affected Latin American economic life greatly.

The other fact common to all of Latin America is the Caudillismo, which still has a bearing on the continent's political life. As Nehemkis (1964) presents it, "independence turned Spanish America into a theatre of guerrilla warfare and fratricidal extermination. Political action degenerated into banditry. . . . The Caudillo—(the big boss, the leader)—was made to order for this violent and primitive environment. As the head of a political faction, a social group, or a family with a network of influential relations, the Caudillo alone could enforce internal order. In effect, he was the government; his word was law. The constitution, if it had any meaning, spoke through him" (49). Nowadays there are a great variety of government styles in Latin America, but the Caudillo still leaks through in many respects. Even though many Latin American countries now have a democratic presidential government, two images haunt the political scene of the region: the "militares" and the revolutionarists. We will not describe either of these two groups in depth, we will only show their personalities briefly, as they have influenced the continent greatly. As for the militarists, Nehemkis (1964) claims:

> If there can be said to be any unifying thread which binds the officer corps it is an instinctive hostility to the democratic processes. In part, this is an outgrowth of lifelong training in a hierarchical organization in which each element is subject to command and obedience. In part—the greater part—it is the result of the conditioning process of belonging to an establishment that has been set apart, enjoys special privileges, and—in some countries is the dominant power structure. (57)

As for the revolutionarists, Rangel (1976) explains the behavior of these groups as follows:

> Millenarian (or revolutionary) sects invariably conceive redemption as absolute, in the sense that, through some transformation, life on earth will suddenly be changed, returned to the perfection it enjoyed before the Fall. Furthermore, millenarian outbreaks have invariably been accompanied by the sudden appearance of prophets and martyrs endowed with special qualities: eloquence, courage, personal magnetism, charisma. No doubt millenarianism and revolutionism do not fit in with

the rationalist spirit in which the West found its greatness. But, on the other hand, they are supremely attractive to all those who feel outcast, marginal, frustrated, beaten, dispossessed of their natural right to enjoy the goods of the earth—with which, it is supposed, the noble savages of America were amply provided before the arrival of the fateful caravels (15–16).

The existence of these personalities is both the result and one of the conditions for the social and economic situation in Latin American countries. In fact, Rangel in his work outlines the theory that the native Latin Americans started by having an image of themselves as good savages (*buenos salvajes*) when they were discovered by the Europeans, later changing in order to become the good revolutionarists (*buenos revolucionarios*).

In each one of the modern capital cities modern architecture and a cosmopolitan environment contrasts with shanty towns. As Nehemkis (1964) points out: "For half a century or more, Latin America's cities have been magnets for a migratory horde from the countryside. . . . Rural migrants are lured to the cities by the tales that percolate into the countryside telling of good jobs at high wages in the factories—and the booming construction industry. The migrants come to escape the bleak poverty and the hopelessness of their lives in the backlands" (184).

This quest for Paradise in the cities, which is now a common practice, has its roots in the past when, as Rangel (1976) states: "A split between urban, commercial centers and rural, producing areas characterized Latin American colonial society and economy, particularly in export production" (206). This condition is linked to the continent's economy.

Among the leitmotivs of Latin American economy we have to mention the following four: agrarian reform, monoculture, industrialization and economic integration. Concerning agrarian reform and land, Nehemkis traces this back to "uneconomical land utilization and antiquated methods of cultivation" (150). Poverty in rural areas and the fact that land is not considered a capital resource and thus is not counted upon in order to derive any return on investment from it, contribute to this state of things. Concerning monoculture, Latin America is dependent in most cases on only a few commodities (chiefly agricultural, such as beef and wheat) that are subject to fluctuations in price on the international markets, as well as to other hazards of international economy and trade. This leads us to the topic of industrialization which would free the continent of the dependency on exports of raw material, but which is subject, among others, to investments and to a sound attitude on behalf of investors, who should reinvest the earnings in the country and not evade fiscal duties. With the new trend toward an information society, however, this model will have to adapt to the new international situation.

Finally, economic integration has to be mentioned. Several tries have been made to create a regional trade organization, starting with the Latin American Free Trade Agreement (LAFTA) in the 1960s and the Andean Pact in the 1970s. Although these have been good initiatives, there are several factors which have not allowed the continent to integrate at this level so far. It should also be mentioned that the relations with the industrialized countries of North America are not always easy. They are humbled by an attitude of mixed feelings which Rangel (1976) describes as a love-hate relationship.

This is, in overall outline, the panorama of the Latin American situation. We will not go into detail about the role of the Catholic church in these countries, nor about the problems of international loans and the drug economy, nor will we focus on widespread corruption, since these are problems requiring deeper study.

But let us now turn to Latin American science fiction to see to what extent the authors reflect some aspects of the continent's situation in their works. Only science fiction writers have been taken into account and not authors who are considered to be borderline in their style, but who do not themselves identify with the genre. For the present study works by authors of Colombia, Cuba, Mexico, Venezuela, Brazil, Argentina, and Uruguay have been taken into account. There is not enough information available about the science fiction of Chile, Peru, Bolivia, Ecuador, and the countries of Central America (except Mexico).

Latin American science fiction is mostly "soft," meaning that it deals mostly with the social sciences and with politics rather than physics—a prime example in English is the work of Theodore Sturgeon. This "soft" condition is due to the fact, first, that a majority of the writers are not scientists but generally have a background in humanities or social sciences. Second, the cultures do not have as extensive a scientific framework as in North America or Western Europe. Latin America is not a producer of technology, but a consumer, and thus the attitude toward technology varies in comparison to the technology-producing countries.

Most Latin American science fiction is brief, embodied in short stories rather than in novels. This is due to the fact that it is more feasible to publish short fiction than to publish longer stories, as the editorial industry as well as the market is limited. With the exception of Jorge Luis Borges, who probably should be classed as borderline, few science fiction writers have attracted enough attention to be translated; hence this reduces the market and the possibilities. This is very much a beginning literature. Finally, Latin American science fiction stories rarely use dates to set the story in time, thus making the stories seem to be atemporal, existing in a generalized Latin America derived from the history and economics mentioned and ranging into the future. If we take the broad outline mentioned above and apply it to representative works in Latin American science fiction we will see some of the themes in more detail. I will evoke each story with a few of its resident Spanish words; eventually we hope for translation of much of this literature and some familiarity with it in the English-speaking world.

The first theme is what I call "integration." The Colombian author Antonio Mora Vélez (1982) uses the notion of "government of the United States of South America," as well as the notion of "Central American and Caribbean Community," in his short story "Crossed Strategies" (Estrategias Cruzadas) (in Souto 1985). Eduardo Goligorsky (Argentina) in " The Last Reduct" (El Ultimo Reducto) (in Souto 1985) mentions the "ships of the World Council." Bruno Henriquez (Cuba), in his short story "Adventure in the Laboratory" (Aventura en el Laboratorio), refers to the "World Scientific Council." In all cases there thus exists the idea of an integration, although neither specifies at what level this integration is to take place.

The next theme is the more common Latin American science fiction theme of "abuses of power." This theme is often dealt with in Latin American science fiction. The abuse can be political, military or of another kind, but it is often shown from the point of view of the victim. Abuse in political power is shown in Luis Britto García's (Venezuela) 1980 short story "The President Is in a Good Mood Today" (El Presidente Amanecío de Buen Humor). This story moreover reflects many of the Latin American situations described above.

This is also the case in "Load" (Carga) by Mauricio José Schwarz (Mexico) (1991). He writes, "About 'before' they only know that men used to kill men. They know that those governing were not trying to govern but to be powerful" (33). On a more daily level, this author in his short story "Abusive" (Abusivo) (1991) shows the violence of the police against the common citizen. Here is a sample of the writing in my translation:

> "Don't get insolent, huh? We want to go to sleep. Just get on the patrol and I'll take your car. . . ."
> "Can you please give me a receipt?" Vladimir asked, seeing that the guy put his personal objects in his uniform's pockets.
> "What receipt, you asshole? Receipt about what?"
>
> The answer was just forming in Vladimir's throat when the first knock came, a right hand directly to one side of his head. He felt his left ear explode. Another blow went to the ribs and a hand grabbed his hair and pulled, bending his head painfully back and prepared him for the kick which hit Vladimir's stomach with an enormous precision. He collapsed panting. He felt he was being pulled and kicked while they took him from the reception area to the cell. Another kick served to deposit him in the patio (16–17).

Uruguayan author Tarik Carson (in Gaut vel Hartman 1987) describes another kind of police violence in his short story "Proyections" (Proyecciones, or Projections)—again in my translation:

> At the Station they identified him by the voice and the hand and brought him to a deserted room. They did not hit him, they just pushed him around. There was some degree of satisfaction in doing this, and every public official who walked past him, pushed him with his shoulder or hand or even with the foot, as if he were a box that was out of place. . . . When the interrogator came in he had already lost the notion of time. . . . "Did you know Aaron Spitzer?" the man said. . . .
>
> "Why were you friends? Did you know his family? Since when hadn't you seen him? What political ideas did he have? And what about the way the system worked? What did he think of Total Freedom?" (159–160).

Angelica Gorodischer (Argentina) (in Souto 1983) also uses the point of view of the victim in "Under the Flowery Jubeas" (Bajo las Jubeas en

179

Flor), a short story in which the captain of a mission is taken prisoner on an alien planet:

> [The director of the prison] pushed a bell to call two uniformed wardens, with whips and pistols. The Director said take him, and so they did. That simply. They put me in a little room and told me to undress. I thought they were going to hit me, and I undressed. But they did not hit me. After looking through my clothes and taking my personal documents, pen, handkerchief, watch, money and all, absolutely all they found, they examined my mouth, ears, hair, navel, armpits, inner part of the thighs, making gestures of approval, and comments on the size, form and possibilities of my genitals (72).

Eduardo Goligorsky (Argentina) treats the topic of propaganda as a part of power in his collection "The Last Reduct" (El Ultimo Reducto):

> In that occasion, a vessel had descended near Tandil, due to a problem in the orientation mechanism. Its tripulation went to look for help and a patrol killed them. The day after a piece of news announced that the security forces had discovered and eliminated a group of foreign subversives. The story turned to be the central theme of the regime's propaganda during a whole year, and after that nobody ever talked about it again (51).

Carlos Gardini (Argentina) (1984) in his short story "Happy Days in Deadtime" (Dias Felices en Tiempomuerte) refers to the topic of military coups and of justice the Caudillo way:

> But everybody, even the youngest colonels of the Palace guard (and the colonels *were* young, because the coup had provoked depositions and quick promotions), had the stern expression on their faces the circumstances demanded. . . . Rather than an execution, it seemed to be the performance of an execution. . . . At the ground the seven executed fell convulsively and the official of the platoon approached them to administer the coup de grace. . . .
>
> Is it true, I asked, that of these seven people only six were accused of being traitors and the other was guilty of a minor delict?

"Seven is a good number for an execution," the polemark replied. "Whereas six. . . . One should never execute six people."

I timidly remarked that in my country this justice criteria would have been considered arbitrary.

"Nevertheless," the polemark smiled, "the recent history of your country has been one of our sources of inspiration. We are not that original" (13–15).

The final theme that I will highlight has to do with the relations with other countries. This theme is also treated in some of the science fiction taken for this study. So for instance in "No Business at All" (Nada de Negocios), Luis Britto García (Venezuela) (1980) presents the difficult trade relation with the United States:

Acceding this high position by the people's will, the day of the proclamation Mister Godwin appears and asks me what I will do with the enormous wells of the Republic, and what can I answer, Mister Godwin, except that I do not know anything about business. Mister Godwin tells me, never mind, I'll exploit them for you. Of course it would be good that for reasons of Development if you granted me the necessary credits with no interests within the Development Plan for the Industry and other things you will show me immediately although you do not know anything of business (64).

Another approach is the one offered by Emilio Eduardo Cócaro in short stories such as "The Dissident" (El Disidente) (1990). "Like many other researchers of his time, Hagen Rodriguez admired the hispanic countries which, only using their vital impulse, had achieved taking control of the government of some countries, among others, of this old empire the symbol of which, an eagle, had come to symbolize the essence of all empires since Rome and until our days" (48). In some cases names in English are used, and in other cases the action takes place in the United States, as though the giant of the north were the Rome of our day.

These are mainly the points in which Latin American reality is reflected in its science fiction. In many cases Latin American science fiction authors avoid topics having to do with internal politics, and rather write about the nuclear war, disarmament, virtual reality, time and other

181

topics which are common in worldwide science fiction. A final characteristic of Latin American science fiction is that the treatment of the topic
is often done with the sense of humor characteristic of the region—such
as the light irony of a Borges that perhaps even derives from the greatest
Spanish ironist of all, Cervantes.

We can thus conclude that Latin American science fiction does not
fail to reflect the continent's reality, although the authors often prefer
being universal. Meanwhile, those "gadget stories" written in Latin
America will probably not be "hard" but rather carry a magical element,
while the continent's political and cultural situations may lead to the
building of interesting utopias and dystopias.

Works Cited

Britto García, Luis. 1980. *Rajatabla.* Caracas: Editorial Ateneo, de Caracas.
Cócaro, Emilio Eduardo. 1990. *Relatos Imposibles.* Buenos Aires: GraFer.
Coligorsky, Eduardo. 1966. *Memorias del futuro.* Buenos Aires: Riesa.
Gardini, Carlos. 1984. *Sinfonia Cero.* Buenos Aires: Riesa.
Gaut vel Hartman, S., ed. 1987. *Fase Uno.* Buenos Aires: Sinergia.
Henriquez, B. 1987. *Aventura en el Laboratorio.* Santiago de Cuba: Editorial Oriente.
Inman, S. G. En Hanke, L. 1959. *South America.* New York: Von Nostrand.
Mora Vélez, A. n.d. *El Juicio de los Dioses.* Monteria: Ediciones El Tunel.
Nehemkis, Peter. 1964. *Latin America: Myth and Reality.* New York: Mentor Books.
Rangel, Carlos. 1976. *The Latin Americans.* New York: Harcourt Brace Jovanovich.
Schwarz, Mauricio José. 1991. *Escenas de la Realidad Virtual.* Mexico: Claves
    Latinoamericanas.
Souto, M., ed. 1985. *La Ciencia Ficcion en Argentina.* Buenos Aires: Eudeba.

Chapter 11

"In Every Revolution, There Is One Man with a Vision"
The Governments of the Future in Comparative Perspective

Paul Christopher Manuel

Although originally written in the 1960s, *Star Trek* did not adopt the economic or cultural determinism of the then-contemporary social science thinking. To the contrary, its episodes, taking politics seriously, often illustrated the dictum that absolute power can and will corrupt absolutely. Story lines warned that nothing would prevent even highly industrialized and literate societies from becoming tyrannical places, absent the political will to the contrary. In other words, *Star Trek* teaches how important political involvement is to society.

Indeed, a theme of comparative interest in the *Star Trek* saga involves the primacy of the political. From Captain Kirk's statement that there is one man behind every revolution, to the new leaders on Ekos asking Kirk to leave them so that they could make their own history, story lines often explored the imprecise and unquantifiable political variables of leadership. Governments in the *Star Trek* world were an end product of the political dynamic, and most certainly did not come into being as a result of deterministic transplanetary historical patterns.

This essay examines the governments of the *Star Trek* future in a search for this admonition toward political involvement. Drawing from the ideal types in Robert Dahl's *Polyarchy*, it will classify and compare the governments found in *Star Trek* according to the following types: I. Democracy, II. Inclusive Hegemony, III. Competitive Oligarchy and IV. Closed Hegemony (Dahl, 6–9). Given the special nature of the governments in some alien worlds, two subcategories were also needed: IV. (A) Computer-Dominated Closed Hegemonies, and IV. (B) Organic-Brain Dominated Closed Hegemonies. Further, a fifth ideal type, called V. Meta-Governmental Societies, was required for those beings who have evolved beyond the need for a government. As indicated in Figure One, these five ideal types, based on the political dimensions of public contestation and participation, set the general boundaries of the governments in the *Star Trek* world.

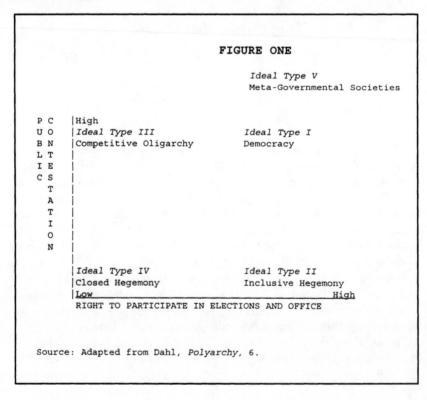

FIGURE ONE

```
                            Ideal Type V
                            Meta-Governmental Societies


   P  C  |High
   U  O  |Ideal Type III              Ideal Type I
   B  N  |Competitive Oligarchy       Democracy
   L  T  |
   I  E  |
   C  S  |
      T  |
      A  |
      T  |
      I  |
      O  |
      N  |
         |
         |Ideal Type IV               Ideal Type II
         |Closed Hegemony             Inclusive Hegemony
         |Low                                          High
          RIGHT TO PARTICIPATE IN ELECTIONS AND OFFICE
```

Source: Adapted from Dahl, *Polyarchy*, 6.

Democracy is a regime in which at least three fundamental conditions are present: (1) extensive and realistic competition among either individuals or organized political groups for all effective positions of power in the government; (2) a very high level of political participation, in which no major adult groups are excluded; and (3) civil and political liberties for all. In other words, a democratic regime allows for full participation and public contestation of all policies; and these characteristics closely follow the definition of democracy in standard works such as Seymour Martin Lipset, Juan J. Linz and Larry Diamond's *Democracy in Developing Countries*. Furthermore, whereas Dahl argues that since no government in the world grants full rights for all of its citizens, the term "polyarchy," or rule of the many, is more accurate. It appears that in the *Star Trek* future, that specification is no longer necessary.

Earth has developed a global democratic system in the *Star Trek* future. It was not an easy transition to global democracy, as Earth suffered a number of horrible wars, including a nuclear holocaust during the Third World War. It appears that global democracy followed this period of war and nuclear devastation. The exact details of the emergence of global democracy are not clear, but it apparently developed from the political organizations of the European Union (noted in the episode, "Up the Long Ladder"). Also, although human nature has not fundamentally changed, a general awareness for the need of human and civil rights seems to have developed in the wake of a Third World War. In the *Star Trek* future, Earth is governed by a constitution similar to the American Constitution, and has entered a into a period of perpetual global renaissance. Alpha III, settled by humans, also has a democratic system. The Statues of Alpha III, cited by Samuel Cogley in "Court Martial," set the precedents for interstellar law, including the formation of an independent star system based on Plato's *Republic*.

Democracy is not an exclusive human product. Alpha Centauri, the first alien planet encountered by Earth explorers, has a global democratic government as well. A founding member of the Federation, it is home to the discoverer of warp speed, Zefram Cochrane, who was introduced in "Metamorphosis." Another alien world, Zeon, also is a democracy. Its effort to spread the democratic values of toleration and respect for others to its neighboring planet of Ekos resulted in a disastrous situation, eventually placing its home world at risk. Zeonian democracy was only saved after the situation at Ekos was resolved, with the help of Captain Kirk ("Patterns of Force").

Omega IV is governed by a document similar to the American Constitution. Its history paralleled Earth's twentieth-century contest between the "Yankees" (Yangs) and the "Communists" (Coms). Unlike on Earth, the Coms won a nuclear war in the past, and had since ruled Omega IV. The Yangs never accepted Com rule, and fought a centuries-long guerilla war against them in the name of the democratic principles enunciated in their Constitution. Over the centuries of armed resistance to the Coms, the Yangs had slurred the original meaning of their Constitution, and begun to consider it not as a political document, but as a sort of holy book, akin to the Bible. Upon their victory (which coincided with the starship *Enterprise*'s arrival at Omega IV), the Yang leadership promised to make their constitution's "holy words" the principles for the new government. However, when Captain Kirk realized that the Yangs intended to construct a limited oligarchical regime from their constitution, which—similar to the American Constitution—started with the words "We the People," he became quite angry. Perhaps in violation of the Federation's Prime Directive, which prohibits all Federation officers from interference in the political and social development of alien worlds, Kirk admonished the Yang leadership for having misinterpreted the meaning of their constitution: "'We the People' . . . are not just words for the chiefs or kings, or the warriors, or the rich or powerful, but for all the people! . . ." And later: "[D]own the centuries you have slurred the meaning [of these words] . . . they must apply to everyone or they mean nothing, do you understand?" ("The Omega Glory").

At that point, the Yangs promised Kirk that, although his interpretation of their constitution was difficult for them to understand, "the holy words" would be respected. It was left for us to assume they would construct a democratic regime. When Mr. Spock suggested that Kirk was in violation of the Prime Directive, he dismissed the criticism, stating that he was merely showing the people of Omega IV the meaning of their long struggle. In his lecture on the meaning of their constitution to the Yangs, Kirk stated that many of the worlds in the Federation also live by democratic rules. In spite of that observation, very few democracies were actually encountered in the *Star Trek* episodes. More often than not, governments on alien worlds fit into one of the other ideal-types.

Inclusive hegemonies are characterized by a high degree of participation in the society, but with low contestation of governmental policies. That is, although most of the population is encouraged by the ruling authorities to participate in the life of the nation, their rights to oppose governmental policies are sharply curtailed. Several of these regimes are members of the Federation.

Vulcan is perhaps the most noteworthy inclusive hegemony. As a result of its particular historical development, governmental rule is based on strict adherence to tradition. When a bloody civil war threatened to end life on the planet in its distant past, the great philosopher and leader, Surak, managed to stop the violence by convincing the warring sides to adopt the discipline of logic. Thereafter, all Vulcans were required to submit their natural emotive tendencies to the rigorous discipline of logic. One need only recall the absolute authority of High Priestess T'Pao to identify Vulcan as an inclusive hegemony. She expected all Vulcans to follow the discipline of logic, and none to question her authority ("Amok Time"). Since no deviance from the norm is allowed, any Vulcan who rejects the way of logic must leave the planet. In fact, the twin planets of Romulus and Remus were colonized by exiled Vulcans, who refused to conform to the discipline of logic, and built a world predicated upon the glory of military conquest. On Vulcan, once emotion was conquered by logic, an enduring global peace was realized.

Like Vulcan, Argelius also faced a bloody civil war in its distant past. A philosophical movement known as "The Great Awakening" convinced the Argelians to replace their brutal ways with the endless pursuit of pleasure. As pleasure became the planet's way of life, Argelius entered into a long period of peace and tranquility. All the citizens were encouraged to live by pleasure, and alien visitors were also welcome to participate in the hedonistic life-style. However, no citizens may question this fundamental tenet of Argelian society: any display of a negative emotion, especially jealousy, can result in severe punishment. Governmental rule is in the hands of a High Councillor, who has absolute power. Since Argelians are only interested in the pursuit of pleasure, the High Councillor has been forced to hire administrative officers from other planets. In the case of a violent crime, the High Councillor relies on the ancient code established before the Great Awakening for punishment, which allows for torture and/or the death penalty ("Wolf in the Fold").

The Ferengis are governed by an inclusive hegemony as well. Governmental rule is in the hands of a traditional leader, known as the Grand Nagus. He has absolute power, and his main responsibility is to expand Ferengi trade opportunities in the galaxy. Further, it is a patrimonial society, in which women are treated as slaves. All Ferengi males live by the "Ferengi Code," which is a set of ethical guidelines, based on the "285 Ferengi Rules of Acquisition." Illustrative of these rules are the following: (Rule 1) Once you have their money, you never give it back; (Rule 6) Never allow family to stand in the way of opportunity; (Rule 21) Never place friendship above profit; and (Rule 62) The riskier the road, the greater the profit ("Rules of Acquisition"). Children are expected to memorize and live by these rules for their entire lives. None are allowed to challenge the rules of social organization, which allocates social position and political power on the basis of personal wealth. Any deviation from the rules can result in serious punishment.

A competitive oligarchy is characterized by a high degree of contestation within the regime, but with restricted citizen participation. In the *Star Trek* world, these regimes tend to be dominated by aggressive military establishments. There are many notable competitive oligarchies in the *Star Trek* saga, and they represent the Federation's fiercest enemies.

The Klingon Empire is ruled by the military-dominated High Council, which excludes the common citizen from any participation. It is a ruthless society, governed by a strict adherence to military discipline. Further, women cannot belong to the High Council. In the movie *Star Trek VI*, Chancellor Gorkon's daughter Azetbur assumed her father's place as Council leader. However, the episode "Redemption, Part I" clearly establishes that women cannot be members of the High Council. The Empire was founded by Kahless the Unforgettable, who assumed power by killing the tyrant Molor in the planet's distant past ("Rightful Heir"). Although the economic crisis which followed the explosion on Praxis led to the improvement of relations with the Federation, Klingon continues to be governed by a competitive, tyrannical oligarchy ("Reunion"; "Sins of the Father").

The Romulus Star Empire is also governed by a competitive oligarchy. The Romulan race, rejecting Sarek's philosophy of pure logic, left Vulcan many years ago and now resides on the twin planets of Romulus and Remus. They are very curious and intelligent beings, governed by their passion. The Romulan leader, the "Praetor," has absolute power, and relies upon the military for his support. The citizens do have an elected body with restricted powers, the Romulan Senate, which is able to offer general recommendations to the Praetor on interstellar issues, but mostly is responsible for domestic concerns ("Balance of Terror"; "Unification, Parts I and II").

The Cardassian Union is also governed by a military-dominated council. Although there is some disagreement within the military establishment over policy issues, Cardassian citizens have been systematically excluded from governmental policy questions ("The Wounded"). In its past, Cardassia was the home to a great civilization, based on peace and spiritual values ("Chain of Command"). For unknown reasons, that civilization collapsed. Lacking natural resources, starvation and disease followed the collapse, and the planet entered into an extended period of decline. At that point the military assumed power, and has since funnelled the planet's meager resources to the effort to conquer other worlds. Millions of Cardassian citizens have died in the war effort.

There are a number of other less known competitive hegemonies in the *Star Trek* saga. Andor, although a member of the Federation, is a closed hegemony. This insectoid-humanoid race is said to make excellent warriors ("Journey to Babel"). The Gorns of Tau Lacertae IX are dominated by their military establishment as well. Although it appears that they were justified in their military attack on the Earth outpost Cestus III, they are a hostile, military-dominated race. Indeed, the Metron who intervened in the conflict between the Gorns and the starship *Enterprise* was quite sure that the Gorn commander would have killed Captain Kirk, if he had won their hand-to-hand combat ("Arena"). The Tholians are also dominated by their military establishment. Little is actually known about the Tholians, but several references to military conquests in the name of the Tholian Assembly have been made ("Tholian Web"; "The Icarus Factor"; "Peak Performance").

The opposite of a democracy, a closed hegemony sharply restricts both public contestation and participation of its citizens. That is, closed hegemonic regimes limit both participation and public contestation. Typically, these regimes are ruled by a dictatorship. Surprisingly, some closed hegemonies are also members of the Federation.

Federation member Ardania is ruled by a small elite class, which lives in the Stratos Cloud City. The working class, which maintains Ardania's economic viability by mining zenite, is forced to live on the planet's cold surface. On the surface, the working class is exposed to a dangerous, natural gas which dulls their mental abilities. Consequently, a clear class distinction has developed based on mental abilities and societal function. The only workers allowed to live in Stratos are those trained to serve the elite class. Opposition to the ruling class is not tolerated, and order is maintained by the arbitrary use of a pain machine. After the intervention of Captain Kirk, some changes may have occurred in Ardania's political life and social organization ("The Cloud Minders").

Gideon is also ruled by a small council which does not tolerate civil opposition. When the Council sought to resolve the planet's overpopulation problem, it did not seek the input of its population. Instead, it decided to set a disease free on the population in order to kill off a portion of it. The dictatorial Council refused other solutions to the problem, such as the resettlement of a percentage of the population to other suitable planets ("The Mark of Gideon").

Three cases of closed hegemonies paralleled Earth's totalitarian past. The planet known as "Planet 892-IV" was ruled by a twentieth-century version of ancient Rome. Unlike on Earth, the Roman Empire did not fall on Planet 892-IV, and was led by a ruthless Proconsul ("Bread and Circuses"). On Ekos, Federation historian John Gill attempted to create a benevolent form of Nazi Germany. Calling it Earth's most efficient society, he sought to recreate a productive form of the regime to develop Ekos. His effort went awry, and an evil dictatorship sprung up. The Nazi leadership dedicated Ekos to the eradication of the people of Zeon, their peaceful neighboring planet ("Patterns of Force"). Earth colony Taurus IV is another example of a closed hegemony. When a food shortage threatened mass starvation there, Kodos, the colony's governor, declared martial law. Reasoning that execution was better than starvation, he decided to execute four thousand colonists. After a Federation supply ship arrived two days later, Kodos disappeared, and eluded capture from the Federation authorities for twenty years ("The Conscience of the King").

Star Trek presents an interesting twist to the classic humanoid closed hegemonic regime model, by adding those dominated by sophisticated machines and/or by computers. These closed hegemonic regimes are characterized by the machine/computer domination of the organic body.

The Borg collective is a closed, machine-dominated hegemony. Born humanoids, cybernetic devices are implanted into the individual Borgs, starting at birth. These devices link all of the Borg to a sophisticated subspace communications network, unifying the organic bodies under the control of the collective mind. Specialized tasks are divided up among the Borg, following the organic model of a body. That is, as the arms and legs have specific functions to enable the organic body to perform, various Borgs perform specialized functions so that the collective can achieve certain tasks. Consequently, all the Borg work as one, and the concept of individual rights is alien to them. Any natural organic instincts are under the control of the machine implants ("Q Who?"; "The Best of Both Worlds, Parts I and II").

The Binars are a humanoid species, who are integrated into a so-phisticated planetary computer network which orients their society and government. They do not function as individuals, but live in pairs, and are electronically connected to one another to quicken the exchange of data among them. They rely upon the computer system for the regula-tion of their government and society, and as illustrated in the episode "11001001," are lost without it.

Beta III is also governed by a complex computer system. De-signed in the planet's past by Beta III's foremost cultural scientist, Landru, the computer system was supposed to help successive gen-erations develop peacefully. Over time, the machine misinterpreted Landru's rules for a proper organization of society, and eventually imposed a social and cultural dictatorship on the people. It main-tained control by forcing all of its people to enter into reprogram-ming booths, where they are programmed to act according to Landru's rules. No deviation from the norm was permitted. The people, unaware that a computer was in charge, de-evolved into a very primitive state ("Return of the Archons").

The citizens of Gamma Tranguli VI worship a computer system named Vaal. This system regulates the planet's climate and food pro-duction on the planet, enabling the people to live thousands of years. Apparently, the computer could turn organic material into energy, which was provided for it by the humanoids of the planet. Under the control of the computer, the citizens were healthy, but their civi-lization was kept in a primitive state ("The Apple").

The Fabrini people are also under the absolute control of a com-puter system. In this case, when the Fabrini's home planet's original sun was about to nova, their ancestors built a spaceship—known as Yonada—to transport the people to a new world. Yonada was constructed to resemble Fabrini in every way, so as not to alarm the people. Some-how, their ancestors managed to board a significant percentage of the population on Yonada without anyone realizing that it was a spaceship, and it left Fabrini on a ten-thousand year voyage to a new and uninhab-ited planet. On board, the computer, called the Oracle, regulated all fac-ets of life, and the people on the ship were neither aware that it was a spaceship, nor that a computer controlled their lives. The Oracle only spoke to the High Priestess, who communicated its orders to the people. Societal order was maintained by a pain-inflicting device, inserted be-neath the earlobe at birth. The Oracle was constantly monitoring the people's thoughts, and any improper questioning was immediately met

191

by intense pain, or by death ("For The Earth is Hollow and I Have Touched the Sky").

There were also a number of highly evolved organic beings that imposed a dictatorship on their subjects. These closed hegemonies forbade participation and contestation.

On Talos IV, a nuclear holocaust had forced these evolved beings to live underground. Their mental abilities were so great that they could control lesser species by making them see, think, experience and hear anything they wanted. This ability became a dangerous narcotic to them: as their minds developed, their bodies weakened. Over time, they lost the abilities to fix the most basic scientific equipment. Since they did not possess the skills to rebuild their planet, they decided to capture alien races and create a "breeding" stock of lesser-evolved races who would be tricked into rebuilding their world. Their plan was exposed by Captain Christopher Pike of the *Enterprise*, and Talos IV was declared off-limits by the Federation. Indeed, the Federation's only remaining death penalty is for those who go to Talos IV ("The Cage"; "The Menagerie, Parts I and II").

The Platonius people were originally from the star system Sahndara. They left their planet as their sun was about to nova, and travelled to Earth around 440 B.C.. On Earth, they studied under Plato, and decided to model life on their new planet, called Platonius, after Plato's teaching. Shortly after their arrival at Platonius, however, they developed extraordinary telekinetic powers, and abandoned the quest for truth and beauty. Instead, the Platonians concentrated on developing their mental powers, and chose a man named Parem to be their leader because he had the strongest powers. No philosopher king, Parem ruled tyrannically, and used his powers to force the weaker minds to tend to his desires. During this time, the Platonians neglected the basic sciences, so when Parem became sick with an infection, they did not know what to do. Fortunately for Parem, the starship *Enterprise* was in their area, and Dr. McCoy was able to treat him. On Plantoneus, Dr. McCoy's research revealed that trace quantities of kironide present in the planet's soil were responsible for the telekinetic abilities of the people. When Parem decided to keep Dr. McCoy as his personal physician—against McCoy's wishes—Captain Kirk and Mr. Spock managed to consume enough of the substance to achieve superior telekinetic abilities than Parem, and gain their freedom ("Plato's Stepchildren").

The Triskelin beings were made up of organic brain materials, and used their great mental abilities to control less-evolved species. They captured alien beings, called thralls, and transported them to their planet by pure thought waves. For entertainment, they bet among each other on forced physical contests involving the thralls. When Kirk, who had been captured as a thrall, realized that the Triskelin beings viewed him the way humans treated, say, race horses, he understood that the only way to gain his freedom was to make a wager with them, and win ("The Gamesters of Triskelon").

The *Star Trek* saga has presented a number of highly advanced, noncorporeal entities, who seem to have no need for government as we know it. These entities, however, do seem to exist in a community of self-governing similar beings, such as Organia, the Metron Civilization, and the "Q" Continuum.

The Organians created the illusion of an ancient village for the use of travellers to their planet. When a war almost broke out on their planet between the Federation and the Klingon Empire, they revealed themselves to be self-governing beings of pure energy. Before explaining any more about themselves, they asked Captain Kirk and Mr. Spock to leave ("Errand of Mercy").

Another noncorporeal race, the Metron Civilization, only presented themselves to the Federation to stop a conflict between the starship *Enterprise* and a Gorn vessel. Captain Kirk was informed the Federation was still too primitive for them ("Arena"). The "Q" Continuum is a mystery as well. "Q" was a very powerful, extradimensional being who appeared regularly to Captain Picard and his crew. Very little is known about the governing structure of the continuum ("Encounter at Far Point, Part I and II"; "Hide and Q"; "Q Who?"; "QPid"; "Deja Q"; "True Q"; "Tapestry"; "Q-Less").

The *Star Trek* saga does not present a deterministic view of politics or history, and suggests no universal patterns for the various forms of government. Rather, and as illustrated in Figure Two, it locates the cause for its various governments in the imprecise and unquantifiable variables of the behavioral style of leaders, their beliefs and personalities, and how they deal with the demands of crisis moments. In that regard, neither advanced technologies nor evolved beings are a guarantor for a civilized, democratic regime. The many computer-dominated closed hegemonies demonstrate that advanced technologies do not guarantee democracy, and as indicated by Talus IV and Platoneus, more evolved species may even be more tyrannical than lesser ones.

FIGURE TWO

CLASSIFICATION OF THE STAR TREK GOVERNMENTS

Ideal Type V
Meta-Governmental Societies
Organia
Metron Civilization
The Q Continuum

```
P C  |High
U O  |Ideal Type III            Ideal Type I
B N  |Competitive Oligarchy     Democracy
L T  | Andor                    Alpha III
I E  | Cardassia                Alpha Centarus
C S  | Tau Lauceratae IX        Earth
  T  | Tholia II                Zeon
  A  | Romulus                  Omega IV
  T  | Klingon Homeworld
  I  |
  O  |
  N  |
     |Ideal Type IV             Ideal Type II
     |Closed Hegemony           Inclusive Hegemony
     | Ardania                  Argelius II
     | Angosia III              Ferengi
     | Capella IV               Vulcan
     | Gideon
     | Eminiar III
     | Ekos
     |
     | Ideal Type IV (a)
     | Computer-Dominated Closed Hegemony
     | Beta III
     | Borg
     | Binars
     | Gamma Tria
     | Yonada
     |
     | Ideal Type IV (b)
     | Organic Brain-Dominated Closed Hegemony
     | Talos IV
     | Platoneus
     | Triskelen
     |
     |Low                                    High
```

RIGHT TO PARTICIPATE IN ELECTIONS AND OFFICE

Source: Adapted from Dahl, *Polyarchy*, 6.

On the other hand, those governmental structures of alien worlds depicted as bleak, military-dominated oligarchies, such as the Klingon Empire, the Romulan Star Empire, or the Cardassian Union, do not have to be that way, and could change. It is conceivable that they could evolve in more peaceful directions, if the military authorities in charge were somehow outmaneuvered by leaders committed to peaceful policies. Conversely, as the evil Federation presented in the episode "Mirror, Mirror" clearly illustrates, democracy on Earth was not inevitable and the Federation did not have to be committed to peace. Further, although *Star Trek* clearly espouses the unabashedly normative position that democracy is the most desirable political system available, democratic regimes do not thrive in the *Star Trek* world. The starship *Enterprise* was far more likely to encounter an alien world based on some sort of dictatorship. In the face of these dim prospects for democracy, Captain Kirk and Captain Picard often lectured alien worlds about the virtues of governmental policies favoring human and civil rights. They have each made the case that the only true guarantee for a democratic regime is the appropriate political will.

Finally, *Star Trek*'s primacy of the political has not only made for intriguing story lines, in which the actions of the actors can make a difference to the outcome, but it also teaches us that our political future is in our hands. Certainly, Captain Kirk's claim that "in every revolution, there is one man with a vision," was well illustrated when Captain Picard sent the Borg known as Hugh—who had been given an awareness of his individuality by the *Enterprise* crew—back into the Borg collective. As we later learned, that one Borg caused even the impenetrable Borg collective to change ("I, Borg"). Indeed, in all of its many incarnations, the *Star Trek* saga has consistently epitomized the point that the political future can be bright or dim, depending on what we do now.

Works Cited

Dahl, Robert A. 1971. *Polyarchy.* New Haven: Yale University Press.

Johnson, Shane. 1989. *The Worlds of the Federation.* New York: Pocket Books.

Lipset, Seymour Martin, Juan J. Linz and Larry Diamond, eds. 1989. *Democracy in Developing Countries.* Boulder: Lynne Rienner.

Okuda, Michael, Denise Okuda and Debbie Mirek. 1994. *The Star Trek Encyclopedia: A Guide to the Future.* New York: Pocket Books.

Schumpter, Joseph A. 1962. *Capitalism, Socialism and Democracy.* New York: Harper Torchbooks.

Chapter 12

Military, Democracy, and the State in Robert A. Heinlein's *Starship Troopers*

Everett Carl Dolman

For who ought to be more faithful than a man entrusted with the safety of his country and sworn to defend it with the last drop of his blood?
                                        Niccolo Machiavelli, The Art of War.

Probably Robert A. Heinlein's most controversial book (Franklin 110), *Starship Troopers* has weathered a storm of adverse protest since it won the Hugo award as 1959's best science fiction novel—a fact "critics and reviewers have been apologizing [for] ever since" (Showalter 113). Jack Williamson called *Starship Troopers* a "dark, disturbing novel, set in a time of vicious space war and devoted to the glorification of the fighting man" (30). The shrillest denunciation may have come from Luc Sante, who claimed Heinlein's work "approaches fascism" and "was a major influence on Charles Manson" (69). Sante condemns the entire body of science fiction, but is particularly vitriolic concerning *Starship Troopers* and its 1961 follow-on *Stranger in a Strange Land*. (Both novels suffer the fascism barb, but it is *Stranger in a Strange Land*, "the bible of psychedelic zealotry" which is singled out as Manson's mentor.) In one of the few published defenses of *Starship Troopers*, Leon Stover suggests "the critics hated it" in part because "it is only by his dislike of the military that the liberal culture critic earns his credentials" (46–8). The latter observation appears as reactionary as any of the hostile critiques, but it serves to focus the debate.

For many of *Starship Troopers'* detractors, the occurrence of democratic and military values in a single state is the embodiment of paradox. These two ideals are thought to be at least contrary, if not mutually exclusive, and denunciations of the political utopia described in *Starship Troopers* are generally variations on this theme. Support for this position is historically naive, however, and is based in subjective perception rather than objective argument. There is ample evidence for a very close and parallel evolution of military structure and democratic values, and this relationship has had enormous impact on the emergence of the modern democratic state (Manicas; Porter 20, 214–5). Max Weber stated the case flatly: "The basis for democracy is everywhere purely military in character" (324). The salient issue becomes not whether military and democratic values can coexist, but can the truly democratic state independently emerge—much less maintain itself—without the democratizing influence of the authoritarianly organized military to nurture it?

Starship Troopers' Terran Federation, Heinlein's last attempt to articulate a perfect government (Smith 159), describes the ultimate embrace of both military and democratic ideals within a single state. This fantasy utopia lends itself to an historical comparison of the positive effects of the military on liberty and personal freedom. Such a comparison will also highlight the inherent potential threat to liberty the military poses simply by its existence (see Finer; Nordlinger; Downing). If, in this idealized state, militarism can be recognized as an ever-present menace, then, *a fortiori*, the danger it represents is even more critical for existing democracies.

Broadly drawn, the Terran Federation is a liberal, representative democracy. All *residents* are protected by the state's constitution, and enjoy the same legal rights and privileges as *citizens* with two exceptions: only citizens may participate in politics—vote and (presumably) hold public office—and only citizens have access to select civil service positions (e.g., state police). Citizenship is open to all, regardless of race, creed, religion, gender, or handicap, but it is not a birthright. It can be acquired only through demonstrated service to the state. A resident, upon reaching the age of eighteen, may formally volunteer for appropriate qualifying service. That service can include any number of rather unpleasant duties, such as mundane labor or clerical chores on a remote research colony, but it is explicitly understood that volunteers unconditionally present themselves for possible military assignment. Of course, the volunteer may request alternate duty, but the needs of the state determine placement. Upon satisfactory completion of two years service (which can be involuntarily and indefinitely extended by the state), the volunteer is discharged and granted suffrage.

Such a simple notion, a test of worthiness in exchange for political franchise, is not without precedent. Proof of residency, poll taxes, property qualifications, and even competency exams have all been employed or proposed to gauge electorate responsibility. Qualifiers such as these have been routinely recognized as acceptable within a democratic society as long as they are applied in uniform fashion. The most basic, the requirement that a citizen must reach a specified age of maturity before being recognized as responsible enough to cast a ballot, is not seriously challenged. The cutoff may be debated (e.g., age eighteen or twenty-one), but the principle is rarely attacked. The citizen who meets community-defined standards of responsibility to—or a vested interest in—the welfare of the body politic, is thought to be more likely to vote responsibly when that privilege is exercised. Heinlein's test of worthiness goes well beyond the quibbling inconvenience of these slight qualifiers, however. It requires real sacrifice, perhaps even the ultimate forfeiture of personal liberty—death.

Despite Heinlein's contention that the vast majority of volunteers will be assigned to non-military service, and those selected for military duty are not forced to serve against their will (indeed, a soldier may renounce his or her quest for franchise by resigning at any time—including the moment before battle), it is this demand that citizenship be integrally linked to military service that concerns the critics of *Starship Troopers*. Alexi Panshin equates *Starship Troopers* to a recruiting film and labels it a "military polemic [, any] other reading is not possible" (94–5). Bruce Franklin flatly states that it "glorifies militarism" (123). While it is true that *Starship Troopers* celebrates the harsh military lifestyle and commends the role of its virtuous alumni in government, it is altogether uncertain that the Terran Federation exemplifies or promotes militarism.

In order to clarify the argument, it is necessary to set some of the terms of the debate. Alfred Vagts's 1937 classic, *A History of Militarism*, begins by distinguishing the "military way" from militarism. The military way is in essence the art of battle, "winning specific objectives of power with the utmost efficiency" (11). It is limited to the functions of war. Militarism, on the other hand, is unlimited in scope and transcends strictly military purposes. Militarism has a tendency to permeate and become dominant over society. In so doing, it takes on the characteristics of "caste and cult, authority, and belief" (11). In order to clarify his definition, Vagts lists several characteristics which distinguish militarism.

The first of these is domination of the military over civilians. This refers to political dominance, official supremacy in which military leaders conduct the affairs of state. Heinlein employs the figure of a wise sergeant lecturing a wayward trainee on the importance of civilian control of the military to dispel any philosophical attachment to this characteristic (*Starship Troopers* 52, 120). Soldiers, he asserts, rightly determine the strategies and tactics of battle, but never the propriety of the fight, nor how far to prosecute that fight once committed. Such decisions belong only to "statesmen" (*Starship Troopers* 52).

Vagts's second characteristic of militarism, an emphasis on "military considerations, spirits, ideals, and scales of value in the life of states" (Vagts 12), is not so quickly dismissed. In *Starship Troopers*, Heinlein's hero revels in his soldierly accomplishments. Pride emanates from the knowledge that he has endured hardships in training most civilians will never approximate. He exults in the camaraderie of friendships formed in battle. He believes his peers are morally superior to civilians because they have fought for their beliefs, and he places loyalty to them above all others. They are men and women of honor. This structurally induced arrogance is without doubt a seed of militarism, but it is still far removed from the militarist state. Military esprit is essential in the development of quality soldiers. Morale is the backbone of battle, and is appropriately stressed in training. Soldiers must be trained to feel they are superior to any force they should encounter on the battlefield as a method of inflaming their passion to fight (*Starship Troopers* 121). The practice is properly part of Vagts's military way.

The continued maintenance of a large standing army in peacetime is Vagts's third characteristic. Militarism, he claims, is concerned with "all the activities, institutions, and qualities not actually needed for war" (Vagts 39). As such, it is more likely to hamper than to hearten the principles of the military way, for it undermines proper military efficiency.

Militarism is thus more likely to surface during peace than war, assuming a large and idle military establishment. Heinlein is not specific on this issue, but it seems clear that he opposes such an institution. His military is never particularly large in relation to the rest of government. Military personnel should comprise less than five percent of the active federal service at any time (argued in a non-fiction essay in Heinlein's *Expanded Universe* 397), and these numbers should never be inflated by non-combat "support" units or a bloated officer corps (*Starship Troopers* 164).

Vagts's fourth characteristic encompasses the first three and is identified as an encroaching military dominion over previously civilian activities. Heinlein's Federation seems to have struck a stable balance between military and civilian functions, and no encroachment is apparent, but the cynic may argue there is simply nothing meaningful left to usurp. Lastly, Vagts warns that militarism can be discerned whenever the military no longer serves the state, and begins to serve only itself. The Oath of Federal Service every *Starship Troopers* volunteer takes upon induction makes it the recruit's sworn duty to obey "lawful" orders of the (civilian) Commander-in-Chief and all military officers of superior rank or position. Lawful means in compliance with the requirement to "protect and defend the Constitutional liberties of all citizens and lawful residents of the state" (30). Throughout *Starship Troopers*, the central character repeatedly professes his pride in serving to uphold the freedoms of the nonmilitary community.

Starship Troopers' Terran Federation, in the context of Vagts's argument, does not evoke a classic definition of militarism. It is reasonable to suspect, however, that the Federation's political stability is fragile, and its present commitment to democracy may someday be undermined by the pressures of a military cadre predisposed to elitism. This is disturbing, and will be addressed later. First, it should prove useful to compare *Starship Troopers'* vision of the military role in government with historical and political references that support the contention the military can, and does, have a positive effect in the evolution of the democratic state. The democratic state, in turn, empowers and enhances the capability of the military force. This dynamic of association was briefly outlined by Otto Hintze, a liberal Prusso-German constitutional historian, in his 1906 essay, "Military Organization and State Organization." Hintze argued that, originally, all political association sprang from the need for collective defensive or offensive action (181). To paraphrase

Charles Tilly, war made the state, and then the state made war. Hintze persuasively charts the concurrent rise of democratic and representational government with the absolute growth in the size of military organizations, and equates this relationship to a recurring historical pattern. Central to his vision is the notion that those who fight for the state rule the state.

Examples from primitive society, when all able-bodied males were members of the warrior class, and more taken from the record of antiquity, when the citizen-soldier became a predominant model, support the Hintzian argument. The subsequent decline of mass representational ideals and corresponding decrease in the size of armed formations in the Dark and Middle Ages are further illuminating. But, it is the irrefutable record of the modern European era which draws the strongest positive parallel between military and state organization. With the passing of the Age of Chivalry, when individual knights on horseback were proven inferior in battle to masses of organized infantry, the population of armies by necessity grew. As their size increased, recruitment bases expanded. The nobility, who fought in exchange for political recognition from their sovereign, supplemented by mercenaries who accepted cash payment for their services, could no longer fill the ranks of military formations. The state looked toward militias of guildsmen, landed peasants, and merchant-privateers to augment its force pool.

In order to coerce large portions of the population to fight for the state, the state was forced to reciprocate by granting or endowing individuals with proportional franchise in the affairs of government. When it matters little who rules—the lot of individuals being such that the replacement of one despotism by another does not materially affect their condition—the individual is poorly motivated to engage in battle to support the existing realm. When an individual has been endowed with certain rights and privileges, and a change in government could alter the relationship of the state and the individual, that person may become highly motivated to participate in war. These newly motivated combatants could in turn be counted on to fight with greater elan than their mercenary counterparts (an argument forcefully made by Machiavelli in *The Art of War*), and thus the democratization of the state plays a role in increasing the effective fighting force of the military.

In a most spectacular example of the growth of military force, J.-B. Colbert, under Louis XIV, and then his son in the next generation and finally Napoleon manipulated the libertine enthusiasm of the French to fashion the largest citizen-army the world had ever known. The source of that growth was a national political awakening, according to Hintze, that came from the "two-sided education" of military service which planted in the soldier's mind an image of the state as "an affair not merely of the rulers but of the ruled and being conceived of as a community" (Hintze 207). David Rappoport concurs, "in all periods of history, [states have] utilized the military experience to educate the citizen to his public responsibility" (Rappoport 80). Faced with the threat of emancipated and armed throngs on their borders, rival European powers were forced to follow the French model and recruit thousands of previously disenfranchised into their own armed forces. Before they could count on the loyalty of these masses, they had to be endowed with some rights of citizenry. Precedent to the establishment of military forces of modern scale came the emancipation of the European population from serfdom (Hintze 212; Andreski 68–70).

The lesson of the French Revolution pertinent to *Starship Troopers'* Terran Federation may be the subsequent history of militarism that flowed from it. Despite the obvious fact that liberating the masses created the Republic, that same action became its downfall. Fisher Ames's famous pronouncement that "a democracy cannot last" is based in his belief that the inevitable result of democracy, by its very nature, must be mob rule, which "dictates that its next change shall be into a military despotism" (Ames 92). In France, the multitudes were moved by their "mobbish" passions to take arms against the monarchy. The leaders of the Revolution, upon seizing power, found that a disciplined force is much easier to control and manipulate than a free mob, and quickly organized the people into formations of national guards. An army thus formed, says Ames, is a "democracy in regiments and brigades," and such "a military government may make a nation great, but it cannot make [its people] free" (95).

The story of the rise of the citizen-army prompts another lesson. By arming the population to defend the state, the state provides the masses with the power to overthrow it and establish a new government. The newly armed citizen-army may now pose a greater menace than any foreign threat to the continued existence of the state. Vagts claims the nineteenth-century Liberal-Tory argument in England was mired in just this dilemma; whether the continually armed masses would gravitate toward militarism and thus become a threat to (Liberal view) or a protection of (Tory view) the institution of liberty (Ames 167).

If arming the population decreases the threat of foreign invasion but increases the likelihood of rebellion, and, conversely, disarming the population, while suppressing the tendency for revolt, invites foreign adventurism (Vagts 168), how can the state preserve itself? Heinlein believes he has solved this dilemma by only arming members of the state who are predisposed to loyalty toward it, evidenced by their willingness to *volunteer* to serve it. In a much-maligned passage, he contends "revolution is impossible" in the Terran Federation because "armed uprising [requires] not only dissatisfaction but aggressiveness. . . . If you separate out the aggressive [members of society] and make them the sheepdogs [through military service], the sheep will never give you any trouble" (*Starship Troopers* 146).

Hintze offers a structural solution. The military can be thought to have two primary roles: defense of the state from external threat and defense of the government from internal threat. The former role is conducive to liberty and democracy, for it protects and nurtures society. Without a military force to protect it, democratic society would fall prey to neighboring expansionist authoritarian states. The latter role is obviously not conducive to liberty and democracy. In effect, the military becomes a tool of oppression. Hintze notes that a military structure dominated by the army is prone to succumbing to the latter role, but a structure dominated by the navy is not. This is because the navy is a poor and inefficient occupier of territory. It has tremendous power projection but little or no ability to sway internal public opinion. For this reason, nations which have traditionally relied on naval power for state security have developed relatively more democratic and libertine constitutions than their contemporaries (213–15, e.g. Britain and the United States; Vagts 13, 356). In *Starship Troopers* the distinction holds, and bodes well for the maintenance of democracy. The Mobile Infantry (MI), despite its appellation as a ground force, is, in the age of interplanetary warfare, a component of the space navy, a military organization of offensive force projection. It concentrates incredible firepower in the hands of a few small units deployed on highly mobile spaceships. Their mission is to go in, create havoc, and get out. Like the navies of nineteenth-century Britain, which controlled the empire by controlling communications and transportation lines (Mahan; Keeghan, 110), the MI secures the safety of the Terran Federation by *forcing the other side* to maintain defensive positions. Heinlein makes a considerable effort to show the folly of a popular call for retreat to a defensive perimeter, which would make the MI an army of occupation and a clear threat to democracy, following the alien enemy's "smear[ing]" of Buenos Aires (*Starship Troopers* 106). Though Heinlein was espousing a military doctrine, it has the effect of conforming to sound policy of antimilitarist civilian control as well.

The macro view of military-democratic interaction, in which the structures of one institution affect the evolution and organization of the other, readily transforms into a micro view, in which a spiraling interaction of individual rights conferred and rights demanded takes place. The military veteran, armed and now steeled in battle, will demand more rights and greater access than previously granted by the state. These demands cannot be ignored by the government, as the soldier has the potential power to take those rights by force, and these demands will continue until the citizen feels completely enfranchised.

This path to franchise is commonly accepted. The notion that a military veteran should enjoy full rights of citizenship is "an implicit social contract" virtually universal in the modern democratic state (Berryman 10; Segal 10). Yet more than just the right to vote (franchise) is implicit in the journey toward citizenship. Equality is the ultimate goal. During the United States Civil War, Joseph Glatthaar writes that "colored" volunteers enthusiastically enlisted to aid in the fight to abolish slavery. After having fought gallantly, they let it be known that "their ultimate goal had been equal rights with whites" (231).

This characterization of the military identifies a pivotal ingredient in the evolution of the democratic state. In a direct metamorphosis, the transformation of soldier to citizen has a leveling effect on society. For example, Charles Moskos emphasizes the military's traditional role as the poor's employer of last resort (136). Individuals too disadvantaged to find respectable vocations within the community have used military enlistment as an outlet for upward social mobility. This function is reinforced by the military's accepted policy of recruiting at the social margin (Moskos 150). Heinlein is acutely aware of this influence. In *Starship Troopers*, the hero's father, a wealthy upper class entrepreneur opposed to his son's enlistment, calls the military "a decidedly expensive way for inferior people who otherwise would be unemployed to live at public expense for a term of years, then give themselves over to airs" (23). In the United States, the issue has been argued since at least the 1814 draft debates when proponents of James Monroe's conscription scheme averred that an all-volunteer force must necessarily cull its recruits from the "dregs of society" (Lacey 200). Indeed, Vagts contends civilianization of the army necessitated the dismantlement of European monarchical systems, as it led to the "intermixture and equalization of the classes" (171).

Heinlein's treatment of equality in the military is quite casual. His hero, Juan Rico, is Hispanic. No attempt is made to explain or justify this decision, and none of the other characters pay any attention to it. This convention is unusual for a 1950s mass-market novel targeted to the young, white, American middle class. It is accepted as a literary given. Fred Erisman has investigated Heinlein's assumption that men and women who train and fight together quickly become comfortable with egalitarianism, and traces this standard to 1948 with the publication of *Space Cadet* (217). This is not to say that Heinlein's characters are color- and gender-blind. Far from it. Heinlein's philosophy is highly individualistic. He takes note of the physical and mental inequalities among peoples while intractably maintaining their equality before the law. His heroes routinely notice and admire the exemplifying characteristics of individuals and social groups, characteristics that enhance their value to society or profession, but never knowingly or maliciously denigrate. Women, for example, make better pilots than men (*Starship Troopers* 8, 161). The duties they perform are different than the duties of men (the combat infantry is apparently all male), but surely no less important. Their status and rank is therefore not parallel (separate but equal) but fully integrated into the military structure (see Tucker 184–85). Nonetheless, Heinlein is an oblivious sexist. He admires the special abilities of women and profoundly believes they should be fully and equitably integrated into society, but he cannot seem to resist attaching a superfluous comment on how "cute" or otherwise attractive the competent woman may be (e.g., "I fully realized that she was really an officer and a fighting man—as well as a very pretty girl" [*Starship Troopers* 139]). He is not, as are most chauvinists, aware of his insulting demeanor, and believes he is being complimentary as opposed to objectifying. This is not a defense of Heinlein's indefensible position, it is intended only to clarify his position.

One of the more salient points in the debate against the use of military service for suffrage hinges on the valid argument that it can automatically disenfranchise those unable to serve, including women and the disabled (Cohen 121–3). But this is an artificial constraint easily removed. Heinlein relieves the Terran Federation of this injustice by requiring the government to find suitable positions for any resident who desires franchise. Once embraced by the system, their gender and handicaps are a descriptive, not an encumbrance. One of Heinlein's fiercer characters is an instructor in the art of "dirty fighting" (an apparently desirable and indispensable military proficiency) who happens to be paralyzed from the neck down. This "minor impediment" (138) may have limited the character's range of employment options, but it certainly did not interfere with his ability to instruct his young charges or his opportunity for dignified status within the system.

True social equality does not come easily in a stratified society. It is one thing to desire integration and another to implement it. Here, too, the military has certain advantages. The rigid disciplinarian and hierarchical structure of the military has been tapped by the democratic state to transform the armed forces into a twentieth-century laboratory of social engineering. Liberal reformers have been able to dictate equality measures to the military that civilian society has been unprepared or reluctant to accept. When it became apparent during World War II that the second class citizenship of black Americans was a national embarrassment, and that it was moreover a cancer on free society (Myrdal), civilian government stepped in to enforce the process of integration. The first arena of social change was the military. From 1939 to 1953, the United States moved from a policy of restricting and segregating black Americans to one of equal opportunity and integration (Dalfume 1). President Truman's Executive Order 9981 (1948), which dictated the integration of the armed forces, preceded the landmark Supreme Court school segregation decision (*Brown vs. Board of Education*) by six years. Having experienced true equality in the army, black Americans returning to their homes in the 1950s could not reconcile their previous position with society's contempt. Truman's order and its rapid and complete compliance within the armed forces was undoubtedly a primary stimulus for the modern civil rights movement. The transformation of the military into an egalitarian core within the whole of society has made it a vanguard of positive social change.

Arguably the most politically suppressed social group in the modern democratic state is women. Whereas minorities defined by race or class have had the advantage of military service to press their claims and polish their credentials for full citizenship, women have traditionally been denied this avenue toward equality. Sue Berryman is explicit: "If women are equally subject to the draft and combat duty, those in power have substantially less moral basis for denying women full political and economic rights in the society" (87; Segal ch. 5). Even with only partial access to combat duties, however, the positive impetus for democracy inspired by military service is notable. Binkim and Bach observe that women in the armed forces can already achieve a social status "far superior to many of their civilian peers" (37–8). The surety in their status that women gain from "egalitarian principles" within their admittedly proscribed military roles make it "conceivable that upon completion of military service, women might be more inclined to participate in the political process" (38).

Unfortunately for society's minorities, the attainment of upward social mobility through the military is not an automatic function of participation. It requires exceptionally valorous service on the battlefield. Cameron and Blackstone reveal that during the 1960s, when 11 percent of the United States population between 18 and 21 years old was black, just 9.8 percent of total service personnel assigned to the Vietnam theater of operations was black, but 20 percent of combat forces and 25 percent of elite combat troops were black (Cameron and Blackstone 1). Stating, "the moral dilemma is obvious," Berryman notes that by 1983, when the American military no longer relied on conscripts but had become an all-volunteer force, 29 percent of all United States combat troops were black (Berryman 82). The obvious fact that minorities are shouldering an unfair burden in the defense of democracy should enhance their rightful claim to full citizenship.

Heinlein is a zealous advocate of the military role in shaping the democratic perceptions of both soldier and society. *Starship Troopers* is, plainly, the story of one young man's entry into government service for the purpose of becoming a citizen and earning franchise. As has been shown, this path to citizenship is acceptable enough; what is distasteful to Heinlein's critics is that he makes it the only route. Still, had this been the core of Heinlein's vision, *Starship Troopers* would have been merely controversial. The charge that inflames is not Heinlein's insistence that only veterans should have the *right* to vote, it is his contention that only those who have served their country through federal service are *worthy* to vote. Heinlein throws down the gauntlet when he has his protagonist correctly answer the question, "What is the moral difference, if any, between the soldier and the civilian?" "The difference," Rico states confidently, "lies in the field of civic virtue. A soldier accepts personal responsibility for the safety of the body politic of which he is a member, defending it, if need be, with his life. The civilian does not" (24; see also 143–5).

Heinlein has insulted the patriotism of every civilian who has not served in the military. Surely *battle* cannot be the only test of loyalty and love of country. The overwhelming negative response *Starship Troopers* received should not have been surprising. Nonetheless, this principle alone is the key to Heinlein's vision of political utopia. Only responsible citizens should participate in politics, and the most sincere demonstration of that responsibility is a verifiable offering of one's life for the benefit of the state. Voluntarism is crucial. Heinlein abhors the use of conscripts, even in war (*Expanded Universe* 397). No other qualifier, not property, nor some test of political acumen, is necessary. Heinlein emphasizes this point by having a physician conducting entrance examinations sarcastically admonish new recruits for desiring to enlist. "Military service is for ants," he declares, young people misguidedly sign on for a "purely nominal political privilege that pays not one centavo *and that most of them aren't competent to use wisely anyhow*" (29, emphasis added).

Heinlein proudly uses his own privileged position as a veteran to belittle the majority who have not served (see "The Pragmatics of Patriotism," *Expanded Universe* 458–70). He disputes the worthiness of their franchise, and, of course, they are compelled to protest. Yet most of those who protest might also grudgingly admit that Heinlein has a point. *Some* qualification for suffrage measured by civic responsibility is rationally desirable. Without it, the masses will rule through passion and not foresight. Plato understood that unqualified and universal democracy is no more than mob rule. How effective is democracy without sacrifice? What is the value of a slothful populace's decision to vote itself bread and circuses, or the usefulness of the decision by mice who vote to bell the cat? (cited in *Expanded Universe* 389; full position in *Starship Troopers* 75–76).

It is extremely difficult to defend Heinlein's position that only veterans are worthy of suffrage; I simply do not subscribe to it. Still, it is undeniable that soldiers have a morally superior position to argue such a point should they wish to do so. This is because the soldier acknowledges upon entrance that he or she willingly relinquishes the rights and privileges of a free citizen in order to guarantee those same rights and privileges for the civilian who is not bound to make such sacrifice. The simple act of enlistment becomes an expression of community altruism. Upon entrance, the soldier becomes subject to military law, a much harsher and restrictive code than that covering society at large. In *Starship Troopers*, the military punishments described are cruel by Terran standards (ch. 5), but considered necessary for proper military discipline. An additional restriction in *Starship Troopers*, unlike contemporary militaries, is that soldiers are not allowed to vote until they retire. This is done so the "idiots" won't vote against going into combat (129), but it is revealing. Soldiers are fighting to protect a privilege of others, one they themselves don't possess but hope someday to hold.

Notwithstanding, it is this notion of supraworthiness of soldiers that is incompatible with the truly democratic state, and makes Heinlein's Federation a fragile political entity. Without question, the military has had a positive reinforcing effect on the establishment and maintenance of democratic values in society, though it is not credible to argue this is the only way such qualities can be sown. At the same time, the military has the dubious and paradoxical quality of being democracy's greatest threat. Power is a tenuous and corruptible force, and a strongly elitist military can quickly slip from an egalitarian to an authoritarian force. The ultimate expression of this kind of change is the military coup—a staple of twentieth-century politics (Nordlinger; Finer). It is the fear of this illegal transfer of power from civilian to military control that is the moral basis for much of *Starship Troopers'* criticism.

The conditions necessary for the emergence of elitism are present in several Terran Federation institutionalized practices, nowhere more clearly than in its over-reliance on veterans in the civil service. Hintze has remarked with some trepidation on the almost universal habit of veterans to entrench themselves in civil service positions upon retirement. In this way, the looming specter of "[m]ilitarism still pervades our political system and public life" (Hintze 211). This phenomenon arises in general because the hierarchical organization of the modern state bureaucracy lends itself to attracting exmilitary (especially clerical) experts. The modern bureaucracy may be most efficient as a military-style organization, but in Hintzian terms, it can be argued that the use of military retirees pressed the development of bureaucracies in that direction. The retirees functioned in the manner to which they had become accustomed, and perhaps the bureaucratic organization evolved differently than it might have. In *Starship Troopers*, the bureaucracy does more than *attract* veterans, specified civil service jobs are "reserved" for them (100). The development of a nonmilitary-style bureaucracy can probably never occur under this condition. Moreover, reserved positions are those required for social control. This includes, of course, the state police. With the establishment of a separate paramilitary internal security force, the democratizing influence of the offensively organized military discussed earlier is summarily negated.

Further, by reserving critical civil service positions, the traditional egalitarian emphasis of the military on society is placed in doubt. The crux of the argument, that the military instills democratic values by intermingling the classes, is offset by the establishment of a privileged class of veterans. The soldier, who has been appropriately trained to feel superior in war, may in peace search out other social groups within the community to dominate. Heinlein suggests the polarization of *Starship Troopers'* society has already begun when he has his hero scoff at the inferior qualities of civilians who don't fight but fill support positions: "Civilians are like beans; you buy 'em as needed for any job which merely requires skill and savvy" (164). The stratification of society which leads to militarism and forces the decay of liberty is in this manner set in motion.

More troubling than the militarization of the government bureaucracy is the notion that if only veterans can vote, then likely only veterans can hold elected public office (Heinlein is not explicit on this, but it is unreasonable to assume anything else). The criteria that only civilians should control the military is crucial to the suppression of militarism. When all civilians of political power are by definition veterans, the distinction is potentially meaningless. Veterans are not, contrary to popular opinion, a bloodthirsty lot. They know first hand the horrors of war and they know the devastation it wreaks on family and friends. It is not the fear of war that causes unease about a veteran-only political hierarchy, it is again the potential that this publicly advantaged group could easily slip into military elitism—militarism—should the noncitizen "residents" of society become unruly or critical of the government's policies.

Yet for the military to dominate, society and the state must provide a suitable environment for the transfer of power. The government must be prone to totalitarianism and society must be conditioned for it. An effective defense against militarism is therefore a constitutionally entrenched democracy (Huntington 163). The practice of accepting any and all residents into federal service (hence into citizenship) blunts the formation of an elitist social order within the Federation. Class-dominant authoritarian society requires at least some stability of the existing social order. Since any resident can become a veteran, and all veterans can remember their own former status as a resident, the possibility that veterans will transform their admittedly privileged positions in government into a permanent social supremacy appears quite remote. Still, in the final analysis, it could happen. Heinlein avers it never would because of the utter disregard most military veterans have for political activity (*Expanded Universe* 385), but that justification is hardly comforting. It means that the social fabric is egalitarian only by the good graces of a class that could, but, as yet, hasn't assumed dictatorial power.

I have labored to show in this essay that *Starship Troopers* does not conform to a classic definition of militarism, and that, consistent with Heinlein's vision, the military can and does help to establish and reinforce democratic values. While it is probably too obvious that I am in general agreement with Heinlein's views as to the merits of military service, I remain concerned with the potential for any military-dominant government to slip into elitism and threaten not only its own members, but its neighbors. On this point, the following excerpt from *Starship Troopers* is especially disturbing: "any breed which stops its own increase gets crowded out by breeds which expand.... Either we spread out and wipe out the [extraterrestrials] or they spread out and wipe us out" (147). The moral authority for humanity's cosmic expansion will be confirmed naturally by its success, "[t]he universe will let us know—later—whether or not Man has any 'right' to expand through it" (211). These lines evoke images of social Darwinism and the geopolitical racist views of Nazi Germany, as espoused by Rudolph Kjellen and Karl Haushofer and brought to life in the rhetoric of *Lebensraum* (see Strausz-Hupe and Dorpalen). At a time when the Federation has managed to eliminate the petty prejudices of humanity, it displays a clear superiority of human over extraterrestrial. Racism, the engine of antidemocratic rhetoric, must be taken in context. When the earth is a closed system, the racist Aryan supremacy of Nazi Germany is undeniable. When the context is galactic, any expansionistic human empire will be ultimately incompatible with the ideals of liberty.

Heinlein is neither a fascist nor a racist. He is an idealist whose conviction is eloquently summed in the statement: "The noblest fate that a man can endure is to place his own mortal body between his loved home and the war's desolation" (*Starship Troopers* 74). Above all he is a marvelous storyteller with few peers, and although *Starship Troopers* reflects his personal preference for responsible government, it had to be crafted in such a manner so as to be both entertaining and consistent to the reader. Heinlein's vision of the ideal state is therefore flawed. He over-simplifies utopia by suggesting democratic government can be perfected if only its citizens can be made responsible for their political actions.

Works Cited

Ames, Fisher. 1982. "Conservative Forebodings." In *The Portable Conservative Reader,* edited by Russell Kirk. New York: Viking Penguin.

Andreski, Stanislas. 1954. *Military Organization and Society.* London: Routledge & Kegan Paul.

Berryman, Sue. 1987. *Who Serves?: The Persistent Myth of the Underclass Army.* Boulder: Westview.

Binkim, Martin, and Shirley Bach. 1977. *Women and the Military.* Washington: Brookings Institution.

Cameron, Colin, and Judith Blackstone. 1970. *Minorities in the Armed Forces: A Selected, Occasionally Annotated Bibliography.* Madison: University of Wisconsin Press.

Cohen, Eliot. 1985. *Citizens and Soldiers: The Dilemmas of Military Service.* Ithaca: Cornell University Press.

Dalfume, Richard. 1969. *Desegregation of the U.S. Armed Forces: Fighting Two Fronts, 1939–1953.* Columbia: University of Missouri Press.

Dorpalen, Andreas. 1942. *The World of General Haushofer: Geopolitics in Action.* New York: Farrar & Rinehart.

Downing, Brian. 1992. *The Military Revolution and Political Change: Origins of Democracy and Autocracy in Early Modern Europe.* Princeton: Princeton University Press.

Erisman, Fred. 1990. "Robert Heinlein's Case for Racial Tolerance, 1954–1956." *Extrapolation* 29: 216–26.

Finer, Samuel. 1976. *The Man on Horseback: The Role of the Military in Politics.* 2nd ed. Harmondsworth, U.K.: Penguin.

Franklin, H. Bruce. 1980. *Robert Heinlein: America as Science Fiction.* New York: Oxford University Press.

Glatthaar, Joseph. 1990. *Forged in Battle: The Civil War Alliance of Black Soldiers and White Officers.* New York: Free Press.

Heinlein, Robert A. 1959. *Starship Troopers.* New York: Berkeley Books, 1984.

———. *Stranger in a Strange Land.* 1961. New York: Berkeley Books, 1968.

———. *Expanded Universe.* 1980. New York: Ace Books, 1991.

Hintze, Otto. 1975. "Military Organization and State Organization." In *The Historical Essays of Otto Hintze,* edited and translated by Felix Gilbert. New York: Oxford University Press.

Huntington, Samuel. 1957. *The Soldier and the State: The Theory and Politics of Civil-Military Relations.* Cambridge: Harvard University Press.

Keeghan, John. 1989. *The Price of Admiralty: The Evolution of Naval Warfare.* Harmondsworth, U.K.: Penguin.

Lacey, James. 1982. "The Case for Conscription." In *Military Service in the United States.* Englewood Cliffs, N.J.: Prentice-Hall.

Machiavelli, Niccolo. 1521. *The Art of War.* Translated by Ellis Farnsworth. New York: Da Capo, 1965.

Mahan, Alfred Thayer. 1897. *The Influence of Seapower on History, 1660–1783.* Boston: Little Brown.

Manicas, Peter. 1989. *War and Democracy.* New York: Basil Blackwell.

Moskos, Charles. 1982. "Social Considerations of the All-Volunteer Force." In *Military Service in the United States.* Englewood Cliffs, N.J.: Prentice-Hall.

Myrdal, Gunnar. 1944. *An American Dilemma: The Negro Problem and Modern Democracy.* New York: Harper.

Nordlinger, Eric. 1977. *Soldiers in Politics: Military Coups and Governments.* Englewood Cliffs, N.J.: Prentice-Hall.

Panshin, Alexi. 1968. *Heinlein in Dimension: A Critical Analysis.* Chicago: Advent.

Porter, Bruce. 1994. *War and the Rise of the State: The Military Foundations of Modern Politics.* New York: Free Press.

Rappoport, David. 1962. "A Comparative Theory of the Military and Political Types." In *Changing Patterns of Military Politics,* edited by Samuel Huntington. New York: Free Press.

Sante, Luc. 1985. "The Temple of Boredom: Science Fiction, No Future." *Harper's* 271, 1625 (October): 69.

Segal, Dennis. 1989. *Recruiting for Uncle Sam: Citizenship and Military Manpower Policy.* Lawrence: University of Kansas Press.

Showalter, Dennis. 1975. "Heinlein's *Starship Troopers:* An Exercise in Rehabilitation." *Extrapolation* 16: 113–24.

Smith, Philip. 1978. "The Evolution of Politics: The Politics of Evolution." In *Robert A. Heinlein,* edited by Joseph Olander and Martin Greenberg. New York: Taelinger.

Stover, Leon. 1987. *Robert A. Heinlein.* Boston: Twayne.

Strausz-Hupe, Robert. 1942. *Geopolitics: The Struggle for Space and Power.* New York: G. P. Putnam's Sons.

Tucker, Frank. 1978. "Major Political and Social Elements in Heinlein's Fiction." In *Robert A. Heinlein,* edited by Joseph Olander and Martin Greenberg. New York: Taelinger.

Vagts, Alfred. 1937. *A History of Militarism: Romance and Realities of a Profession.* New York: W. W. Norton.

Weber, Max. 1927. *General Economic History.* Translated by Frank Knight. Glenco, Ill.: Free Press.

Williamson, Jack. 1978. "Youth Against Space." In *Robert A. Heinlein,* edited by Joseph Olander and Martin Greenberg. New York: Taelinger.

Chapter 13

Gender Identity in *Star Trek*

Kathy E. Ferguson, Gilad Ashkenazi, and Wendy Schultz

Identity is about boundaries. Identities are compelling largely through their ability to mobilize or demobilize available self-understandings concerning what is "me" and what is "not me." Boundaries between "me" and "you" or "us" and "them," like distinctions between an "old me" and a "new me," must be constituted—they are not self-evident or natural. Often identities are constituted along lines that make them appear to be natural, such as those between visibly different types of bodies. But bodily differences become marked with significance through processes more political than biological—processes that name some distinctions as crucial to identity and order while relegating others to the sidelines. Boundaries become naturalized when this process of naming becomes invisible, when the act of making the distinction disappears and only the distinctions themselves remain. In this way boundaries take on an air of inevitability—it becomes possible to think of them as having no history and requiring no explanation, as simply "the way things are."

In the original *Star Trek* and in *Star Trek: The Next Generation* potent notions of identity and difference are brought into play. Some common distinctions between self and other, or within aspects of self, are called into question, while others are relegated to the taken-for-granted background of the social order.

In the original *Star Trek* the boundaries that separate racial and class identities, and sometimes species identities as well, were frequently denaturalized. But conventional gender identity generally went unchallenged: men were men, and women were women, usually with all the accouterments of traditional gender practices to accompany those identities—scanty clothing, emotional outbursts, and ultimate capitulation to the desires of men being the primary lot of women, while strength, reason and autonomy were reserved for males.

In *The Next Generation*, this has changed in many respects. While some aspects of the tone of gender presentation in the original series reappear in the sequel—for example, Deanna Troi's skintight uniform and plunging neckline, or the periodic camera angles emphasizing the breasts or buttocks of female characters—less traditional and more creative presentations of gender identity also made an appearance. Perhaps owing to the influence of twenty years of feminism in the society (and on the writers), or perhaps to the greater availability of postmodern ideas about the loosening of the categories of identity, *The Next Generation* often plays with conventional gender boundaries and practices in unconventional ways. This denaturalizing move has interesting implications for encouraging and legitimating a more feminist, more postmodern turn in popular culture; while its limits have equally interesting implications for the curtailment of cultural criticism in commercial spaces.

Identities are built upon layers and layers of habitualized gestures, postures, expressions, responses, attitudes, descriptions and anticipations. These layers readily become more or less frozen into place, a compacted composition which Judith Butler calls a sedimented corporeal style (Butler 139–140). The "doing" of them disappears; they appear to be only a "being." To denaturalize some dimension of identity and difference requires patient attention to identity as something one does, not simply as what or who one is. Such denaturalization has important political and cultural implications in that conventional arrangements come to be seen as amenable to change; the social world comes into focus as a place that has been made, not simply discovered, and possibilities for remaking that world can be imagined.

The original *Star Trek* brought this attentive focus to the boundaries of racial identity practices, as well as to those involving class and species. Spock's ancestry, half human and half Vulcan, suggested the possibilities of connections across species differences, as well as providing a site for ongoing identity disputes within an individual. The episode "The Cloud-Minders" was sharply critical of a society in which an absolute distinction between workers and thinkers/artists was held to be natural, and introduced a device capable of providing "equal opportunity" across class boundaries (although not of eliminating the class system itself). Most prominently, the boundaries maintaining separate racial identities were brought under critical scrutiny. There was a certain amount of racial diversity among the crew, which included a black woman and an Asian man on the bridge and several other people of color in the background. There was the simmering erotic connection between Kirk and Uhura, which surfaced in "Plato's Stepchildren" in the first on-screen kiss between a black woman and a white man in television history, according to McDonnell (55). And there was the memorable episode "Let That Be Your Last Battlefield," in which beings who maintained an absolute sense of racial otherness are sharply criticized. Similarly, in "Balance of Terror" prejudice against the enemy Romulans, and against the Vulcans who physically resemble them, is reputed, and the Romulans are reconsidered as beings not reducible to a uniformly evil "them."

In contrast to the vigorous playing with boundaries of color, class and species in the original series, conventional gender distinctions and self-understandings were consistently reproduced. Gender was implicitly presented as a natural phenomenon, one that has no history, requires no explanations, and resists any efforts at restructuring or even reimagining. The female crew members' costumes, in contrast to the ordinary work clothes of the men, were generally miniskirts and go-go boots, apparel less than fully practical for space exploration. The leadership of the *Enterprise* and her fellow spacecraft was unrelentingly male, with women found in traditional pink collar or helping professions.

For all her visibility on the bridge of the original *Enterprise*, Uhura's position as communications officer was a cross between secretary and telephone operator (although she did occasionally repair her own communications panel). While Uhura's character is attractive, her humor, competence, and loyalty shine through more by force of personality (the character's and the actress's) than by dint of opportunities to act. Nurse Chapel's position is even more limited: professionally subordinate to Dr. McCoy, emotionally subordinate to Mr. Spock. Yeoman Rand, Kirk's "right-hand woman," was most restricted of all; she was labelled by actress Grace Lee Whitney who played her as "a space geisha" (McDonnell 18). Uhura as doorwarden; Rand as chatelaine of the castle;

Chapel as acolyte worshipping at the feet of mystery/Mr. Spock—none of these portrayals brings women very far out of the category of passive object or supportive subordinate, recipient of the male gaze, the looked-at rather than the one who looks and acts.

Captain Kirk's traditional sailor behavior left him with a woman in every port, and female guest stars often portrayed his "guest lays" as well. While some of the female characters were professionally competent women, they were largely restricted to the "soft sciences": psychology (Dr. Helen Noel in "Dagger of the Mind"), history (Lt. Marla McGivers in "Space Seed"), anthropology (Lt. Carolyn Palomas in "Who Mourns for Adonis"), and not well represented in the areas of "hard" knowledge or command authority.[1] In "Mudd's Women," an episode boasting a plot line reminiscent of Levi-Strauss's anthropology, women are the goods traded between two male worlds. No one on the *Enterprise* questions the validity of this arrangement, only its particular terms. Kirk makes sure that "his" woman is not swindled and that she makes a satisfactory deal, but her coming-to-consciousness about some of the limits of the traditional feminine role is his accomplishment, not hers.

Frequent comments are made by the male leads about women's irrationality, their mysteriousness, their inexplicable feelings and behavior. While Kirk bedded or bested (or both) most feminine life forms crossing his path (evidently with no concern for interstellar venereal disease), the women are seldom worthy enemies or steadfast friends. While Areel, the lawyer unwillingly prosecuting Kirk in "Court Martial," was portrayed as a competent lawyer and supportive friend as well as former lover, most of Kirk's relationships are the love 'em and leave 'em (or, in the case of the exotic Elaan in "Elaan of Troyius," spank 'em and leave 'em) variety. Kirk was always able to triumph over the relational distractions the women represented to his primary love affair with his ship. Kirk's promiscuity was most often merely physical; he actually fell in love only a few times: with Edith Keeler, the angelic social worker in "City on the Edge of Forever," with the young android "Reena" in "Requiem for Methuselah," with the lovely Indian maiden Mirimanee in "The Paradise Syndrome." (All three women conveniently died at the end of their respective episodes.)

While McCoy, Spock, and Scotty seldom "got the girl," when they did the relationships were usually portrayed as deeply personal, mutually enhancing, and seldom fatal (Spock with Leila in "This Side of Paradise" and with Zarabeth in "All Our Yesterdays"; McCoy with the image of Nancy Crater in "The Man Trap" and High Priestess Natira in "For the World is Hollow and I Have Touched the Sky"; Scotty with the young Argelian dancer in "Wolf in the Fold" and with the continually fainting Lt. Mira Romaine in "The Lights of Zetar") in comparison to Kirk's more casual or dangerous liaisons.

Full-fledged loving relationships between men and women, or between adults and children, were generally forbidden on the *Enterprise* itself. (Intimate relations among men, in contrast, are the show's central theme, with the homoerotic implications properly subdued.) Marriage was for people who had nothing to lose: the dying Zephram Cochran of "Metamorphosis," the paraplegic Captain Christopher Pike in "The Menagerie, Part II" (see Selley). The few children in the series were completely outside of ordinary life. Usually they were dangerous: possessing uncontrolled powers in "Charlie X," or manipulated by a malevolent alien in "And the Children Shall Lead," or mutating into murderous savages in "Miri" (Selley, 7). The *Enterprise* was involved with children only to rescue them. Kirk's nephew Peter is somewhat of an exception, in that he was not dangerous; however, he did require rescuing ("Operation: Annihilate"). Kirk's brother, sister-in-law, and nephew appeared only long enough to establish the captain's isolation and necessary lack of family life. Childbearing was something that happened on primitive planets (Leonard James Akaar in "Friday's Child"), and the best mother in the entire series was the Horta, a silicon-based life form scurrying around the tunnels in "The Devil in the Dark." The women who fell in love usually died, saw their lovers die, or had to leave. Perhaps they were considered to be Kirk's potential harem, so punishment followed if they strayed in their affections; or perhaps the show's limited vision of interpersonal dynamics restricted its relational energies.

Even in episodes in which some fairly nonconformist behavior seems to be occurring with regard to gender identity, conventions are defied only to be more firmly reestablished in the end. In "Turnabout Intruder" a nefarious and irrational woman exchanges bodies with Kirk in order to pursue her (nefarious and irrational) dream of becoming a starship captain. It is, of course, her impulsiveness and lack of self-restraint that reveals her crime and reestablishes Kirk as legitimate leader. While the presence of a man in a woman's body, and vice versa, suggests some interesting disconnections of bodies and identities, the two categories of bodies, male and female, are themselves held quite stable and unchanging. The original *Star Trek* did not challenge the categories of masculinity and femininity even when it allowed some unusual traffic between them. Paralleling the creation of the characters, the gender coding of the practice of space exploration itself in the original series suggests a patriarchal orientation. Star Fleet was portrayed as an odd amalgam of the Navy and NASA, including strict hierarchy of rank and authority (which Kirk could often flaunt, of course, but only because he was always right) and a preference for representing relationships within an offensive/defensive matrix. While there was the occasional peaceful and modest encounter with otherness, as in young Ensign Bailey's first contact with an alien species in "The Corbonite Maneuver," or the overt critique of war offered by the more advanced species in "Errand of Mercy," more often the Prime Directive was made to be broken and intervention with all guns blazing was the favored response.

Three further considerations need to be brought to bear on questions of boundaries and otherness in the original series. First, *Star Trek* was made during the late 1960s, in the context of the civil rights movement and the black power struggles. The times were relatively receptive to reconsidering racial otherness in light of claims to equality. Nichelle Nichols, who played Lieutenant Uhura, remembers that Martin Luther King commented to her that her role as a major character in a television series was a very important role model for African-American youth. In contrast, "the times," especially as mediated by the always conservative television networks, were not yet sufficiently agitated by the demands of the still nascent women's movement to provide a hospitable context for a parallel questioning of conventional gender arrangements. Creator Gene Roddenberry originally cast a woman as "Number One" (second-in-command, played by Majel Barrett, whom he later married) in the pilot episode "The Cage," and then was forced by NBC to back away from such untraditional casting. Barrett was recast in the more acceptable role of nurse (McDonnell, 10).

Second, while conventional gender boundaries are ruthlessly maintained in most aspects of the original series, the categories nonetheless managed to leak in other ways. The Kirk-Spock-McCoy triangle was, in an indirect sort of way, a gendered relation: Spock's hypermasculinity, ostensibly devoid of emotions and devoted to linear reason, pursued a love-hate relation with McCoy's disguised femininity. McCoy was a "feminine" presence in his frequent emotional tirades, his suspicion of Spock's sterile logic, his attunement to the emotions of the others, his devotion to concrete life as opposed to universal abstractions. McCoy introduced some dimensions of a "feminine" presence into the battlefield-oriented male bonding of the trio. Yet his authority was ultimately legitimized by his maleness and the access to power that it offered.

219

As a study in the elemental construction of character, the three personified archetypical subsections of one complete man: the logician/mystic; the healer/nurturer; the warrior/procreator; or, brain, heart, and balls. But because the three categories are externalized in three different people (with the partial exception of Spock's bispecies identity struggles) it became difficult for any of them to have very complex reactions to situations, and the dialogue tended to fall into familiar patterns. Spock's gender coding was the most complex: his extreme devotion to reason and self-control were frequently disrupted by factors such as his interstellar mindmelding (a sort of emotional promiscuity, set against Kirk's more conventional kind), his helplessness in the face of Vulcan reproductive drives, or his vulnerability to alien spores. Spock's passion for science indirectly sabotages the emotion/reason opposition, undermining the strict dualistic coding of masculine and feminine on some levels, while reestablishing it on others.[2]

Third, identity as a whole is consistently treated as a rather fixed set of traits lodged in a stable entity called "personality." In the notable episode "The Enemy Within" Kirk is forced to acknowledge and reintegrate his "bad side" back into his "good side," but the idea of identity as a permanent and unchanging foundation remained. Spock's embedded head/heart contradiction was often externalized as the disharmonious meeting of his "human half" and his "Vulcan half," suggesting two fixed categories with stable boundaries and firm anchors. It was left to the writers and producers of *Star Trek: The Next Generation* to begin reordering identity into something more mobile, more temporal, less a base from which one acts and more an outcome of what one does.

Like its predecessor, *The Next Generation* holds some conventions of identity and otherness stable in order to call others into question. Unlike its predecessor, gender falls more frequently into the latter category. Significant elements of patriarchal gender conventions remain, particularly with regard to the "tits and ass" factor: Troi's painted-on clothing; the outfits worn by the women crewmembers in the first year of the series, reminiscent of the original go-go boots and miniskirts; frequent camera shots of Lieutenant Yar's bouncing breasts; a hierarchical leadership structure still largely male.

But more interesting are the ways in which the sequel moves away from these sure-sell (to heterosexual men, at least) conventions into gender practices that are more imaginative, less predictable, more promising for a feminist, postmodern politics. Perhaps reflecting the influence of feminism and postmodernism in the larger society, women's roles in *The Next Generation* have moved beyond the erotic/exotic in several ways.

Before exploring further the constellations of gender in *The Next Generation*, it is important to note some other contexts in which boundary questions are addressed. While Captain Picard makes frequent reference to the progress made by earth toward justice and equality, this progress is not readily detectable in either the racial makeup of the crew or the thematic content of the show. Two members of the main cast are black (LeVar Burton as chief engineer Geordi LaForge, and Michael Dorn as Klingon security officer Worf). A few of the background characters are people of color, including Whoopi Goldberg's character Guinan, who appears infrequently but is often central to the story line when she does. In the main, *The Next Generation* seems to be on hold when it comes to race.

In contrast, the boundary between human and machine is frequently challenged, as is that between species. Data, the android, is an obvious example of the blurring of distinctions between human and machine, as are Geordi La Forge's prosthetic visor and the spooky mechanized humanoids called the Borg. People fall in love with holodeck images, suggesting a different sort of commerce between human and machine: Geordi first becomes involved with Leah Brahms (whom he later marries, according to the final episode) on the holodeck ("Booby Trap"), and Riker falls for the holographic Minuet whom he has special-ordered from the Binars ("11001001"). Data's sexual liaison with Lieutenant Yar in "The Naked Now," and his experiment in romance with security officer Jenna D'Sora in "In Theory," forges links between organic and mechanical life forms.

Troi continues Spock's split identity across species (half human, half Betazoid) as does Worf's mate, K'Ehleyr (half human, half Klingon). If one thinks of species differences as metaphors for racial differences, then the field opens up a bit: Worf and Ensign Ro could then be thought of as people of color, although it's clear that Bejorans are played by Caucasian actors. The sexual relation between Troi and Worf in the final episode could, in this light, be seen as a racially mixed relationship.

While these examples highlight a few instances of racial nonconformity, in general racial differences are not central to the plot lines and character development in *The Next Generation*. One could speculate on reasons for the relative absence of color-challenging practices, compared to those regarding gender: perhaps "the times" have tired of racial more than sexual politics; perhaps the networks feel that feminism sells better than antiracism. For whatever reason, the treatment of identity within and across gender boundaries presents much more food for thought than that regarding race.

Traditional gender boundaries are frequently rearranged in *The Next Generation* through a process of reversal, in which women and men are found thinking, feeling, and acting in ways traditionally associated with the other gender. While gender reversals may unwittingly reinforce gender coding by holding on to the very categories that divide life forms into male and female, nevertheless such reversals often succeed in expanding the boundaries of the life worlds of women and of men.

Perhaps most obviously, in the sequel women are often found in authority. Tasha Yar's early role as chief of security casts her in a traditionally male position: not only does she wield considerable authority; she also is in control of the legitimate use of violence. Women make frequent guest appearances as high ranking officials within Star Fleet Command, most notably Admiral Nechaev, Picard's nemesis-turned-ally, and the Admiral who welcomed her grandson back to earth in "Suddenly Human." Women command other space craft, including the courageous Captain Garret from the past in "Yesterday's Enterprise" and the young black woman introduced as "the youngest captain in the Fleet" in "Conspiracy." Young Commander Shelby ends up in charge of Federation defenses against the Borg in "The Best of Both Worlds" (see Wilcox). These women are not brought on as erotic interests for the captain (although the first officer has his share of guest lays). They are by and large accorded the authority, rationality, autonomy (and clothing) that accompanies their positions.

The *Enterprise* frequently encounters worlds where women rule, including the rather heavy-handed reversal of earth's traditional gender categories in "Angel One," in which the larger, stronger, more rational and intellectual women dominated the smaller, weaker and less intelligent men. When patriarchal worlds appear, as in "Suddenly Human," the situation is presented as quite foreign to earth, allowing Lieutenant Worf (himself a Klingon raised by human parents) to declare that "among humans, the woman can do anything the man can do." Ensign Ro is both a strong female figure and a kind of intergalactic Palestinian, raised in the Bejoran labor camps under Cardassian occupation. The young Bejoran ensign who gambled her life for a good cause—and lost—in "Lower Decks" was a gallant and admirable officer. Tasha Yar's daughter, the Romulan commander, was a worthy enemy; her sister Ishara, who doublecrossed the *Enterprise* crew in support of her faction on her home world in "Legacy," was an intriguing combination of fanaticism and vulnerability.

Women are commonly seen in engineering, the hard sciences, and defense/security: the young engineering ensign who spills cocoa on Picard; Leah Brahms, starship designer; numerous unnamed women on Worf's security teams; the unidentified black woman sitting in Wesley Crusher's old seat on the bridge in later episodes. Perhaps most memorable were the two shape-shifters who took female form in "The Dauphin": the young one taught Wesley something about maturity and responsibility, while the old one made a big impression on Worf. Certainly one could wish for more development of some of these characters, or a happier fate for others; but none of them are reducible to thin feminine stereotypes. *The Next Generation* has been much more flexible than the original show in placing women in a variety of situations and allowing them a fuller range of initiatives and responses.

In light of this diversity and depth, it is much more noticeable when a woman character is brought on exclusively as a love interest or is set up to fail. K'Ehleyr, Worf's mate, was a trained diplomat and a specialist in Klingon culture. She was the logical one to come up with the solution to the *Enterprise*'s conflict with the Klingon ship from the past in "The Emissary." She not only failed to do so, she obstructed Worf's efforts to solve the problem, did a lot of ranting and raving, and finally stood back admiringly while Worf saved the day. Perhaps the writers could not imagine K'Ehleyr succeeding and still maintaining Worf's erotic attention, Klingon male pride being, no doubt, very delicate. K'Ehleyr's character invited consideration of numerous tensions—between human and Klingon identities, between love and work, between parental and erotic love. *The Next Generation* writers could have recovered K'Ehleyr and made her character a site of female agency and development, but they killed her off instead.

The leading female characters following Yar's demise as security chief—Dr. Beverly Crusher, Counselor Deanna Troi, and Guinan (the bartender)—combine some traditional with some unconventional characteristics. In *The Next Generation*'s first two years they were accorded little serious character space. Their presence as feminine archetypes— Troi as the emotional, exotic beauty, Crusher as the mother of the savior, Guinan (or perhaps the *Enterprise* computer itself, voiced by Majel

Barrett) as the wise crone—was uncomplicated by the crosscurrents necessary to give a character depth and range.

But this changed as the show developed. While the three women
are found in positions generally associated with conventional femininity—as healers, counselors and listeners—they frequently exercise considerable authority within those positions, and they are not exclusively
confined to them. Both Troi and Crusher are promoted to command rank
in the show's final year. Their presence in conventionally female occu-
pations could be read, not as diminishing the women by limiting them
to lower status work, but as elevating the work by featuring it as central
to the full and balanced functioning of the ship. Troi exercises command
of the *Enterprise* in "Disaster," and goes underground among the
Romulans in another episode. Crusher solves the mystery of her own
disappearance in "Remember Me," takes the lead in solving the problems she and the captain face when they are taken captive, assumes temporary command of the *Enterprise* while the rest of the crew searches for
Data among the Borg, and in the final episode, "All Good Things," cap-
tains her own ship under her married name, Picard. Guinan's mysterious and always successful influence over Captain Picard, as well as her
intelligent advice to others, often puts her in the position of final authority, most notably in "Yesterday's Enterprise" and "The Measure of a
Man." In some ways Guinan is the most interesting and least conventional of the female figures—the only woman of color, her authority and
status come from her personal power and history rather than any official position. (Bartenders do not rank particularly high in the hierarchy
of Star Fleet.) All three women are accorded considerable dignity and
authority, even though the official top chain of command (Picard—
Riker—Data—La Forge—Worf) remains exclusively male.

Increased flexibility in gender roles is made available to the men as
well as to the women of *The Next Generation*. In the early years of the
show the men, like the women, seemed to represent fairly straightforward Jungian archetypes: Riker as warrior/procreator; Worf as warrior/
primitive unconscious; Geordi as mystic/inventor; Data as logician;
Picard as interrelator/ego/synthesis. As the show developed, the men
developed a greater variety and range of character traits. Often this
greater emotional range comes from encounters with children. Worf,
Data, Riker and Picard all become parents: Worf keeps Alexander with
him, and accepts his son's uniqueness, after being visited by the

Alexander from the future. Worf also takes young Jeremy Aster into his family, via the Klingon R'uustai ceremony, after Jeremy's mother died on an away mission commanded by Worf ("The Bonding"). Riker parents briefly with an alien illusion while being held captive by a lonely child, and Data sees his daughter born, come to maturity, and die in "The Offspring." Picard's brief encounters with the young human male in "Suddenly Human," with his own "son" (conjured up by a vengeful Ferengi), with the frightened children in the turbolift in "Disaster," with the son and daughter of his parallel life in "Inner Light," and his long and complex relationship with Wesley Crusher (whose stepfather he eventually becomes) all stretch him out of his command mode, into a more relationally attentive way of being. The men's relationships to hierarchy also undergo some re-evaluation: Data opposes Star Fleet authority to keep his daughter with him, and Picard opposes that same authority out of a newly learned respect for android parenting. Even Riker, usually a bastion of conventional masculinity, comes to value his rewarding relationship with the *Enterprise* crew over career advancement.

The Jungian coding of gender was brought out most overtly in "Loud as a Whisper," in which a deaf-mute negotiator with a telepathically linked "chorus" is brought on board to initiate peace talks with a society convulsed by civil war. The negotiator's chorus explicitly express and act out the interaction of the rational/philosophical self, the feminine/nurturing/creative self, and the warrior/protective/sensual self. While one could quarrel with the gender coding of the categories (why should the rational voice and the warrior voice be male? the nurturer, female?) the episode insisted that a balanced and secure psyche includes all of these dimensions.

There is somewhat greater equal opportunity within sexuality itself in *The Next Generation*; while Riker remains the king of the casual encounter, Troi ("The Price") and Crusher ("The Host") also have passionate affairs with strangers passing through. Neither of the women are "punished" for their sexual explorations. On the rare occasion when Picard is romantically involved, his partner is always portrayed as a strong, intelligent woman with a life of her own: the irrepressible Vash, the Judge Advocate General in "The Measure of a Man," the talented pianist who directs stellar cartography for a time on the *Enterprise*. Most importantly, the sexual tensions among the main crew—between Crusher and Picard; between Yar and Data; between Troi and Riker; in the final season between Troi and Worf—do not destroy the positive working relationships that the crew sustain with one another. In *The Next Generation* women and men can work together with affection, regard and humor, can respect one another for their skills, can find a strong sense of belonging together—without destroying their teamwork with distracting sexual liaisons.

The boundaries between adults and children are flexible and complicated. In a great leap forward, *The Next Generation's Enterprise* has families on board, and Star Fleet officers who do not "have time" for families are chastened, as Picard is by the human boy's adoptive father in "Suddenly Human," or changed, as is Worf when Alexander comes back into his life. Childbearing seems to be something people do on a regular basis, as a part of ongoing relationships (Worf and K'Ehleyr's son Alexander, Miles and Keiko O'Brien's daughter Molly), or as a result of adventures with extracorporeal aliens (Deanna Troi's short-lived son), or as an experiment in understanding the meaning of being human (Data's daughter Lal). Young Wesley Crusher assumes adult responsibilities, while the omnipotent "Q" is remarkably childlike. In "Disaster" Worf served as midwife at the birth of Molly O'Brien. On one occasion several crew members, including Picard, Guinan, Ro and Keiko O'Brien, became children again and as children defeated the Ferengi. On another, all the crew except Data and Picard de-evolved into primordial forms, and the solution depended on Data's cat giving birth for inspiration and on the recently promoted Lt. Agawa's pregnancy for implementation.

Similarly, childrearing is included as a part of the lives of Star Fleet officers, who are either parents themselves or who interact with children simply because they are there. When Dr. Crusher left for her post at Star Fleet Medical, the rest of the crew divided up the parenting responsibilities, with Worf in charge of bedtime. Picard's initial discomfort with children gradually evolves into a competent and loving relationship, most notably when he is stranded in a malfunctioning turbolift with three scared kids in "Disaster." Space exploration itself is less ruthlessly masculine and interventionist. For starters, the introductory speech has been changed: instead of boldly going where no man has gone before, the galaxy-class *Enterprise* is enjoined "to boldly go where no *one* has gone before" (emphasis added). While Star Fleet is still organized on a military model, Picard's leadership style is portrayed as somewhat collaborative, especially in comparison to other, more hierarchical commanders or to Picard's own alter ego in "Yesterday's *Enterprise*." Picard's work as an amateur archeologist links command more with scholarship than soldiering. The Prime Directive is taken seriously as a major pivot for several plots, and the captain's immediate predilection is for negotiation or mediation rather than war. The claim to be on a peaceful mission of exploration is more believable for the *Enterprise* of *The Next Generation*. In the world of prime-time television, these are no small accomplishments. They confront the traditional world of gender with some bold reversals. But *The Next Generation* willingness to contest the boundaries of gender goes even further than simply reversing the usual arrangements, sometimes even addressing the nature of identity itself in relation to the gendered body. The best examples of this more radical contestation of gender are "11001001," "The Host," "Liaisons," and the problematic "Outcast."

In "11001001" the gender mixing goes on in the background, subsidiary to the main plot. An unusual species called the Binars is presented primarily as beings who are intimately intertwined with computers. Their activities—enhancing the *Enterprise*'s holodeck facilities, hijacking the *Enterprise* through manipulating its evacuation procedures, merging the ship's main computer with their own in order to save their homeworlds—all emphasize the blurring of the boundaries between life and machine more than between male and female. Yet the latter set of distinctions are also called into question. The Binars are introduced to the *Enterprise* crew as "neither male nor female" but "a unified pair." While the nature of this unity is left unspecified, it is suggested that together they include both male and female, but apart they are neither. Their appearance confounds earth's gender expectations—they are small, dainty, bald, flat-chested. Riker exemplifies this confusion by insisting on referring to them as "gentlemen"; his categories do not fit, but he clings to them nonetheless.

The connection of gender to identity is questioned more directly in "Liaisons" and "The Host." In "Liaisons" the alien Ambassador Voval from the planet Eyar wants to experience the human emotion of love. His bodily form is male, by human standards; unbeknownst to the *Enterprise* crew, his is a species of shapeshifters. Voval selects Picard for his experiment in human eros and affection (meanwhile his two colleagues have selected to explore the pleasures of gluttony with Deanna Troi and of anger with Worf) and transforms himself into Anna, a human female. Anna tries aggressively to win Picard's affections, then finally gives up

227

and turns back into the male body of the Ambassador. A man turns into a woman in order to love a man. Picard's response is significant: he expresses surprise at the unexpected transformation, and anger at being manipulated, but no repulsion or aversion at having been kissed by a woman who was "really" a man. And the alien's ready ability to transform throws doubt on the idea that it is "really" male at all; its initial maleness, like its transformation into Anna, could have been in cooperation with human convention, rather than reflective of its species's realities. There is no obvious foundational gender state.

In "The Host," Beverly Crusher falls in love with an alien whose basic identity, its sense of itself as a being with a stable identity continuing through time and across space, has no relation to the gendered body in which the earthlings (also the Betazoids, the Klingons, and other humanoids) anchor their sense of themselves. Crusher's encounter with this alien, who moves from the male body in which she originally encounters it, into a different male body (Will Riker's), then into a female body, illustrates the difficulty that earthlings have in conceiving of identity independent of the gendered body: Crusher cannot "keep up," that is, cannot adjust to the changes that, while insignificant to the alien, are overwhelming to her. The alien finds Crusher's unwillingness to pursue love and passion across the shifting lines of bodily self-presentation to be equally puzzling. Beverly's hurt and confused question to her lover is primarily one of identity, not behavior: "Who are you?" . . . "I don't know who you are!" Crusher responds to the final caress she receives from the alien (now in a female body) with a look of recognition; she is not repulsed or offended by the intimacy with another woman, only saddened at the loss.

Through these encounters *The Next Generation* opened up the possibility of loosening the hold that masculinity and femininity have on identity, of imagining a sense of identity uncoupled from an unchanging and unambiguously gendered body. Gender becomes at least partly denaturalized; it becomes a phenomenon that requires an explanation, that is capable of having a history and a geography, rather than an unquestioned manifestation of the natural order of things. These brief deconstructions of conventional gender make us long for more. Crusher's recognition of her inability to transcend the accustomed boundaries of eros and identity could be an unwitting admission of the show's inability to get past those same barriers, and thus a critique of contemporary social limitations.[3] As a kind of self-critique and apology, it is both moving and frustrating.

That same frustration is overwhelming in "The Outcast." The *Enter-prise* encounters a planet where the people have no gender. The androgy-nous Jenai, predictably, make Riker and Worf nervous. The main character's sexual frankness—"Commander, tell me about your sexual organs. . . . I'm interested in your mating practices"—is disconcerting. An erotic attraction between this character and Riker develops; Soren "comes out" to Riker as a member of the minority of her people who have a gender: "I have had to live a life of pretense and lies. But with you I can be honest." Soren is found out by the Jenai authorities, taken into custody, and given ominous sounding "psychotechnic treatments" to "cure" her. Riker's and Worf's attempts at a rescue are thwarted by Soren's own transformation into a "normal" Jenai.

This episode hums with interpretive tensions, with political oppor-tunities advanced and not pursued. On one level it is a story about ho-mophobia and sexual authoritarianism; it could also be a larger tale about otherness and sameness. The Jenai police identity ruthlessly, rooting out nonconformity and "fixing" it. Soren's stirring speech to the court de-fends the right to difference:

"I am tired of lies. I am female. I was born that way. I have had those feelings, those longings, all my life. It is not unnatural. I am not sick because I feel this way. I do not need to be helped. I do not need to be cured. What I need, and what all of those who are like me need, is your understanding and your compassion. We have not injured you in any way. And yet we are scorned and attacked. And all because we are different.

What we do is no different from what you do. We talk and laugh. We complain about work and we wonder about growing old. We talk about our families and we worry about the future. And we cry with each other when things seem hopeless.

All of the loving things you do with each other; that is what we do. And for that we are called misfits and deviants and crimi-nals. What right do you have to punish us? What right do you have to change us? What makes you think you can dictate how people love each other?"

"The Outcast" is intriguing in its politicization of a society's claims to "normality." The whole idea of normality is thrown into question by the vicious policing that it entails; the viewer is encouraged to think about her or his own society's policing practices, to imagine the pain they inflict and the rigid enforcement they require. History can no longer masquerade as nature: if the Jenai's prevailing social arrangements were truly written into nature, they would not need constant scrutiny. Normality becomes hegemony, a cultural practice demanding conformity and policing difference.

But this episode's bold venture into the politics of otherness and difference is closeted by its insistent rooting of difference itself back into nature.[4] "I was born this way," Soren insists. Sexual difference is explained genetically, without any reference to patriarchy, hierarchy, or desire. Soren's demand for acceptance slides into a plea for compassion, suggesting an "I can't help it so don't hurt me" defense. Further, the plot completely confuses gender (the social roles, behaviors, and attitudes associated with women and men) with sexual orientation (an erotic preference for a particular sex). Soren's identity with the female gender seems to lead her "naturally" to a preference for men. Why couldn't she think of herself as a woman and fall in love with, say, Beverly Crusher? The writers and directors of the show seemed to feel the need to reassure the audience that the boundaries of heterosexual desire were in no danger of transgression. Soren's "androgyny" is thoroughly coded feminine: she is slender, small-boned, delicate; those familiar camera angles give us a quick look at a very round ass and the suggestion of breasts. Soren could have had any number of bodies; why choose one that so clearly resolves her gender uncertainty in the direction of femaleness? Why make her femaleness so similar to ours? The limit of "androgyny" is that it does not so much confuse gender categories as it reinscribes them; it is constituted in relation to the settled categories of male and female. The more robust gender bending offered in "The Host," "Liaisons," and "11001001" is suggested by the premise of "The Outcast" and then withdrawn by the terms of its resolution.

The dance of denaturalization is a delicate one. It must take some familiar categories for granted in order to throw others into question. Yet the familiar readily reaches out and recolonizes the unconventional, folding it back into the territory of comfortable assumptions. *The Next Generation* sometimes succeeds in setting a stage that allows for the denaturalization of conventional gender boundaries and identities, providing a discursive space for imagining a differently gendered world. At other times it takes away the very social critique it seems to be offering.

What to make of this ambivalence? Given the usual constraints of popular television, the series offers significant openings for feminist and postmodern ideas about shifting gender boundaries to make their appearance and do their work. Yet *Star Trek* as a commodity depends on titillating, and then reassuring, consumers whose values have been and continue to be structured by, among other sources, the medium of television itself. The show's demographics show *Star Trek* viewers to be skewed toward young, white, middle-class, well-educated males. (Although it is our informal impression that a strong subgroup of feminist viewers is underestimated, and underappreciated, by the network.) It is arguable that *Star Trek* 's relatively liberal bent has been defended to the sponsors as producing and maintaining the continued interest of those middle- and upper-middle class educated viewers—an elite market niche, and very attractive to advertisers selling high-quality, high-priced, technologically sophisticated goods. That is, attractive to advertisers which can pay premium rates for prime time spots, a concept network executives also applaud. If the show's design and production team were independent filmmakers, we could expect a lot more in the way of social critique. They aren't, and we can't.

Star Trek: Deep Space Nine offers some interesting possibilities for further exploration of identity and difference. Sometimes the spin-off show frames gender difference in conventional, commercial terms (Major Kira's body-hugging costumes, for instance, or the "T and A" contributions of Quark's dabo girls) but often it throws conventional gender boundaries, as well as racial and species distinctions, into disarray. Dax's species, the Trill, are a fascinating site for unknitting and reknitting identity practices. Jadzia Dax, the current female host of the Dax symbiot, both is and is not the "same person" as Curzon Dax, the former male-bodied union, and the other previous hosts. Jadzia is clearly female, yet she retains Curzon's loyalties to his former comrades and lovers. Odo, the shapeshifter, also offers many productive confusions: why is he in a male body? Why is he white? How does he mate? The ruthless patriarchy of the Ferengi (and implicitly, of the viewers) has been consistently challenged by the strong female characters in the show, who show little need for male supervision and a predilection to stay clothed. Commander Sisko's dark skin is a major deviation from the largely white authorities on the *Enterprise,* and his mysterious selection by the Bejoran prophets as their "Emissary" undermines distinctions between secular and spiritual as well as between Bejoran and human. Sisko's pride in his culinary skills, and his close relationship with his son Jake, fold domestic and familial labor into his life as commander.

Star Trek: Voyager continues to open up the world of identity practices in numerous ways. Captain Kathryn Janeway's command authority is exercised with both firmness and compassion. The senior officers include a Native American man, a Korean man, a dark-skinned Vulcan male, and a woman who is half Klingon, half human. The initial friction between Janeway and Belana Torres (the Klingon/human chief engineer) develops into a relation of respect and trust, based in part on their shared personal strength and their expertise in science. Janeway's reliance on her Vulcan officer Tuvok for advice reveals a longstanding friendship; when Tuvok admits to violating the captain's orders in an effort to help her, there is a range of emotion in Janeway's response that includes anger, disappointment, perhaps gratitude, certainly the willingness to openly need another. A similar range of emotions characterizes her response to alien dangers, her respect for all life forms, her concerns about her crew. She acknowledges responsibilities to life forms inadvertently harmed by her ship or her crew, while offering strong resistance to actual dangers that *Voyager* encounters.

The newest spin-off series also complicates human/machine boundaries through the interesting figure of the holodeck doctor. The doctor's increasing responsibilities on the ship test the limits of his programing, while his sympathetic relation with the young telepathic alien Kess features his similarities with humanoid life forms. The first season's episodes also highlight interesting conflicts and contrasts between the organizational structure and function of Star Fleet, and the looser guerilla organization of the Maqui. Janeway's crew includes several Maqui members, whose standard operating procedures and historical loyalties complicate the Star Fleet chain of command.

Because *Star Trek* is an ongoing text, endlessly emerging in new books and series as well as in less official channels, it offers complex possibilities. Unfortunately for the future of gender exploration, Gene Roddenberry's original idea is now a copyrighted image of the future owned by Paramount. This ownership expands commercial control of *Star Trek* themes: for example, Paramount may censor additions to the *Star Trek* repertory, controlling writers who seek to expand the universe of identities and boundaries within which the *Star Trek* narratives re-side.[5] Yet the self-organizing practices of writers and fans may undermine commercial control. Activities among *Star Trek* USENET news groups, conventions, discussion groups, readers and viewers indicate an extraordinary level of cultural, educational, and economic resources that could boldly go where no commercial network would dream of setting foot.

Notes

1. Tom Lalli points out that Dr. Noel is one of the few women in James Kirk's life who was "at once attractive, strong-willed and professional." She is sexually assertive without being "ruled by her passions" (45). Lt. McGivers falls is love with Khan, but stops to save the *Enterprise* before leaving with him; while she is more properly described as "ruled by her passions," she also has some lasting loyalty to Kirk. Lt. Palomas is coached by Kirk in how to be seductive toward a male god, which suggests an interesting combination of projection and narcissism on his part.
2. It is fascinating that the Leonard Nimoy Fan Club, one of the first and largest of all the fan clubs for the actors in the original series, is 95 percent female (Blair 294).
3. This comment was offered by Annette Gardner during a seminar on "Gender Identity in Star Trek" in the Department of Political Science, University of Hawaii, spring 1994. Our thanks to all the participants in that seminar for their comments and insights.
4. Our thanks to Diane Maluso and Bernice Lott for their insightful interpretations of this episode.
5. According to information gleaned from the USENET newsgroup rec.arts.startrek, and confirmed via e-mail by Timothy Lynch.

Works Cited

Blaire, Karen. 1993. "Sex and Star Trek." *Science Fiction Studies* 10: 292–297.

Butler, Judith. 1990. *Gender Trouble: Feminism and the Subversion of Identity*. New York: Routledge.

Lalli, Tom. 1990. "Same Sexism, Different Generation." In *The Best of Trek*, edited by W. Irwin and G. G. Love. New York: Penguin.

McDonnell, David, ed. 1991. *Star Trek 25th Anniversary Special*. Paramount Pictures.

Selley, April. 1992. "'Whom Gods Destroy': Family Members and Romantic Partners in Star Trek." Paper presented at the Annual Meeting of the Popular Culture and American Culture Associations. Louisville, Ken. March 18–21.

Wilcox, Clyde. 1992. "To Boldly Return Where Others have Gone Before: Cultural Change and the Old and New Star Treks." *Extrapolation* 33, 1: 88–100.

Chapter 14

"We Owe It to Them to Interfere"
Star Trek and U.S. Statecraft in the 1960s and the 1990s

Mark P. Lagon

The original *Star Trek* television series explored numerous twentieth-century social problems through metaphors. One of the most frequently addressed social problems was the proper role of the United States in the world. Particularly through the device of the Prime Directive—restricting interference in the internal affairs of other planets—*Star Trek* explored the moral dilemmas faced by American foreign policy makers. By stressing interesting plots rather than plausible or aesthetically-pleasing special effects, this television series of the late 1960s created a superb metaphor for problems in American statecraft through science fiction.

The creators of *Star Trek* consciously addressed several problems and themes in United States foreign policy in the period when the series originally aired. Perhaps even more startling, there are intriguing metaphors for new problems faced in United States foreign policy today, in a post-Cold War era. The latter were not intended to comment on U.S. foreign policy at the time of the show, but they aptly confront new problems for the United States in the global context twenty-five years later.

To explore these intended metaphors for American foreign policy in the 1960s and the unintended metaphors for United States foreign policy today, two episodes provide superb illustrations. The episode entitled "The Apple" explores how Captain Kirk and a landing party overthrow an idyllic system on Gamma Trianguli VI where natives never age, die, or need to mate and experience love because they worship and feed a machine called "Val" which provides for their welfare and stability. "A Piece of the Action" may be the old *Star Trek* at its funniest, in presenting the story of how Kirk, Spock, and McCoy set out to create order in a society modelled on Chicago's mobsters. These two episodes are full of intended and unintended metaphors for United States foreign policy.

There are five central themes in *Star Trek* meant as commentary on American foreign policy at the time the series aired. First, the zealous desire of James T. Kirk, as the hero of the original *Star Trek*, to spread the Federation's way of life serves as a mirror to observe the American style of foreign policy. The missionary zeal of Kirk reflects an aggressiveness in United States Cold War policy which bordered on what Kenneth Waltz called a "rage to rule" (Waltz, 1992). The American culture's moralism is seen in two sides of American foreign policy. On the one hand, Americans are isolationist, fearing entangling alliances and being tainted by less pure cultures abroad. Once this insularity is transcended through times of crisis, American moralism is translated into a missionary zeal, seeking to vanquish nondemocratic foes (Dallek 1983). This is why Theodore Lowi has noted that United States statesmen have had to exaggerate external threats to transcend the isolationist form of moralism (Lowi 1969). This moralism also explains why Americans prefer doctrines declaring generalizable moral principles as a rationale for involvement in world affairs (Crabb 1982).

Second, the series intentionally provided metaphors highlighting how the United States routinely breaks the norms of nonintervention and international law which it established and celebrated rhetorically. The Prime Directive represents the idea of the sovereign equality of nations and the presumption against intervening in the internal affairs of sovereign nations which the United States vested in international law and organizations as the primary architect of the United Nations. The United States routinely violated those norms in the era in which the show aired—for better and for worse. Whether criticizing the human rights record of sovereign nations or invading a nation in the name of security, the United States broke its own Prime Directive. Scholars and

policy makers alike have formulated elaborate pretexts for this hypocrisy, such as John Norton Moore's defense of American aid to the Contras
on the basis of the Sandinista complicity in trying to unseat other sovereign nations and upset "world order" (Moore 1987).

Third, the old *Star Trek* explored the views of American elites about
political development in the Third World. Debates conducted between
Kirk, Spock, and McCoy over the respective social systems and paths to
development and growth of other planets reflect similar concerns on
the part of foreign policy elites. Furthermore, the visual similarity of
aliens to humans (unlike *Star Trek: The Next Generation*) and the frequent
carbon copies of chapters in Earth's history either by contamination or
spontaneous parallel development (e.g., the Roman empire, 1920s Chicago, and Nazi Germany) reinforced the American notion that all nations develop in the same unilinear pattern. As Robert Packenham noted,
liberal American elites in government and in the academy tends to think
that the successful aspects of Western political and economic development naturally coincided. They believed "all good things go together"
(Packenham 1973).

A fourth intended critique of U.S. foreign policy in the old *Star Trek*
was the symbolic role of small planetary powers who served as clients
of the Federation. The crew of the *Enterprise* went to great lengths to
manipulate indigenous leaders on planets by dressing up in disguise in
their clothing and taking on their way of speaking. The manipulation of
leaders on planets as surrogates for Federation reflected the moral
conundra faced by the United States of utilizing often unsavory clients
in the East-West conflict. Through military and economic aid, the United
States acted as patron to numerous Third World clients in a effort to add
to the pro-Western coalition in the zero-sum competition of the Cold
War. Sometimes these surrogates for American power were sitting governments (such as the Salvadoran government) and sometimes they were
insurgents (such as the Contras). In particular, the United States nur-
tured patron-client relationships with Central American nations
(Gasiorowski 1986). The chief client the United States was working with
at the time of the show's original broadcasts was the government of
South Vietnam. The fifth aspect of American foreign policy explored by
the old *Star Trek* was the American intervention in Southeast Asia and
its intrusive efforts at nation-building in South Vietnam. The Vietnam
War must have been very much on the minds of the writers of the show,
given its development at the very same time as the show aired. The

certainty with which Kirk entered into conflicts on planets and the ambivalence expressed by Spock about the logic of doing so reflected a debate among "the best and the brightest" elites in the Kennedy and Johnson Administrations about United States involvement in Vietnam (Halberstam 1969). Those elites developed the military doctrine of "flexible response" and Vietnam was the test case they sought (Gaddis 1982). In the process, these elites cast doubt upon the efficacy of American internationalism due the failure of that test case (Hatcher 1990).

How are these five themes explored in the two episodes selected as case studies? One sees references to the missionary zeal of the United States in Kirk's behavior in "The Apple." When Spock is hit by the projectile spores of a deadly plant, Kirk orders his crew to go on "security alert." This aggressive reaction to an apparently inanimate threat symbolizes the obsession with national security which the moralistic American culture produced during the Cold War. Later, Kirk sneaks up on the native who has been tracking them through the jungle, and punches him. As the native, Akuta, is horrified by having been struck, Kirk says "I won't hurt you," and "We come in peace." The juxtaposition of Kirk's words and deeds acts as a metaphor for American aggressiveness in the East-West conflict, despite peaceful intentions and rhetoric.

In "A Piece of the Action," the crusading style of American foreign policy is explored through Kirk as well. When Kirk and Spock seek to confront the gang boss Jojo Krako, a boy offers to help them make "the hit" by creating a diversion. Spock, ever logical, is concerned about involving the boy in a potentially violent situation. Kirk is not, using the boy as part of a ruse to see Krako, and offering him an unspecified percentage or "piece of the action." Kirk later has Scotty use the *Enterprise*'s phasers to stun battling gangsters in a one-block radius of a meeting of mob bosses he arranged as a show of might. Both these aggressive moves mirror American demonstrations of force and resolve in confronting the Soviet Union and its allies in the Cold War.

American hypocrisy in setting up international law and norms of behavior restricting interference in the internal affairs of sovereign nations is explored in both episodes. In "The Apple," McCoy sets the tone of the episode by saying "It's a shame to have to intrude" in the first moments, preparing the viewer for the moral dilemma to come. Spock and Kirk address this dilemma when they later say, in debating whether they should upset the balance of the society on the planet in its mindless service of Val:

Spock: If we do what it seems we must, in my opinion, we will be in direct violation of the Noninterference Directive.

Kirk: These people are not robots. . . . They should have freedom of choice. We owe it to them to interfere.

In "A Piece of the Action," Kirk blatantly violates the Federation's self-imposed norms not to interfere in other planets' affairs (despite a loophole suggested in the episode that the planet was contaminated by a Federation visit before the Prime Directive went into effect). Krako says, "I thought you guys had laws—no interference." Kirk responds, "Who's interfering? We're taking over." Though Kirk never intends to take over, his bravado shows how American foreign policy first violated international norms and ultimately could be quite imperial.

The two episodes also explore American beliefs and prejudices about political and economic development in the Third World. The atmosphere of the jungle and the primitive village in "The Apple" set the scene for an exploration of American views of underdevelopment. The debate over whether other nations will follow a similar path of development to that of the West is captured by a heated exchange between Spock and McCoy as they observe natives feeding Val, the machine which protects them:

Spock: In my view, a splendid example of reciprocity.

McCoy: It would take a computerized Vulcan mind such as yours to make that kind of statement.

Spock: You insist on applying human standards to nonhuman cultures. I remind you that humans are only a tiny minority in this galaxy.

McCoy: There are certain absolutes, Mr. Spock. And one of them is the right of humanoids to a free and unchained environment— the right to have conditions which permit growth.

Spock: Another is their right to choose a system which works for them.

I suspect the show's authors sympathize with Spock's moral relativism, despite Kirk's ultimate overthrow of Val. McCoy's view embody the 1960s beliefs among elites that development and growth were essential to lesser developed countries (LDCs) and that political and economic freedom in the form of democracy and capitalism provided the only road to that end. Evidence in the intervening quarter century bears out McCoy's thesis. Spock and McCoy revive the issue the end of the episode:

Spock: Captain, I'm not at all certain we did the correct thing on Gamma Trianguli VI.

McCoy: We put those people back on the normal course of social evolution. I see nothing wrong with that.

McCoy's statement mirrors the certainty of American leaders that the one unilinear path to development should be promoted globally.

Views of development are explored in "A Piece of Action" as well. In his first communication with Bela Oxmyx, Kirk is asked why a radio message from a ship that visited Sigma Iotia II took one-hundred years to get to Earth and how the landing party would beam down. He responds twice, "I'll explain it in more detail when I see you." This language, like that of an adult seeking to avoid explaining a complex concept to a child, reflects how Americans have at times looked down upon the leaders of Third World nations as unsophisticated thinkers. The previous visit of a Federation ship, the *Horizon*, occurred at the beginning of industrialization on Sigma Iotia II, reinforcing the theme of economic development. The references to the Iotians as imitative refer to efforts of the United States to get LDCs to copy its pattern of political and economic development. The following hilarious exchange is crucial:

Krako: What do you think, we're stupid or something?

Kirk: No, no. I don't think you're stupid. I just think your behavior is arrested.

Krako: I've never been arrested in my whole life.

Kirk thinks the Iotians are in an arrested state of development, and they must be helped—just as the United States has tried to manipulate internal affairs in LDCs to promote their development.

The issue of American clients in the Third World during the Cold War is also explored in "A Piece of the Action." Bela Oxmyx symbolizes the kind of unsavory Third World clients the United States had to court in the Cold War. When asked if he headed the government within his territory, Oxmyx responds, "What government? Like I told you, I got the territory and I run it, that's all." Oxmyx wants "heaters" (weapons) to eliminate his rivals for power, a motivation animating many Third World despots who received foreign aid from the United States. Pointedly, the episode features oscillation between the crew of the *Enterprise* being taken hostage by Oxmyx and Krako and the crew bullying the indigenous leaders. This oscillation highlights the ambiguous mutual leverage in Cold War era patron-client relations between the United States and Cold War allies.

Spock reflects the American rationalization for the need for order to prevent Communist revolutions in allied Third World countries. "We may quarrel with Mr. Oxmyx's methods, but his goal is essentially the correct one. This society must become united or it will degenerate into anarchy." Spock relates his sympathy for Oxmyx's aims only to be faced with the moral dilemma of relying on brutal clients and surrogates:

> Spock: You yourself have stated the need for unity of authority on this planet. We agree.
>
> Oxmyx: Yeah, but I've got to be the unity.

Spock reflects the necessity for the United States to rely on clients by explaining to McCoy why he must take Oxmyx at his word: "If we are to save the Captain without blatant, forceful interference on this planet, Doctor, we must have the assistance of someone indigenous. We are therefore forced to trust Mr. Oxmyx."

Ultimately, Kirk takes clothes from Oxmyx's henchmen and takes on their hard-boiled vernacular to get the indigenous leaders to do as he wishes. He decides to talk in terms they will understand: "The planet, uh, is being taken over by the Federation. But we don't want to come in here and, uh, use our muscle, you know what I mean? That ain't, uh, subtle. So what we do is, we, we help one guy take over the planet. He pulls the strings and then we pull his. Heh heh heh heh." No better explanation of American patron-client relations with Third World dictators in the Cold War could be articulated. Kirk forms a syndicate of indigenous leaders, calling for a 40 percent cut for the Federation. At the end of the episode, Spock and Kirk discuss the ethical problems of Kirk's solution.

Spock: I do have reservations about your solution to the problem of the Iotians.

Kirk: I understand that. You don't think it is logical to leave a criminal organization in charge.

Spock: Highly irregular to say the least.

Similarly, "kleptocratic" leaders who plundered their populations through their penetration of the business communities in their nations—such as Anastosio Somoza or Ferdinand Marcos—were American allies of convenience in the Cold War.

Finally, both episodes exhibit intentional commentary on the Vietnam War. "The Apple" features a planet that appears to be a paradise until crew members are rapidly killed by a deadly plant, lightning, and an exploding rock (a land mine of sorts). Kirk establishes the parallel to Vietnam in calling the planet "a Garden of Eden with land mines." Kirk regrets not having extricated himself from this quagmire, where the energy is being sucked out of the *Enterprise* by Val, the crew cannot be beamed away from the hazardous environs on the planet, and the ship is being pulled slowly toward the planet risking its ultimate destruction. These are metaphors for how the United States was stuck in a conflict it did not relish in Vietnam. Kirk blames himself for not avoiding the danger to his crewmen, and Spock consoles him.

Spock: You were only following Star Fleet orders.

Kirk: I have the option to disregard orders if I consider them hazardous.

Paralleling American elites who blamed themselves for getting into Vietnam, such as Robert McNamara, Kirk repeats his self-criticism about endangering his crew on the *Enterprise*: "400 people. They'll die because I could not see a warning sign. I had to follow orders—always orders."

The reference to following orders parallels the discussion during the Vietnam War of excessive violence by American forces, particularly after the My Lai incident. Some claimed Americans had committed war crimes for which the pretext of following orders was no more convincing than when Nazi officers used that defense in the Nuremburg trials (Lewy 1978).

"A Piece of the Action" also addresses the Vietnam War. It explores the United States treatment of the South Vietnamese government as its client. Kirk reflects the ruthlessness of this treatment in one statement, even though Kirk was play-acting: "The Federation is moving, we're taking over. You play ball, we'll give you a piece of the pie. You don't, you out. All the way out, you know what I mean?" The alleged CIA orchestration of Ngo Dinh Diem's assassination when he became a hinderance to the Kennedy Administration's policy in Vietnam bears an uncanny resemblance to the fate of being "all the way out" to which Kirk refers.

The old *Star Trek*, epitomized by these two episodes, not only reveals lessons about American conduct in world politics concurrent with the run of the show in the 1960s. It also provides lessons for United States statecraft in the 1990s. Five further lessons applicable to the changed circumstances of today are apparent in the old *Star Trek*.

First, the old *Star Trek* reveals the perspective of Earthlings who have gotten beyond the Cold War. Frequent references in the series to the aggressive era of thermonuclear weapons in the late twentieth century in the original *Star Trek* are cast as expressions of thankfulness for having transcended a period of pointless conflict. The implications of the Cold War's demise are the subject of some of the most heated discussions among scholars and policy analysts. Some identify the end of the Cold War not only as the passing of an unfortunate era, but a watershed representing more or less the triumph of democratic capitalism over all other ideologies (Fukuyama 1989). Others worry that the simplicity of the bipolar standoff in the Cold War will be replaced with unstable uncertainly (Mearsheimer 1989).

Second, one can see in the dominance of the Federation and, moreover, of Earth within the Federation in the old *Star Trek* a parallel to today's post-Cold War distribution of power in the world. Some internationalists today note that with the disappearance of the Soviet Union as a superpower—and as a nation for that matter—we have a one superpower world. As a result, they argue they the United States should unabashedly act as the world's policeman and use its hegemony to impose cooperation between small nations where it might not otherwise arise. For example, the columnist Charles Krauthammer has titled articles "Universal Dominion" (Krauthammer 1989–90) and "The Unipolar Moment" (Krauthammer 1990–91) with both descriptive and prescriptive meanings in mind.

On the other hand, one also sees in the old *Star Trek* a third phenomenon pertinent to the United States's situation in the world today. Characters in the old *Star Trek* express fear of the Federation being overtaken by rival powers. Today, there is a growing fear of Japan or a unified European Community overtaking the United States. Political scientist Robert Gilpin has noted that hegemonic powers inevitably experience hegemonic decline due to the burdens of maintaining regimes of cooperation which they created, due to domestic preferences for consumption over investment, and due to diffusion of technology (Gilpin 1981). These factors appear to many to be verified respectively by American difficulty in maintaining the Bretton Woods monetary regime and the General Agreement on Trade and Tariffs (GATT) trade regime, United States consumption eclipsing its investment in the 1980s, and Japanese success in marketing technology invented by the United States. The theme of inevitable decline due to "imperial overstretch" was popularized by historian Paul Kennedy (Kennedy 1987). Some critics of the decline school reject the idea of inevitable "imperial overstretch" as too determinist (Harries 1988), and others claim that the United States will remain a key leader despite relative decline (Nye 1990). The anxieties lying at the heart of this debate are portrayed in the zero-sum logic of Kirk in *Star Trek*.

Fourth, Kirk's passion for flagrantly and repeatedly violating the Prime Directive reflects a concern for promoting democracy and American values as relevant today as it was in the Cold War context at the time *Star Trek* first aired. The American missionary sentiment that "we owe it to them to interfere" remains a powerful rationalization for intervention. While the United States might hypocritically ignore tenets of international law providing for nonintervention in other nations's affairs, it does so in the name of promoting democracy. A number of policy analysts have argued that the United States should promote democracy as the natural, positively defined purpose to follow the negatively defined anticommunism of the Cold War. From the conservative American Enterprise Institute (Muravchik 1991) to the centrist Democratic Leadership Council (Diamond 1992) to Harvard's Kennedy School of Government (Allison and Beschel 1992), one finds advocates of United States promotion of democracy. Some question the sincerity of the United States' prodemocracy rhetoric in the past, especially in Latin America (Lowenthal 1991; Carothers 1992), hoping that without the Soviet threat, democratization will no longer be jettisoned in favor of convenient clients.

This concern with errors of the past points to the fifth lesson to be found in the old *Star Trek* relevant to United States foreign policy today. In *Star Trek* it was said that the Prime Directive could be ignored if intervention involved righting past wrongs, or if the Federation distorted development on a nation before to Noninterference Directive went into effect. Similarly, if Western intervention in the Third World occurred at a time when no stigma was attached to interfering other cultures' affairs then new intervention to rectify past inequities might be justified. The United States is likely to concern itself with righting past wrongs in dealing with the nations of the South. Examples include the Panama invasion aimed at removing Manuel Noreiga as a former American client, and the proposal of Richard Feinberg and Delia Boylan that the United States should help fund a multilateral fund to aid war-torn nations trying to recover from Cold War era regional conflicts in countries like Angola (Feinberg and Boylan 1991).

How are these five contemporary problems illustrated by the two episodes of *Star Trek* studied here? The theme of the cold war being over is seen in "The Apple" in the form of Ensign Pavel Chekhov. Chekhov's presence on the *Enterprise* crew reinforces the image of Earth transcending the Cold War, a change the creators of the show hopefully anticipated. The fact that Chekhov works for Kirk, an American, as his superior officer, also symbolizes the situation where the United States prevailed in the Cold War. Under Foreign Minister Andrei Krozyrev, Russia has sought to be part of the West, just as Chekhov submits to Kirk's leadership. Furthermore the motif found in many episodes of Chekhov's Russian nationalism—now transformed into a benign joke—is seen in his attribution of historic human achievements to Russia. In comparing the pastoral splendor of Gamma Trianguli VI to the Garden of Eden, he claims the latter was located just outside of Moscow. Kirk, as ever, is amused by this harmless nationalist barb. The Cold War is indeed long over.

The passage from a warlike era into a more peaceful one is explored in "A Piece of the Action." Upon seeing the inhabitants of Sigma Iotia II toting machine guns, McCoy says, "I've seen pictures of the old days which looked like this." In a warlike environment very different from the apparent paradise of Gamma Trianguli VI, the *Enterprise* crew appreciates the new pacific situation *their* world enjoys in comparing it to the warlike "old days" brought to life by the *Iotian* world.

The second factor relevant to United States foreign policy today—the circumstance of a unipolar world—is reflected in "A Piece of the Action" as well. Kirk takes advantage of Federation power to force the warring parties to cooperate in establishing a power-sharing arrangement and, hence, order. When Kirk cannot persuade through the force of his arguments to sit down "and talk about it like reasonable men," he resorts to using Federation power to coerce them into cooperating. This is precisely the kind of order United States power would allow in a unipolar world, according to hegemonic stability theory (Gilpin, 1981). Using superior military technology (phasers) to intimidate the bosses and superior nonmilitary technology (the transporter) to bring them to the table with one another, Kirk forces them to cooperate. The dominance of the Federation is clearly the facilitating factor, as seen in the exchange between Krako and Kirk.

Krako: I thought you guys had laws—no interference.

Kirk: Who's interfering? We're taking over.

The ease with which this response falls from Kirk's lips may be an indicator of the frequency with which the United States will discard international norms of nonintervention, and take over processes to impose cooperation between weaker actors in a unipolar world.

While the United States may act as the sole superpower in the world, as it did in the Persian Gulf War, it is not without its anxieties about being overtaken by other powers. "A Piece of the Action" reflects the concern Americans experience in observing the rapid growth of Japan and the newly industrialized countries (NICs) of East Asia, which have so successfully copied American technology and prospered in marketing them. McCoy expresses concern over leaving his communicator in Oxmyx's office after the *Enterprise* leaves its orbit around Sigma Iotia II. Kirk and Spock note that as a highly imitative people (like Japan and the NICs) the Iotians would discover the translator resting within the communicator, which is the key to the Federation's technology. Kirk expresses the fear of being overtaken:

Kirk: It upsets the whole percentage.

McCoy: How do you mean?

Kirk: In a few years, the Iotians may demand a piece of *our* action.

Kirk expresses the implications of the "diffusion of technology" which scholars like Gilpin identify: United States decline (Gilpin 1981).

The problems involved in promoting democracy and Western values in American foreign policy is apparent in analogous dilemmas explored in both episodes. In "The Apple," the landing party is indignant when they learn that Val forbids love, takes over procreation ("replacements" in their words of the natives), and requires natives to feed it at regular intervals in a sacrificial ritual when it "hungers." The landing party, and Kirk and McCoy in particular, disapprove of values and habits different from their own, and openly seek to spread the Federation's brand of freedom, must like the United States seeks to spread its brand of freedom. Having destroyed Val and Gamma Trianguli VI societal system as the natives have known it, Kirk makes a speech: "You'll learn to care for yourselves, with our help. . . . You'll learn to build for yourselves, think for yourselves, work for yourselves, and what you create is yours. That's what we call freedom. You'll like it a lot." Like American foreign policy after the Cold War, the Federation attempt to introduce their system of freedom is very noble, and indeed justified. Nevertheless, the caveat "with our help" points to a set of complicated questions for U.S. policy: How long and at what cost will others societies require help to introduce democracy? Must they conform to our variety of democracy (limiting government intervention in economic affairs, based on a presidential rather than parliamentary system, and based on single member districts rather than proportional representation)? Should the United States use force to promote democracy?

In "A Piece of the Action," the landing party discovers that Iotian politics are based on values they do not approve of. Oxmyx's henchman Kalo explains the complaints of two women about street lights and the lack of laundry pick-ups, saying "They pay their percentages and the boss takes care of them." Not only does this statement bring to mind Mafia protection, but the client system which the United States has confronted in many Third World countries, especially in Latin America and East Asia. In introducing democracy, the United States has and will continue to face informal systems of political leaders delivering services and benefits (taking care of them) to citizens in return for political support (paying their percentages). For democracy to take root, the United States must be patient in seeking to displace such indigenous values in other nations. At the end of the episode, Kirk explains to Spock what is to become of the 40 percent cut for the Federation he demanded from the Iotian bosses to demonstrate he meant business. He suggests the money should go into the planet's treasury for future: "Despite themselves, they'll be forced to accept conventional responsibilities. Isn't that logical?" Promoting the Western model for development will likely serve American interests and those of its recipients, but the United States must find ways to get LDCs to accept "conventional responsibilities" according to that model "despite themselves." There is a fine line between a benign Pax Americana where U.S. interests and those of LDCs are not mutually exclusive, and a condescending and domineering imposition of our standards.

Finally, the righting of previous wrongs as a justification for American intervention in Third World countries' internal affairs is reflected metaphorically in the two shows' plots. In both episodes "contamination" of the indigenous cultures of planets symbolizes the previous wrongs requiring further intervention. When Chekhov kisses Yeoman Martha Landon, two eavesdropping natives mimic their embrace. The contamination of an insular culture, in which Val forbids love, moves the plot of "The Apple" towards its denouement. Val subsequently introduces murder to the blissfully ignorant natives in ordering the landing party clubbed to death. The landing party is not responsible for introducing murder to Gamma Trianguli VI (as Spock implies), but their intrusive role forces a confrontation between their values and indigenous ones to come to a climax. Val and the landing party seek to destroy one another, with the latter winning out. American involvement in developing nations in the past often necessitates further intervention to bring an incomplete introduction of Western values in the past to full fruition.

In "Piece of the Action," contamination in the past plays an even more central role to the plot. The *Enterprise*'s mission on Sigma Iotia II is to assess the *Horizon*'s effect when it visited before the Nonintervention Directive was promulgated. As the usual antagonists, Spock and McCoy spar in defining their mission.

McCoy: So we're going down to recontaminate them.
Spock: The damage has been done, Doctor. We are here to repair it.

It turns out that the *Horizon* left a copy of a book titled *Chicago Mobs of the Twenties* on the planet. Humorously, they note that the book was published in 1992. The contamination was based on the imitative Iotians setting up a social system based on this book. The book is their Bible, as McCoy observes, explaining a society mirroring the influence of gangsters in Chicago's most anarchic decade. Kirk decides they must act: "If this society broke down as a result of the *Horizon*'s influence, then the Federation is responsible. We've got to do something to straighten this mess out."

How will the U.S. select cases in which it feels responsible for interfering in other nations to right past wrongs, to "recontaminate them?" No doubt the legacy of Western colonialism, past U.S. intervention, and disruptions wrought by the superpowers in Cold War regional conflicts will rightly justify United States involvement, but how often and how much?

In sum, "The Apple" and "A Piece of the Action" reveal the conscious commentary on United States statecraft in the 1960s woven into *Star Trek* by its creators. Both episodes serve as allegories which reveal the zealous missionary style of U.S. foreign policy; the pattern of U.S. violation of norms of nonintervention it established in international law when higher values are at stake; American notions about political and economic development; American use of clients and surrogates in the world; and dilemmas faced in the Vietnam War. Much of this commentary remains pertinent today.

While this intended commentary is interesting, the old *Star Trek* proves even richer than the series' writers might have imagined in the late 1960s. One can actually see several problems the United States faces in an utterly different international context in the 1990s in looking at the behavior of Kirk, the *Enterprise* crew, and the Federation in the two episodes. The United States must craft policy which suits an era where the Cold War is transcended, but instability and conflict have not ended. The United States now acts in a one-superpower world, and must determine how to use that unipolar dominance and how not to. And despite this unipolar moment in the immediate aftermath of the Soviet Union's demise as a superpower, the United States will face rising powers which claim a piece of the action. The United States will now be able to promote democracy without the compromises and diversions of Cold War strategy, and must face complex questions in doing so. And finally, despite the Cold War having passed from the scene, the United States will be driven to intervene in countries to right past wrongs for which it may or may not have been at fault.

The original *Star Trek* series is so rich that in pointing to the compulsion of American foreign policy makers to feel that they owe it to other countries to interfere in their affairs, it yields lessons beyond the context existing when it aired. These additional problems which *Star Trek* unintentionally highlights in the contemporary post-Cold War environment merit our attention a quarter century after Gene Roddenberry and his compadres brought them to life in the NBC series.

Works Cited

Allison, Graham T., Jr. and Robert P. Beschel, Jr. 1992. "Can the United States Promote Democracy?" *Political Science Quarterly* 107: 81–98.

Carothers, Thomas. 1992. *In the Name of Democracy*. Berkeley: University of California Press.

Crabb, Cecil V., Jr. 1982. *The Doctrines of American Foreign Policy: Their Meaning, Role, and Future*. Baton Rouge: Louisiana State University Press.

Dallek, Robert. 1983. *The American Style of Foreign Policy: Cultural Politics and Foreign Affairs*. New York: Alfred A. Knopf.

Diamond, Larry. 1991. "An American Foreign Policy for Democracy." *Progressive Policy Institute Policy Report*. 11.

Feinberg, Richard and Delia Boylan. 1991. In *Eagle in a New World*, edited by Kenneth A. Oye, Robert J. Lieber, and Donald Rothchild. New York: HarperCollins.

Fukuyama, Francis. 1989. "The End of History?" *The National Interest* 16: 3–18.

Gaddis, John Lewis. 1982. *Strategies of Containment*. New York: Oxford University Press.

Gasiorowski, Mark. 1986. "Dependency and Cliency in Latin America." *Journal of Interamerican Studies and World Affairs* 28: 47–66.

Gilpin, Robert. 1981. *War and Change in World Politics*. New York: Cambridge University Press.

Halberstam, David. 1969. *The Best and the Brightest*. New York: Random House.

Harries, Owen. 1988. "The Rise of the American Decline," *Commentary* 85: 32–36.

Hatcher, Patrick Lloyd. 1990. *The Suicide of an Elite: American Internationalists and Vietnam*. Stanford: Stanford University Press.

Kennedy, Paul. 1987. *The Rise and Fall of the Great Powers*. New York: Random House.

Krauthammer, Charles. 1989–90. "Universal Dominion." *The National Interest* 18: 46–49.

———. 1990–91. "The Unipolar Moment." *Foreign Affairs* 70: 23–33.

Lewy, Guenther. 1978. *America in Vietnam.* New York: Oxford University Press.

Lowenthal, Abraham F., ed. 1991. *Exporting Democracy: The United States and Latin America.* Baltimore: Johns Hopkins University Press.

Lowi, Theodore J. 1969. *The End of Liberalism.* New York: W. W. Norton.

Mearsheimer, John. 1990. "Back to the Future: Instability in Europe After the Cold War." *International Security* 15: 5–56.

Moore, John Norton. 1987. *The Secret War in Central America.* Frederick, Md.: University Press of America.

Muravchik, Joshua. 1991. *Exporting Democracy: Fulfilling America's Destiny.* Washington: AEI Press.

Nye, Joseph S., Jr. 1990. *Bound to Lead: The Changing Nature of American Power.* New York: Basic Books.

Packenham, Robert A. 1973. *Liberal America and the Third World.* Princeton: Princeton University Press.

Waltz, Kenneth N. 1991. "America as a Model for the World? A Foreign Policy Perspective?" *PS* 24: 667–670.

Star Trek episodes "The Apple" and "A Piece of the Action."

Index

CPSIA information can be obtained at www.ICGtesting.com
Printed in the USA
237143LV00008B/2/P

9 781570 038471